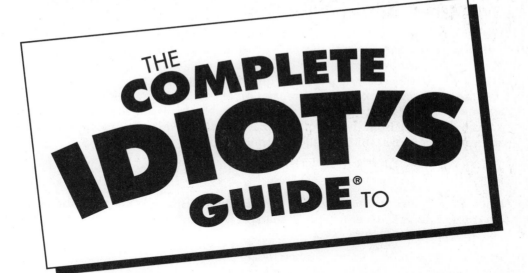

THE COMPLETE IDIOT'S GUIDE® TO

Tax

Deductions

by Lisa N. Collins

alpha books

A Division of Macmillan General Reference
A Simon & Schuster Macmillan Company
1633 Broadway, 8th Floor, New York NY 10019

Alpha Development Team

Publisher
Kathy Nebenhaus

Editorial Director
Gary M. Krebs

Managing Editor
Bob Shuman

Marketing Brand Manager
Felice Primeau

Editor
Jessica Faust

Development Editors
Phil Kitchel
Amy Zavatto

Production Team

Development Editor
Scott Warner

Production Editor
Christy Wagner

Copy Editor
Martha Thieme

Cover Designer
Mike Freeland

Photo Editor
Richard H. Fox

Illustrator
Jody P. Schaeffer

Designer
Glenn Larsen

Indexer
Riofrancos & Co. Indexes

Layout/Proofreading
Ellen Considine
Laura Goetz
Pete Lippincott

Contents at a Glance

Contents

4 Even Better Than Deductions—Tax Credits   41

5 Pay Yourself First and Lower Your Taxes   59

17 Travel, Meals, and Entertainment 235

18 Education Expenses 253

Foreword

Our government is constantly changing the tax laws in this country. There has been a tax bill in nearly every year since 1986, and most of the bills have made substantial changes effecting individuals filing tax returns. I've also found that each time Congress wants to encourage social change (i.e., save more for retirement by adding Roth IRAs) or close a perceived loop hole (i.e., limiting deduction of business meals because too many people don't really do business) they can't make a law administratively simple but rather add way to many ifs, ands, or buts. It appears they intend on making sure those "deemed" too well off can't take advantage of it, or those not very well off can't get too much of a good thing. Those of us in the tax profession have had to commit significant hours each year to studying the changes in order to keep up with the changes.

The plunging cost of computers is causing more and more families to have one in their home. In addition, the advancements in making computer software easier than ever to use is providing more and more individuals the courage to tackle their own personal tax returns. However the old adage "garbage in, garbage out" was never more applicable. If you don't understand the rules of what can be deducted and what can't be deducted you will either take deductions you are not entitled to, and possibly be subject to back taxes, penalties, and interest, or miss out on the opportunity to legally reduce your taxes to the fullest extent possible. Even if you have someone else prepare your tax return, you need to have a good understanding of what is and isn't deductible to insure your tax advisor is maximizing your deductions. Too often the right questions are not asked, or information volunteered, and deductions are missed.

Lisa Collins has done a phenomenal job in writing this book and providing you with a comprehensive and easily understood explanation of the many deductions an individual can avail themselves of. Upon reading Lisa's book I understand why she is consistently rated one of the top instructors to Certified Public Accountants in this country, as she has the ability to take difficult subject matter and make it easily understood by all. Lisa provides many practical sidebars that explain technical concepts in layman's terms. She also gives many practical planning ideas that anyone could implement to increase the deductions allowed on one's return. This book provides wonderful advice that even many professionals could use.

Todd A. Jackson, CPA, MBT
Tax Partner, McGladrey and Pullen, LLP

Introduction

"Death and taxes and childbirth! There's never any convenient time for any of them!"
Margaret Mitchell, in *Gone with the Wind* (1936).

It was true in 1936, and it's still true today.

Taxes are essential, but they are a real frustration. You can argue that the system is too complicated. You can argue whether our money is spent wisely. You can argue until you're blue in the face, but you still have to pay your taxes.

Having said this, you also have the right to use deductions and credits to legally reduce your tax bill. There are only two reasons you wouldn't take a legitimate tax deduction or credit:

> ➤ You didn't know about the deduction or credit you could have taken
> ➤ You didn't keep the right records

Don't lose out on tax savings for either reason. Find all the deductions you can and be prepared to document, document, document.

This book was written to help show you how to find ways to save money on your tax return. The book is divided into four parts.

Part 1, "Getting to Know Your Tax Return," will walk you through your tax return to show how it all works. We'll talk about some deductions and credits that may lower your tax bill.

Part 2, "Itemized Deductions," will explain each of the deductions to take if you itemize. Big tax savings are found in itemized deductions and you don't want to miss any of them.

Part 3, "Business Expenses," is for anyone who spends money to make a living. Whether you are an employee or you own your own business, you probably have to spend some money on the job. We'll help you discover which business expenses you can deduct on your tax return.

Part 4, "Deductions Even If You Don't Itemize," explains how you can use deductions to cut your tax bill whether you itemize or not. IRAs are hot again, and we'll talk about them, including the new Roth IRA.

Extras

To help you along the way, this book gives you quick pointers. Look for these helpful information boxes:

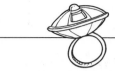

Your Decoder Ring

These boxes help you make sense of the tax lingo. By knowing the language, you can use the tax rules to your advantage. Our tax laws really are written in English, but you sometimes need a translator.

Paper Trail

Keeping records is an important part of your tax strategy. We'll give you tips on records to keep and which forms to fill out.

Red Flag

Pay attention to these information boxes to avoid tax traps and tangles with the IRS.

This Book Is for You

Even if you use a CPA to prepare your tax return, you may save money by learning more about the tax process. Your CPA can only use the information that you provide. Learn what deductions you might have been missing.

If you prepare your own tax return, it's completely up to you to know the tax rules. Tax preparation software is extremely helpful, but you still need to know what deductions you can take. It's your tax return and your money.

A Word of Caution

No tax book can cover every situation. This book provides general information about a variety of tax topics. We can't cover all of the topics that you might need to consider and we can't cover all of the details that you might need in your own situation. This book should not be relied on as tax advice. If you need help with a tax situation, use a qualified tax professional.

Tax laws are also constantly changing. Some of the information in this book could have already changed. That's just the nature of income taxes; they are a moving target. When you prepare your tax return, be sure to read your instruction booklet. It's not the most exciting reading, but the IRS does point out some of the changes. They won't cover them all, of course, but they hit the highlights.

Acknowledgements

I am very grateful for the kind words of encouragement that I have received from so many wonderful people. My clients, friends, partners, coworkers, and family have all been terrific.

There are some people in your career that can make a real difference. I'm fortunate enough to have known two such people. I can't say thank you enough to Dick Shymanski and Sid Kess.

My sincere thanks to Brenda Wallace, who took care of my clients while I stole away for some quiet writing time and to my parents for providing the place to which I could flee.

My dear husband, John, and my kids, Ian and Arlie, are my greatest supporters. It's a real treat to work on a project that your kids are proud of. They're great kids, and I'm thankful for their humor and kind words.

Special Thanks to the Technical Reviewer

The Complete Idiot's Guide to Tax Deductions was reviewed by an expert who double-checked the accuracy of what you'll learn here, to help us ensure that this book gives you everything you need to know about tax deductions. Special thanks are extended to Todd Jackson, a partner with McGladrey and Pullen, LLP.

McGladrey and Pullen, LLP is the nation's seventh largest certified public accounting and consulting firm and among the 40 largest consulting firms serving American business. McGladrey and Pullen serves clients from 63 offices nationwide and is linked with 86 independently owned CPA firms in the United States and Puerto Rico through the McGladrey Network. Internationally, McGladrey and Pullen is known as RSM International, the world's ninth largest accounting and consulting firm, with 400 offices in more than 75 countries.

For more information about McGladrey and Pullen you can visit our web site at www.mcgladrey.com.

Part 1
Getting to Know Your Tax Return

If you've ever felt frustrated by your tax return, you are certainly not alone. Our tax system is a patchwork quilt of special rules. Unfortunately, it looks like a quilt made of scraps.

Even putting political debate aside, there are many ways that our tax system could be simplified. Right now, though, we have to work within the system that we have. There is no other option. This means that each of us has to understand our own tax return.

Our goal is to pay the least amount of tax required under the law. To meet this goal, you don't want to miss out on any deductions or credits that will cut your tax bill. Knowledge is power when it comes to saving taxes. Catching all of your deductions saves you money. Don't miss out. Read on so you can learn how your tax return works and what kind of deductions and credits you can take.

Chapter 1

The Mechanics of Your Tax Return

> ### In This Chapter
>
> ➤ Knowing how your tax return works
>
> ➤ Deducting from your taxable income
>
> ➤ Finding your tax rate
>
> ➤ Calculating the tax savings from a deduction

Tax deductions can be your ticket to a higher refund. There are a lot of tax-saving opportunities, but the rules are confusing and frustrating.

Taxes are expensive. Many families spend more money on taxes than any other budget item. Unfortunately, a lot of us pay more income tax than we need to. By knowing the rules, you can take advantage of tax-saving deductions.

Through deductions, you can legally lighten your tax load. But how much will a deduction save you? Is it worth spending money to get a tax deduction?

The Big Tax Picture

Your personal tax return is divided into sections. Each section has a different purpose. By the time you work your way through the sections, you have completed your return.

The following are the sections of your Form 1040 tax return:

1. The Income section, where you add up your income to calculate total income.
2. The Adjusted Gross Income section, where you subtract certain deductions to calculate adjusted gross income. These are often called the *above-the-line* deductions.
3. The Tax Computation section, where you subtract itemized deductions (or standard deduction) and personal exemptions to get taxable income. These deductions are called the *below-the-line* deductions.
4. Income tax calculation section.
5. The Credits section, where you subtract credits, and the Other Taxes section, where you add other taxes.
6. The payments section, where you subtract your tax payments and withholdings to get your refund or the balance due to the IRS.

Your Decoder Ring

Adjusted Gross Income (AGI) and **taxable income** are important tax terms. AGI is a step in the path to taxable income. Some deductions can be taken before AGI (called **above-the-line**). Other deductions, such as itemized deductions and personal exemptions, are taken after AGI (called **below-the-line**).

Deductions Come in Different Flavors

Not all deductions yield the same tax savings. Some deductions save you more than others will. In general, deductions taken earlier on the return (above-the-line) are more valuable than those taken later on the return (below-the-line).

Above-the-line deductions are taken off your income to calculate your adjusted gross income (AGI). AGI is a stop that is mid-way to your taxable income. Below-the-line deductions (itemized deductions and personal exemptions) are taken away from AGI to calculate your taxable income.

You can't just pick and choose how you will claim a deduction, though. There are rules to follow, of course.

There are basically four types of deductions:

➤ Business, farm, or rent expenses (above-the-line)
➤ Above-the-line deductions other than business, farm, or rent
➤ Itemized deductions or standard deduction (below-the-line)
➤ Personal exemptions (below-the-line)

Business, Farm, or Rent Expenses (Above-the-Line)

If you own your own business, you have several forms to chose from. Your business could be a corporation, a partnership, or a sole proprietorship, to name a few. If your business is neither a partnership nor a corporation, it is most likely a sole proprietorship.

You report your net business income from a sole proprietorship on a Schedule C. The net income is then included in the Total Income section of your tax return. Your business deductions are claimed directly on Schedule C.

Farm income and expenses are claimed on Schedule F. Partnership income and expenses are reported on Schedule E, as are rent income and expenses.

Above-the-Line Deductions Other Than Business, Farm, or Rent

These above-the-line deductions can be taken even if you don't itemize. These deductions are valuable because they reduce your adjusted gross income (AGI).

Many tax advantages are available only depending upon your AGI. The larger your AGI, the less likely you are going to be able to enjoy a tax deduction or credit. This is Congress's way of guaranteeing that tax benefits are enjoyed only by lower- and middle-income taxpayers. High-income taxpayers are denied many tax advantages. AGI is often the measuring stick used for allowing tax deductions or credits.

Paper Trail

If you have a Schedule C business, a farm, or rent property, you might be able to claim expenses against these activities. A deduction taken on Schedule C saves more taxes than that same deduction taken as an itemized deduction. Tax return preparation fees are an example.

For example, medical expenses are deductible to the extent that they are more than 7.5% of your AGI. The lower your AGI, the more medical expenses you can claim. Another example is Social Security benefits. If your AGI is less than a threshold amount, your Social Security benefits are tax-free. As your AGI increases, more of your Social Security benefits are taxable.

In both of these examples, a deduction against AGI is valuable. If your AGI is lower because of a deduction, your medical expense deduction will be greater, and less of your Social Security benefits might be taxable. These are just two of many tax benefits that depend on your AGI.

The following are the above-the-line deductions:

➤ IRA contributions

➤ Student loan interest (new for 1998)

➤ Medical savings account deduction

➤ Moving expenses

➤ Half of self-employment tax

➤ Self-employed health insurance premiums

➤ Retirement plan contributions for the self-employed person

➤ Penalties on early withdrawal of savings (CDs)

➤ Alimony

These deductions are discussed in later chapters.

Itemized Deductions or Standard Deduction

Every taxpayer is entitled to claim a standard deduction. The dollar amount of the standard deduction is determined by your filing status. Standard deductions are discussed in Chapter 3, "Your Tax Freebee—The Standard Deduction."

You can claim itemized deductions instead of the standard deduction. If your itemized deductions are greater than your standard deduction you would choose to itemize. These deductions are claimed on Schedule A (see Appendix A, "IRS Forms").

Paper Trail

Claiming the standard deduction doesn't require any special record keeping. If you itemize, though, be sure you can support your deductions. Without support, a deduction can be taken away by the IRS.

Many people refer to itemizing their deductions as "filing a long form." There is no reason to resist or avoid itemizing, but some people fear filing the long form. If you can itemize, but choose not to, you are paying more tax than needed.

Deductions that you can itemize include the following:

➤ Medical expenses

➤ Taxes

➤ Interest

➤ Charitable contributions

➤ Casualty and theft losses

➤ Job expenses and miscellaneous deductions

Part 2 of this book discusses each itemized deduction in detail.

Personal Exemptions

We can take a tax deduction for each person that we support (including ourselves). This deduction is called a personal exemption. Read more about this in Chapter 2, "Personal Exemptions." Personal exemptions are taken even if you don't itemize.

Since each exemption will reduce your income taxes, you can cash in on the tax savings by having your employer withhold less income tax from your pay. When you fill out your withholding form for your employer (Form W-4), you can take credit for all of your exemptions. Your tax withholding is reduced for each exemption that you claim.

You might not want to reduce your withholding, though. If you are married, for example, you might need to have more taxes taken out of your pay. This is because your tax rate might be boosted higher when you combine your income with your spouse's income. You don't have to claim all of your exemptions on your withholding form. It's up to you how to fill out the form. You can still claim all of your exemptions on your tax return. Your withholding form only serves to instruct your employer how much taxes should be held out from your pay.

What Is My Tax Bracket?

After you have added up your income and taken all of your deductions, you have calculated your taxable income. The next step is to calculate your tax. There are two ways to calculate your tax. You will either use the Tax Table or the Tax Rate Schedule.

The instructions to the Form 1040 will tell you which way you should calculate your tax. It depends on your taxable income. High-income people use the rate schedule. Everyone else uses the tax table.

The Tax Table is a chart (included in your Form 1040 instruction booklet). By finding your taxable income on the chart, you can find your income tax. It's an easy chart to use, but you can't tell what your tax rate is. How do you know your tax rate?

By using the Tax Rate Schedules, also found in your Form 1040 instruction booklet, you can find your tax rate. The 1998 Tax Rate Schedule for married individuals filing jointly looks like Table 1.1.

Red Flag

Believe it or not, finding the incorrect tax on the tax tables is one of the most common mistakes. Double-check your tax. A mistake will delay your tax refund.

Table 1.1   1998 Tax Rate Schedule for Married Individuals Filing Jointly

If Taxable Income Is Over	But Not Over	Tax Is	Of the Amount Over
$0	$42,350	15%	$0
42,350	102,300	6,352.50 + 28%	42,350
102,300	155,950	23,138.50 + 31%	102,300
155,950	278,450	39,770.00 + 36%	155,950
278,450		83,870.00 + 39.6%	278,450

Our tax system is based on "graduated" tax rates. The higher your income, the higher the tax rate. The alternative to graduated tax rates is a flat tax rate. Although there has been a lot of talk about flat taxes, our system still relies on the graduated tax rate schedules.

Our tax rates are built up in layers. The first layer of income is taxed at 15%, the second layer taxed at 28%, and so forth. Even if you reach the highest tax rate of 39.6%, part of your income is still taxed at each of the lower tax rates.

It is a common misconception that adding taxable income pushes up the tax rate on all of your income. In truth, if you add more income, the new income is taxed at your highest rate. Your other income stays down in the lower tax rate levels. The other income doesn't move up to a higher tax rate if you add taxable income. This layering is the backbone of our graduated tax rate system. It protects us from getting gouged with high tax rates if our income increases slightly.

For example, let's say you are married and you have taxable income of $41,000. Your employer gives you a $3,000 bonus. What is your tax rate on that bonus? The first $1,350 will be taxed at 15%. The remaining $1,650 will be taxed at 28%. How was this calculated? The 15% bracket applies to taxable income up to $42,350. Without the bonus, your taxable income was $41,000. You still had $1,350 left in the 15% bracket. So $1,350 of the bonus is taxed at 15%. The rest of your bonus, $1,650, moves up to the next tax bracket and is taxed at 28%.

Your highest tax bracket is called your "marginal" tax rate. If you want to know how much tax you will pay on that next dollar of income, you use your marginal tax rate. It is the highest rate of tax you pay. In the same way, you use the marginal tax rate to find out how much a tax deduction saves you. In our example above, a $100 deduction would save you $28. Your top tax bracket (your marginal tax rate) was 28%. The deduction would come out of your 28% bracket.

Filing Status Matters

Your filing status has a big impact on your tax return. There is a different tax rate schedule for each filing status. Choosing the right filing status can make a big difference in your tax return. Your filing status choices are:

➤ Single
➤ Married filing jointly
➤ Married filing separately
➤ Head of household
➤ Qualifying widow or widower

You don't have to be unmarried for an entire year to have a single filing status. If you are not married on December 31, the IRS considers you not married for the whole year. If you are getting divorced, you are considered unmarried for the whole year if the final divorce decree is obtained by the last day of the year. If a decree of separate maintenance is in effect by December 31, you are also treated as unmarried for the whole year.

Regardless of when you are married during the year, you can file as married filing jointly. You are considered married for the whole year if you are married by the last day of the year. If your spouse dies, though, you will still be treated as married for the whole year and can file jointly.

Even if you are married, you can choose to file separately from your spouse—married filing separately. Some people file separately for legal reasons. If you file separately, you won't be responsible for your spouse's taxes. Although it is a rare situation, some couples can save taxes by filing separately.

Paper Trail

Planning a year-end wedding? Some couples can save taxes by delaying nuptials until January. Other couples can save taxes by getting married in December. It's not too romantic, but run the numbers both ways to see if it makes a difference for you.

If you qualify for head of household status, your tax rate will be much lower than the single tax rates. You qualify if you meet all of the following criteria:

➤ You aren't married

➤ You pay more than half the cost of keeping up a home

➤ A relative lives with you

Your home has to be the principal home of your relative. In other words, the relative has to live with you more than half of the year. If your relative has to be away from home for a temporary absence, that time away won't count against you. Temporary absences might include hospital stays or time away at school.

Even if you are married, the IRS will consider you to be unmarried if you meet some tests. By being considered unmarried, you might qualify as head of household. This is a beneficial form of tax trickery. You will be considered unmarried if you meet all of the following criteria:

➤ You don't file a joint return with your spouse

➤ You paid more than half the cost of keeping up your home for the year

➤ For the last six months of the year, your spouse did not live with you (temporary absences don't count)

➤ Your dependent child, stepchild, adopted child, or foster child lived in your home for more than half of the year

Paper Trail

You get a special break if you support a parent. If you pay more than half of your parent's expenses, you can qualify as head of household even if your parent doesn't live with you.

If your child was your dependent, but you released the dependency exemption to your spouse in writing, you will still be considered unmarried to qualify as head of household. You will also be considered unmarried if your spouse is a nonresident alien. If you don't choose to treat your spouse as a resident alien and you meet the other head of household tests, you can qualify as an unmarried head of household.

In the year that your spouse dies, you can file jointly with your late spouse. If you have a dependent child living with you, you can use the qualifying widow or widower status for two years after your spouse dies.

For example, let's say your husband dies in 1998, and you have a child living at home with you. In 1998, you can file jointly with your late husband. In 1999 and 2000, you can use the qualifying widow filing status if your child still lives with you and you have not remarried. The qualifying widow(er) tax rates will save you significant tax dollars.

Red Flag

Head of household rules are tricky. Each year, read the rules in your tax instruction booklet carefully to see if you qualify. It can be a big benefit, and you don't want to miss out.

Kiddie Tax

Some children have to pay tax at their parents' tax rate. We call this the *kiddie tax*. A child pays kiddie tax if he or she meets both of the following criteria:

➤ The child has not reached age 14 by the end of the year.

➤ He or she has unearned income of more than $1,400.

Unearned income includes interest, dividends, capital gains, and rents, to name a few examples. Essentially, any income other than the child's own wages or self-employment income is unearned income.

The first $700 of unearned income is not taxable at all. It is eliminated by the child's standard deduction. The next $700 of unearned income is taxed at the child's tax rate. Any unearned income above $1,400 is taxed at the parents' top tax rate. Form 8615 is used to calculate the kiddie tax.

Parents can, in certain situations, choose to include the child's income on their tax return. This choice might be easier than calculating the kiddie tax. You can elect this option if the following conditions are met:

➤ The child's income is from interest and dividends only.

➤ The child's gross income is more than $700 but less than $7,000.

➤ The child has not paid any estimated taxes and has had no taxes withheld from interest or dividends.

The child's dividend income might include capital gains distributions. That will not cause you to fail these requirements. Even though the dividends are taxed as capital gains, they count as dividend income. You can still elect to include the child's income on your tax return.

Determining the tax rate for your child might prove to be more complicated than you thought if kiddie tax applies. Remember that after a child reaches age 14, kiddie tax doesn't apply any more. Choosing investments that will defer taxable income until a child is age 14 might be a smart move.

Paper Trail

To complete the tax return for a child who pays kiddie tax, the parents' tax return must be completed first. If there is more than one child subject to the kiddie tax in your family, all of the children's tax returns will have to be prepared simultaneously.

Don't Forget Your State Taxes

Most states have some type of income tax. Only Alaska, Florida, Nevada, South Dakota, Texas, Washington, and Wyoming don't have a state income tax. A tax deduction might save you state taxes in addition to the federal tax savings. Each state has different tax rules, though. Some states follow the federal tax rules. Most states start with the federal rules and add their own special blend of seasonings to the mix.

For example, Indiana has a 3.4% income tax. The Indiana income tax is applied to adjusted gross income. An above-the-line deduction, such as alimony, will save Indiana state taxes of 3.4%. An itemized deduction, such as mortgage interest, will save nothing on an Indiana return.

To know the value of a deduction on your state return, you need to know the following:

➤ Can I take the deduction on my state return?

➤ What is my marginal state tax rate?

Put It All Together— What Do You Save?

To know what a deduction is worth, you will apply your marginal federal and state tax rates. Let's go through a couple of examples.

How much will an IRA contribution save? Consider the following situation to work through an example:

Your Decoder Ring

Each of us has a state of **domicile**. This is the state we call home. It is where we file our resident state tax return. Each state has domicile rules. Changing domicile from one state to another can save taxes, but the move has to be legitimate. A paper move won't work. If you have a question of domicile, check with your attorney or your CPA.

➤ Greg Charnes is single.

➤ He doesn't own his own home.

➤ He never has enough deductions to itemize.

➤ Greg is thinking about making an IRA contribution because his employer doesn't have a retirement plan.

➤ Greg's top tax rate is 28%. His state tax rate is 5%. An IRA contribution will be deductible on his state return.

A $1,000 IRA contribution will save Greg:

Federal taxes	($1,000 × 28%)	$280
State taxes	($1,000 × 5%)	50
Total savings		$330

Will a home equity loan save taxes? How much? Consider the following situation to work through as an example:

➤ Marcia and David Forston are married.

➤ They itemize their deductions.

➤ Marcia and David are planning to add on to their home and are considering a home equity loan. The interest would be deductible on their federal and state returns.

➤ Their federal tax rate is 31%.

➤ Their state rate is 4%.

➤ The home equity interest in the first year will be $3,000.

The home equity interest will save Marcia and David:

Federal taxes	($3,000 × 31%)	$930
State taxes	($3,000 × 4%)	120
Total savings		$1,050

Your state tax savings might vary from our example. It depends on your state tax rate. It also depends if your state allows you to claim a deduction or not. We have 50 states in the union and 50 different sets of tax rules.

These examples show that deductions can be of great value. Spending money just to get a deduction is seldom a wise choice, however. People who lose money just to get a tax write off are only cheating themselves.

Don't be afraid to take deductions. Each deduction that we can take is in the tax law for some reason. Charitable contributions can be taken so that charities will have the funds to provide valuable services. Home mortgage interest is deductible to encourage and support home ownership.

By the same token, take the tax laws seriously. Claiming deductions that you are not entitled to take is a serious matter. Most of us don't look too good in stripes, and going to jail for tax offenses just isn't worth the money you save.

The Least You Need to Know

➤ Deductions are your ticket to paying lower income taxes. By claiming deductions, your taxable income is reduced.

➤ There are different types of deductions. Some deductions can be taken only if you itemize. Other deductions can be taken even if you don't itemize.

➤ To know the value of a tax deduction, you need to know your tax rate.

➤ Your filing status is important. It sets your tax rate.

➤ Tax deductions might reduce your state income taxes. States vary in which deductions they allow.

➤ Spending money just to get a tax deduction is not a good strategy.

➤ Respect the tax laws, but don't be fearful of claiming deductions to which you are legally entitled.

Chapter 2

Personal Exemptions

In This Chapter

➤ Claiming others as dependents

➤ Calculating whether you support someone

➤ Determining who claims the children in a divorced couple

➤ Losing exemptions because of high income

A personal exemption is a deduction. You get one personal exemption deduction for yourself. Your spouse gets one personal exemption deduction for himself or herself.

You can also claim a deduction for each person that you support. This deduction is called an *exemption for dependents.* An exemption for a dependent is worth the same dollar amount as a personal exemption. There are tests that must be met to claim an exemption for a dependent.

In this chapter, we'll discuss when you can claim personal exemptions and exemptions for your dependents. We will use the term *personal exemption* for both types of exemptions.

In 1998, you can deduct $2,700 for each personal exemption. Every year, the exemption amount is increased by inflation. The exemption deduction can be taken even if you don't itemize. To know how much an exemption saves you, multiply your tax rate by $2,700. If you are in the 15% bracket, each exemption will save you $405 of income tax. If you are in the 28% bracket, each exemption will save $756 of income tax.

Exemptions can be valuable, but some people can't take advantage of their exemptions. People with high income can lose the benefit of their personal exemptions. Other people are not even able to claim themselves on their own return.

Making Your Claim

You can usually take a personal exemption for yourself and for your spouse. There is, however, a one person/one exemption rule. A person can't be claimed more than once.

Depending on Others

If you are single and someone else claims you as a dependent, you can't take a personal exemption for yourself. For example, let's say you are a 20-year-old college student. You have a job, but your parents provide more than half of your support. Since your parents can claim you as a dependent on their return, you can't claim a personal exemption for yourself on your own tax return.

Unfortunately, there is no personal choice. If someone else is eligible to claim you, the dependency exemption belongs to the other person. You can't choose to take your own exemption, even if the other person agrees to not claim you.

Red Flag

The IRS can match up dependency exemptions. If a person is claimed more than once, a notice will be sent to both people who claimed the exemption. Someone will have to budge.

If you are married and someone else can claim a personal exemption for you, you have two choices. You can either:

➤ File a joint return with your spouse. You can claim your own personal exemption on a joint return even if someone else qualifies to claim you. The other person will not be able to claim you then. Remember the one person/one exemption rule.

➤ File a separate return from your spouse. You won't be able to claim yourself. The other person who is eligible to claim you will take the dependency exemption.

If you file a joint return, you can always claim an exemption for your spouse. If you file separately from your spouse, chances are good that your spouse will claim himself. It is possible for you to claim your spouse on a separate return, but only if your spouse had no income for the year and your spouse could not be claimed by anyone else as a dependent.

Death and Taxes

When an unmarried person dies, a final tax return must be filed. For example, if your sister dies in 1998, her final personal tax return must be filed for 1998. The obligation to pay taxes lives longer than we do!

After you die, someone needs to take care of your final financial matters. Your will might appoint an executor or a personal representative. If you don't have a will, the court will appoint a personal representative. Your final tax return can be signed by your personal representative.

All income and deductions through the date of the death must be reported on the final tax return. A full personal exemption for the deceased can be claimed on the final tax return. So, even though the year may be shortened by the death, a full $2,700 exemption is allowed.

When a married person dies, the surviving spouse can file a joint return for the year of death. All of the surviving spouse's income and deductions for the whole year are reported on the joint tax return. The deceased spouse's income and deductions up to the date of death are reported on the joint return also. A full $2,700 personal exemption is claimed for the deceased spouse in the year of death.

For example, if your husband died January 1, 1998, you can still file a joint 1998 tax return. Only one day's income and deductions are reported for your husband on your joint tax return. You will claim a full personal exemption for your husband even though he lived only one day in 1998.

Paper Trail

Do you have a power of attorney? It is smart to appoint a power of attorney. This person can handle financial matters, including your tax return, if you become too ill to take care of them yourself. An attorney can draft a power of attorney document for you.

The income earned after death is still taxable. No such luck of a reprieve here! After you die, your assets will either go to your estate or to someone else that you name. The after-death income is reported either by your estate or your heirs.

For example, you leave a rental house to your daughter in your will. There will be a period of time after you die that your estate will not be settled. The house will then be transferred to your daughter. The rent received before death is reported on your final tax return. The rent received after death but before title passes to your daughter will be reported by your estate. Your estate will have to file a tax return. The rent received after your daughter takes title will be reported by her.

What if your wife dies in 1998 and you remarry in 1998? You can file a joint return with your new wife, but you can't claim a personal exemption for your deceased wife. Even if you provided all of the support for your late wife, you lose her dependency exemption if you remarry in the year she dies.

Divorcees

If you are divorced, you cannot claim a personal exemption for your ex-spouse. You can't take the exemption even if you provided all of the support for your ex-spouse for the whole year.

Children and Other Household Pets

A dependency exemption can be taken for people that you support. Remember that if you are eligible to claim someone, that person can't claim himself. There is no opportunity to choose who gets the exemption.

You can claim someone if you meet five tests. You must meet all of these five tests, discussed in the following sections:

1. Gross income test
2. Support test
3. Relationship or member of household test
4. Joint return test
5. Citizenship test

Your Decoder Ring

Who is **divorced** by IRS standards? When a final decree of divorce or separate maintenance is obtained, you are considered divorced. If you are divorced by the end of the year, the IRS considers you divorced for the entire year.

Gross Income Test

To claim someone as your dependent, the person must have less than $2,700 of gross income in 1998. Each year, the gross income test amount changes. The gross income test amount is the same as the personal exemption dollar amount.

Almost every tax rule has an exception. True to form, there are some dependents who don't have to pass the gross income test. Your child can have any amount of income and still be claimed by you if he or she is younger than age 19 at the end of the year. You do still have to pass the other four tests to get the exemption, though.

The gross income test also doesn't apply if your child is younger than age 24 at the end of the year and is a student. To be considered a student, your child must be enrolled full-time in school for some part of five calendar months. The months don't have to be consecutive. What is full-time enrollment? Call the school. The school can tell you how many hours must be taken to be considered full-time in their program.

These exceptions to the gross income test apply to your child, stepchild, legally adopted child, a child placed with you for legal adoption, or a foster child placed in your home the entire year. If a person doesn't qualify for a "child" exception, the gross income test must be met.

Any taxable income is counted as gross income. Some examples of gross income include the following:

➤ Interest on a checking account
➤ Dividends from stocks or mutual funds
➤ Capital gains

➤ Wages
➤ Gross business income
➤ Unemployment benefits
➤ Rent income (gross rent—do not deduct rent expenses)
➤ Scholarships for room and board
➤ Share of gross partnership income

Examples of income that doesn't count as gross income are:

➤ Tax-free municipal bond interest
➤ Social Security benefits that are tax-free
➤ Scholarships that are tax-free
➤ Sheltered workshop wages earned by a disabled person (this is a special exception)

Support Test

The support test is the most difficult of the five tests to apply. To pass this test, you must provide more than half of the person's total support for the year.

To apply the support test, you first calculate the person's total support. Second, calculate how much support you provided. Third, calculate if your contributions make up more than half of the total support? If so, you pass the support test.

This might seem easy enough, but how do you measure "total support"? How do you measure how much support you provide? How do you measure putting a roof over someone's head?

Let's start with "total support." Total support includes:

➤ Food
➤ Lodging
➤ Clothing
➤ Education
➤ Medical and dental care
➤ Recreation
➤ Transportation

Use the cost of providing food to measure total support. If you are buying food for more than one person, you should allocate the cost. For example, if your mother lives in your home with you, your husband, and two children, you will buy groceries for five people. In measuring your mother's total support, one-fifth of your grocery expenses would count toward her total support.

All other expenses, except lodging, are also measured using cost. This would include clothing, education, medical and dental expenses, recreation, and transportation expenses.

Lodging, on the other hand, is measured by the fair rental value of the living quarters. If you pay rent for the home occupied by your dependent, it is easy to measure the fair rental value. The rent that you pay is the value of the lodging.

If a dependent lives in a home or apartment that you own, ask yourself how much you could expect to receive if you rented the property out. This rental value is used in determining total support. You can add utilities and furnishings to the rental value, but you cannot add real estate taxes, insurance, mortgage payments, or appliances.

Let's go over an example using the following assumptions:

➤ Your sister lives in a home that you own.

➤ Your sister doesn't pay you rent, but the home would rent for $500 a month.

➤ Your sister pays for the utilities, which are $1,800 a year.

➤ You pay for the taxes and insurance, which are about $1,500 a year.

➤ About half of the furniture in the house is yours. Your sister owns the other half of the furniture. If you were to rent furniture for the house, it would cost about $1,800 per year.

Table 2.1 lists the household expenses for determining support.

Table 2.1   Example of Support Calculation

Item of	Provided by You	Provided by Sister	Total Support
Lodging	$6,000	0	$6,000
Furnishings	900	900	1,800
Utilities	0	1,800	1,800
Total	$6,900	$2,700	$9,600

Let's try another example. Your grandmother lives in your home with you and your son. She insists on paying $100 a month toward her lodging, but you pay all other household expenses. You live in an apartment that you rent for $500 a month unfurnished. Your monthly utility bills are $200 a month. If you were to rent furnishings, it would cost about $200 a month.

Your monthly lodging, utility, and furnishings cost is $900. One-third ($300) is included in your grandmother's total support. You contribute $200 per month ($2,400 per year) to her lodging. Your grandmother contributes $100 per month ($1,200 per year) to her own lodging.

Once you have determined a person's total support for a year, you must determine if you contributed more than half. In measuring support contributions, you must count how much a person actually spends toward support. How much a person could spend is not important.

In the example above of your sister, you provided 71.9% of her support ($6,900 divided by $9,600). You provided more than half, so you satisfy the support requirement. In the case of your grandmother, you have also met the support requirement since you provided 66.7% of her total support.

You may have to pay for someone to stay in a nursing home. Some living facilities will allow you to make a lump-sum payment in exchange for a promise to care for your relative for life. If you make this payment, you can count a portion of the lump-sum payment each year as support. To calculate the annual support you provide, divide the lump-sum payment by the life expectancy of your relative. If the life expectancy is 10 years, one-tenth of your lump-sum payment will count each year toward providing support. Paying lump sums is a gamble. If the person dies before the life expectancy has expired, you have spent support dollars that will give you no tax benefit. On the other hand, if the person lives longer than their life expectancy, you have made a good deal with the nursing home, but your support dollars for tax purposes have run out.

Paper Trail

So often people make the mistake of adding up a person's income to determine support. Remember that support is not how much you make, it's how much you spend.

If your child receives a scholarship and is a full-time student, you can't count the scholarship toward support. If the school gives a $10,000 per year scholarship, it will not count in total support for your child. Since it won't be included in total support, it is less likely to disturb your dependency exemption.

What if no person meets the support test? It is possible that nobody provided more than half the support on his own. What do you do? For example, if three adult children equally contribute to the support of their father, no one person has provided more than half of the father's support. It would appear that nobody gets the dependency exemption. There is an option, however. You can choose who gets the exemption. You can make this choice if:

➤ More than one person contributes to the support but no one person provides more than half.

➤ The other four dependency exemption tests are met.

➤ Each person who contributed more than 10% signs Form 2120 Multiple Support Declaration.

By using the Form 2120, you can choose who will be able to take the dependency exemption. Some families take turns by rotating the exemption from year to year. Other families give the exemption to the person who gets the most tax benefit.

Relationship or Member of Household Test

To claim an exemption for someone, he or she must either be related to you or be a member of your household for the entire year. The following are considered related to you:

➤ Your child

➤ Your legally adopted child

➤ Your stepchild

➤ Your grandchild, great-grandchild, and so on

➤ Your brother, sister, half-brother, half-sister, stepbrother, or stepsister

➤ Your parent, grandparent, great-grandparent (but not your foster parent)

➤ Your stepmother or stepfather

➤ Your aunt or uncle

➤ Your niece or nephew

➤ Your mother-in-law, father-in-law, son-in-law, daughter-in-law, brother-in-law, or sister-in-law

You can claim these relatives if you meet the other four dependency tests. These relatives do not have to live in your home to be claimed as your dependent. If someone is not your relative or a relative not on this list, they have to pass the member of household test.

If you are in the process of adopting a child, there will probably be a period of time that the child is living in your home, but the adoption isn't final. If the child was placed in your home by an authorized agency, you can treat the child as your relative. This means that you can claim the child even if he or she didn't live in your home the entire year. If you did not use an authorized adoption agency, the child will not pass the relationship test. To claim the child, he or she must live in your house the entire year.

If you have a foster child or a foster adult in your home, he or she will not be considered a relative. You can take the exemption for a foster child or adult only if the foster child or adult lives with you the entire year and you receive no payment from a government agency or tax-exempt placement agency for being a foster parent.

What if you support your wife's aunt? Your wife is related to her aunt, but you are not related to her. You provide the support, not your wife. The aunt doesn't live with you. If you file a joint return with your wife, it doesn't matter if you provided the support or she provided the support. If you or your wife meets the relationship test and one of you provided the support, you can claim the exemption. As a word of caution, filing jointly or separately really matters in this case. If you file separately from your wife, neither of you will qualify to claim her aunt. You will fail the relationship and member of household test, and your wife will fail the support test.

If someone is not your relative, you can still pass this dependency test if he or she is a member of your household. To be a member of your household, a person must live with you in your home for the whole year. This doesn't mean that you have to see the person 365 days of the year. If your dependent is away from home for special reasons, you can still meet the member of household test. Temporary absences for special reasons include the following:

➤ Being away at school
➤ Being in the hospital or another facility for medical treatment
➤ Being away from home on business
➤ Going on vacation
➤ Being away from home due to military service
➤ Being in a nursing home (if it is a temporary stay for medical reasons)

Paper Trail

If one of your dependents dies, you can still take the exemption in the year of death. Even if the person only lived one day of the tax year, you can take the exemption, assuming you meet all of the five tests. If a child is stillborn, you will not be able to claim an exemption for the child. However, if a child is born alive, but dies shortly after death, you can take a dependency exemption. This is true even if the child only lived for a brief moment. State or local law will determine if the child was born alive.

If your dependent died during the year, the member of household test will be met if the person lived with you until the time of death. If there is a hospital or nursing home stay before death, the person is still considered to be living with you. Even if a person spends all of the year in the hospital or medical facility for medical treatment, the test can be met. Likewise, if a child is born during the year, you can meet the member of household test if the child lived with you after birth. Time spent in a hospital will count as time spent with you.

Sorry, but pets never qualify as dependents. Our pets can require a lot of care, give a great deal of pleasure, and are very much a part of our family, but we can't claim an exemption for beings other than the human variety. (Teenagers can be questionable on this requirement, but they do count.)

Joint Return Test

If your dependent files a joint return with his or her spouse, you can not claim the dependency exemption. Even if all four other tests are met, you lose the exemption.

For example, your son, who just graduated from college, gets married in December of 1998. His new wife graduated in the spring of 1998 and is working in her new career. Your son will begin his new job in January, after the honeymoon. You supported your son (provided more than half his support) for 1998. He is a U.S. citizen. He has gross income less than $2,700 in 1998. He can file a joint return with his new wife since they were married before the end of 1998. If he chooses to file a joint return with his new wife, you cannot claim your son as a dependent. You meet four of the exemption tests, but you fail the joint return test.

There is, of course, an exception to the rule. If your son and his wife have no tax liability and are filing a joint return just to get a refund of taxes, you can still claim your son. In our example above, let's say that the new wife is also graduating in December. She had less than $2,700 of income in 1998. The new couple isn't required to file a tax return. They will have no income tax in 1998, but there were taxes withheld from your son's pay for his summer job. Your son can file a joint return with his new wife to get his withholding refunded to him. Since there is no income tax liability for 1998, you can still claim your son.

Citizenship Test

To claim a person as your dependent, the person must meet one of the following requirements:

➤ He/she is a U.S. citizen

➤ He/she is a U.S. resident

➤ He/she is a resident of Canada

➤ He/she is a resident of Mexico

What if you have legally adopted a child who is not a U.S. citizen? First, you must meet the other four tests (gross income, support, member of household, and joint return). Second, your home must have been the child's main home for the entire year. If these requirements are met, you can claim the child.

Your natural child might have been born outside the United States or might be living outside the United States. If you were a U.S. citizen when your child was born, chances are likely that your child is also a U.S. citizen. Even if your child lives outside the United States, Canada, or Mexico, the citizenship test will still be met if your child is a U.S. citizen. If you meet the other tests (support, gross income, and joint return), you will be able to claim your child as a dependent.

Foreign exchange students are usually not U.S. citizens. If you have a foreign exchange student in your home, you will most likely not meet the citizenship test. There is a charitable contribution deduction that you might be able to claim, though. Check this out in the charitable contributions chapter.

Divorced Parents

Dependency exemptions for children of divorced parents can be a source of bitter dispute. Even if the parents are cooperative, determining who gets the exemption can still be a challenge. For the divorced parent rules to apply, the parents must be either divorced or legally separated. The parents must also have provided more than half of the children's support. If someone other than the parents provided the children's support, neither parent will be able to claim the children. The general rule is that the custodial parent will get the dependency exemptions for the children. Even if the noncustodial parent provided more than half of the children's support, the custodial parent will get the first shot at the exemptions.

It can be a challenge to determine who has custody. Let's review a couple of examples.

Mandy and Nathan were divorced in 1997. Under the divorce decree, the children live with Nathan nine months of the year, and they live with Mandy three months of the year. Nathan is eligible to claim the children since he is the custodial parent. Even if Mandy provided more support than Nathan, he has the first shot at the exemptions.

During 1998, Pamela Folz shared custody of her children with her ex-husband. The children spent half of their time with Pamela and half of their time with their father. In November, Pamela was granted full custody under a new custody decree. For the last two months, the children lived with Pamela full-time. Since Pamela had custody more than half of the year, she is considered to have provided more than half of the children's support. She will be able to claim the children on her tax return.

Paper Trail

If you are in the U.S. military, your children might have been born outside the United States. The children might also be living outside the United States. The children's other parent might not be a U.S. citizen. As long as the children are U.S. citizens, they will meet the citizenship test.

Your Decoder Ring

Who is the **custodial parent**? The parent with whom the child lives for more than half the year is the custodial parent. Often, custody arrangements provide for sharing time with the child. You must determine who has the child in his or her home for more than half of the year. This person is the custodial parent for tax purposes.

There are situations where the custodial parent may get less tax benefits for claiming the children than the noncustodial parent. There is a remedy available.

A custodial parent can give up the right to claim the exemptions for the children. By signing a release, the custodial parent can grant the exemptions to the noncustodial parent. How do you do this? You complete a Form 8332, Release of Claim to Exemption for Child of Divorced or Separated Parents. You can also sign a written declaration that releases the exemption, but using the form is a much safer approach.

The custodial parent can release the exemptions for one year, for a fixed number of years, or for all future years. How should it be done? It depends on the circumstances. If you are the custodial parent, you might not want to give up the exemptions for all future years. If you are the noncustodial parent, you will want the release signed for all future years. Otherwise, you have to get your ex-spouse's signature every year on a new form. These are not easy situations if there is any bitterness between the parents.

The Form 8332 or the signed declaration must be attached to the noncustodial parent's tax return. If the exemption is released for one year, the original signed form or statement must be attached to your return. If the exemption is released for more than one year, the original is attached the first year. A copy can be attached in later years.

Red Flag

On your tax return, you have to disclose if your children live with you or not. This is the IRS's cue to check for a Form 8332. This is one case in which following the IRS instructions *exactly* can avoid hassle. Using Form 8332 is a safer bet than drafting your own statement. Making sure the form is completed and signed properly is essential. Making a mistake on the form can cost you the exemption.

There are two exceptions to the "custodial parent gets the exemption" rule. As discussed in the following sections, these depend upon when the divorce was finalized.

Divorces After 1984

You don't have to be the custodial parent if you meet the following tests:

➤ You were divorced or separated after 1984.

➤ Your divorce decree or separation agreement states that you can claim the exemptions for the children.

➤ There are no conditions that you have to meet to claim the children. For example, if you are given the right to the exemptions only if you pay child support, you fail the test.

If you claim your children under a post-1984 agreement, attach a copy of your divorce decree or separation agreement to your tax return. Highlighting the paragraph that gives you the exemptions won't hurt. Remember that the people reviewing your tax return at the IRS can't read your mind. It pays to make your tax return as thorough and easy to follow as possible.

Divorces Before 1985

If you were divorced or separated before 1985 and you still have dependent children living with you, the old rules still apply. Under the old rules, the noncustodial parent would get the dependency exemption for the children if the following is true:

➤ The decree or agreement states that the noncustodial parent is entitled to the exemption.

➤ The noncustodial parent provides at least $600 for the child's support during the year.

For example, Suzanne and Todd were divorced in 1984. They had an infant daughter at the time of their divorce. The daughter is now 14 years old and lives with Suzanne. Suzanne provides more than half of her daughter's support. The divorce decree states that Todd is unconditionally entitled to the dependency exemption for his daughter. If Todd pays at least $600 in 1998 for his daughter's support, he can claim the dependency exemption. If Todd doesn't provide at least $600 of support in 1998, he loses the right to claim the exemption. Suzanne can then claim her daughter.

The noncustodial parent can satisfy the $600 per year support rule by either paying for support items directly or by paying child support to the custodial parent. Even if the custodial parent chooses not to use the child support payments for the child, the payments are treated as if they were used to support the child.

What if payments are in arrears? Let's say that you didn't make your support payments in 1997. You can't claim your child in 1997 because you didn't satisfy the $600 support rule. If you pay your 1997 child support in 1998, it won't count for 1998 support either. If you catch up for 1997 in 1998 and also pay your 1998 payments, you are back in the program and can claim your child in 1998.

Red Flag

Before you launch into a battle over exemptions for your children, evaluate if you can get any benefit from the exemptions. Some people will fight for the exemptions only to learn that their income is too high to get benefit of the exemptions. This is one time that being stubborn can needlessly cost tax dollars.

High-Income People Beware

Contrary to popular belief, there are a lot of tax benefits that high-income taxpayers cannot use. The use of personal exemptions is one of those benefits. Each year, a "threshold amount" is published by the IRS. The threshold amount is different for each filing status. If your adjusted gross income (AGI) is less than the threshold amount, you can claim your personal exemptions. If your AGI is more than the threshold amount, you can't deduct all of your personal exemptions. You have some calculating to do. The following are the threshold amounts for 1998:

Joint or Surviving Spouse	$186,800
Head of Household	$155,650
Single	$124,500
Married Filing Separately	$93,400

If your AGI is more than the threshold amount, follow the following schedule for calculating your 1998 exemption deduction.

1. Multiply your number of exemptions by $2,700 _____
2. Enter your AGI _____
3. Enter your threshold amount _____
4. Subtract line 3 from line 2 _____
5. Divide line 4 by $2,500 ($1,250 if married filing separately); if the result is not a whole number, round it up to the next whole number _____
6. Multiply line 5 by 2% (.02) _____
7. Multiply line 1 by line 6 _____
8. Subtract line 7 from line 1 _____

Your Decoder Ring

We hear a lot about **marriage penalty** these days. The threshold amounts for personal exemptions are a perfect example of a marriage penalty. If a couple is not married, they could have $249,000 of AGI and still deduct all of their personal exemptions. A married couple loses deductions at $186,800, which is $62,200 less than two single persons' limit.

The result is your deduction for exemptions. What you have done is reduce your personal exemptions by 2% for each $2,500 (or part of $2,500) by which your AGI exceeds the threshold amount. If you are married and file separately, you will reduce your exemptions by 2% for each $1,250 (or part of $1,250) by which your AGI exceeds the threshold amount.

This calculation is pretty tricky, so let's work a couple of examples.

Susan and Jim are married and file a joint return for 1998. The adjusted gross income on their joint tax return is $205,000. Susan and Jim have three children who live at home. They are entitled to five personal exemptions. Their deduction for personal exemptions is calculated as follows.

1. Number of exemptions (5) times $2,700 — $13,500.00
2. Adjusted gross income — 205,000.00
3. Threshold amount — 186,800.00
4. Subtract line 3 from line 2 — 18,200.00
5. Divide line 4 by $2,500 and round up to the next whole number — 8.00
6. Multiply line 5 by 2% (.02) — 0.16
7. Multiply line 1 by line 6 — 2,160.00
8. Subtract line 7 from line 1 — 11,340.00

Betty is married, but files separately from her husband. Her 1998 AGI is $150,000. The deduction for her personal exemption is calculated below.

1.	Number of exemptions (1) times $2,700	$2,700.00
2.	Adjusted gross income	150,000.00
3.	Threshold amount	93,400.00
4.	Subtract line 3 from line 2	56,600.00
5.	Divide line 4 by $1,250 and round up to the next whole number	46.00
6.	Multiply line 5 by 2% (.02)	0.92
7.	Multiply line 1 by line 6	2,484.00
8.	Subtract line 7 from line 1	216.00

Social Security Numbers for Dependents

You and all those you claim as dependents must have Social Security numbers in order to claim a dependency exemption. To get a Social Security number, file Form SS-5 with the Social Security Administration. It will take a couple of weeks to get the number. If you don't have it by April 15, file an extension (Form 4868) for your tax return. Do not file your tax return without the Social Security numbers.

If you had a child that was born alive but died in 1998, attach a copy of the child's birth certificate to your return. Also, enter "DIED" in the place on your Form 1040 that you would enter the child's Social Security number.

If you are adopting a child, you might not know his or her Social Security number. You can file Form W-7A, Application for IRS Adoption Taxpayer Identification Number.

You might have a dependent that is not a U.S. citizen but is a resident of Mexico or Canada. If your dependent lives in Mexico, you can enter "MX" on your Form 1040 in the place that you would enter the Social Security number.

Red Flag

The Form 1040 refers to a worksheet that you can use to calculate your personal exemption amount. This is the only clue on the form that a limitation might apply. It is easy to miss the limitation, so be alert.

Red Flag

Other tax benefits can be denied without a dependent's Social Security number: Head of Household status, Child Care Credit, and Earned Income Credit to name a few. It is vital to have the Social Security number.

Likewise, if your dependent lives in Canada, you should enter "CN." This entry on your form will be adequate to claim the exemption.

Some persons, such as resident aliens, may not be eligible to get Social Security numbers. In these situations, the IRS will issue an Individual Taxpayer Identification Number (ITIN). You can get an ITIN by filing Form W-7. It will take about a month to get the ITIN from the IRS.

The Least You Need to Know

➤ A personal exemption can be claimed for you and each person you support.

➤ There are five tests you must meet to claim an exemption for your dependent. All five tests must be met.

➤ Care must be taken in divorce situations. The rules covering children of divorced parents are very specific and must be carefully followed.

➤ If you have high income, you might not be able to deduct all of your personal exemption amount.

➤ Social Security numbers are a must when claiming dependents on your tax return.

Chapter 3

Your Tax Freebee— The Standard Deduction

In This Chapter

➤ Determining who has to file income tax returns

➤ Calculating how many standard deductions you can take

➤ Figuring out who can take more than the full standard deduction

➤ Finding who can take less than the full standard deduction

Most of the time, you have to spend money to get a tax deduction. There aren't very many tax freebees. The standard deduction is an exception. You don't have to spend any amount of money on any particular expense to get a standard deduction. The amount of your standard deduction is determined by your filing status. You don't have to keep receipts or cancelled checks to support your standard deduction. It is there for the taking.

There is an alternative to the standard deduction. If your itemized deductions are more than your standard deduction, you can choose to itemize instead. Chapter 1, "The Mechanics of Your Tax Return," discusses the different types of itemized deductions that are available.

For a lot of people, the standard deduction is more than their itemized deductions. For example, if you don't own your own home, it might be difficult for you to scrape up enough deductions to itemize. If your home is paid for, you also might not be able to itemize. Don't fret. You can take the full standard deduction anyway.

On the other hand, if you have a home mortgage or large charitable donations, look into itemizing. By the time you add in your state income taxes, you just might be able to itemize. It's worth checking out.

Give Me a Break! Who Has to File?

There are some people who don't even have to file a federal income tax return. If you combine the standard deduction and personal exemption, you get a fixed amount of deductions that you can take. If your income is less than your fixed deductions, you are not required to file a tax return. The rules can be tricky, so pay close attention.

You Don't Have to File If. . .

Use Table 3.1 to see if you have to file a 1998 tax return. You can only use this table if you can't be claimed as a dependent on someone else's tax return.

Table 3.1   Filing Requirements
(If you are not someone else's dependent)

Filing Status	Age	Gross Income
Single	under 65	$6,950
	65 or older	$8,000
Head of Household	under 65	$8,950
	65 or older	$10,000
Married, Joint Return	both under 65	$12,500
	one 65 or older	$13,350
	both 65 or older	$14,200
Married, Separate Return	any age	$2,700
Qualifying Widow(er)	under 65	$9,800
	65 or older	$10,650

If your gross income is less than the amount on the table, you don't have to file a federal income tax return.

When you use this table, include any income that would be taxable on your return. For example, include wages, interest, dividends, pension income, and so on. Do not include nontaxable income such as municipal bond interest and Social Security benefits.

Even if you don't have to file a federal tax return, you might still have to file a state income tax return. Each state has its own tax rules. It would be nice if the states would get together and make the rules consistent from state to state, but that isn't likely to happen.

Even though you don't have to file a tax return, you still might choose to file. Why would you do this?

➤ To claim a refund of taxes withheld

➤ To claim a refund of taxes paid

➤ To claim your earned income credit

➤ To establish a loss that can be carried back to a prior year or over to the next year

➤ To avoid administrative problems if your state requires you to file a tax return

In a perfect world, only people who have to file would file a tax return. It wastes time and money in the IRS service centers processing unnecessary returns. Some taxpayers find themselves in a letter-writing loop if they skip a year filing a tax return, though. If your income dips below the filing level for one year, but will rebound the next year, you might want to file anyway just to stay current in the IRS computer system.

Who Else Has to File?

Even if your income is below the amounts in Table 3.1, you still might have to file an income tax return if any of the following applies to you:

➤ You have self-employment income of $400 or more

➤ You took a distribution from your IRA or retirement plan before age $59^1/_2$ and you owe a penalty

➤ You reported tips to your employer, but Social Security taxes were not withheld from the tips

➤ You have tip income that you did not report to your employer

➤ You have wages from a church that is exempt from Social Security and Medicare taxes

➤ You received advance Earned Income Credit payments from your employer

Your Decoder Ring

The IRS has a funny way of counting your **age**. If you turn age 65 on January 1, 1999, you are considered to be age 65 for 1998. Talk about an early birthday present!

Paper Trail

Social Security benefits can be taxable. If your income is low enough that you don't have to file a tax return, don't worry about Social Security benefits. If you have to file a tax return, check your tax booklet. In it is a worksheet to calculate how much of your benefits are taxable.

Paper Trail

You get a letter from the IRS. Are you going to be audited? No. The IRS sends a notice if it suspects something is wrong with your tax return. Don't assume the IRS is always right. You should respond with a letter if you think your tax return is correct.

➤ You owe tax on your Medical Savings Account

➤ You owe alternative minimum tax

➤ You have to repay a tax credit to the IRS (investment credit, low-income housing credit, electric vehicle credit, and so on)

No Breaks for Kids and Other Dependents— When Do They Have to File?

If you can be claimed as a dependent on someone else's tax return, your filing requirements can be a bit complicated. Let's try to make it simple (you're supposed to laugh on that cue!). Review Table 3.2 for the rules that affect those who can be claimed as dependents.

Table 3.2 Filing Requirements for Dependents

Married?	Age 65 or Blind?	You Must File If You Have
No	No	Any unearned income and total income of more than $700.
No	No	No unearned income and earned income more than $4,250.
No	Yes	Earned income more than $5,300. If both age 65 or older and blind, have earned income more than $6,350.
No	Yes	Unearned income more than $1,750. If both age 65 or older and blind, have unearned income of more than $2,800.
Yes	No	Income of at least $5, you file a separate return, and your spouse itemizes.
Yes	No	Earned income more than $3,550 and no unearned income.
Yes	No	Any unearned income and your total income of more than $700.
Yes	Yes	Income of at least $5, you file a separate return, and your spouse itemizes.
Yes	Yes	Earned income of more than $4,400. If both age 65 or older and blind, have earned income of more than $5,250.
Yes	Yes	Unearned income of more than $1,550. If both age 65 or older and blind, have unearned income if more than $2,400.

Now, isn't that an easy table? I don't think so! This is one of the many provisions in our tax system that could use some serious simplifying. It just is not easy to tell if you have to file a tax return if you can be claimed as someone's dependent.

We will talk about a dependent's standard deduction later in this chapter. By then, this chart should be clear as a bell. If you still have doubts, be on the safe side and fill out a tax return. If you have any income tax calculated on your return, you have to file.

Your Standard Deduction

Let's say you have to file a tax return. This isn't a stretch of the imagination for most of us. You are deciding if you should itemize or not. To do this, you have to know the amount of your standard deduction.

So, How Much Is Your Standard Deduction?

Your standard deduction depends on your filing status. The following are the standard deductions for each filing status in 1998:

➤ $4,250 if you are single

➤ $7,100 if you are married and file jointly

➤ $7,100 if you are a qualifying widow or widower

➤ $6,250 if you are head of household

➤ $3,550 if you are married and file separately

Your Decoder Ring

There is no reason to dread the **long form**. What is it? It is the Form 1040. You use it if you itemize your deductions. Your other options are the 1040A and 1040EZ.

You might have noticed that marriage penalty again. Two single people have total standard deductions of $8,500. A married couple can take a $7,100 deduction. The married couple has $1,400 lower standard deduction than two single people.

You also might have noticed how favorable the head of household standard deduction is. Compared to a single taxpayer, a head of household can deduct a full $2,000 more. Don't miss the head of household status. If you qualify, it can really cut your tax bill.

Every year, the standard deductions are changed. The deductions are increased by a cost of living factor. Every now and then, Congress also changes the standard deduction. Any time the standard deduction is increased, fewer people have to file tax returns. This is one way that our tax system ensures that low-income people don't get burdened with income taxes.

Claiming Your Standard Deduction

If you file a Form 1040, there is a line that you use to enter either your standard deduction or your itemized deductions. The standard deduction amounts are printed right on the form.

If you file a Form 1040A, there is also a line for your standard deduction. The amount of the standard deduction is printed right on that line also. It's a pretty easy step.

If you file a Form 1040EZ, the IRS has made it even easier for you. The standard deduction is built into the tax tables. You don't even see the standard deduction at all. It's in there, but you don't have to do a thing to get the benefit.

Some People Get More

Congress gives a special tax break to the elderly and the blind. This break is an increased standard deduction. You can't claim the additional standard deductions if you itemize your deductions. As you get older, your perception of age changes. What seems elderly to a 20-year-old might seem young to a 90-year-old. Fortunately, Congress tells us who gets the break for the elderly. You might not agree with their definition of elderly, though! You get an additional standard deduction if you are age 65 or older. If you turn age 65 on January 1, 1999, you are considered age 65 at the end of 1998.

You also get an additional standard deduction if you are blind. Who is blind? You can benefit from the additional standard deduction if you are totally blind or partially blind on the last day of the year. Either of the following conditions define partial blindness, as defined by the IRS:

➤ You can't see better than 20/200 in the better eye with glasses or contact lenses.

➤ Your field of vision is not more than 20 degrees.

The IRS wants you to explain why you are eligible to claim the blindness deduction. So you must do the following to get this deduction:

Paper Trail

The IRS will send you a tax form, but if you want to use a different form, that's okay. You can get forms at IRS offices, many banks, post offices, libraries, by fax, and off the Internet. The IRS fax number is (703) 368-9694. See your instruction booklet for fax instructions. The IRS web site is www.irs.ustreas.gov. You might also be able to get state tax forms over the Internet. Check your state tax booklet for your state's Internet address.

➤ Attach a statement to your return explaining that you are totally blind. You can write this statement yourself. It doesn't have to come from a doctor.

➤ If you are partially blind, you need a doctor's statement. Attach to your tax return a certified statement from your eye physician or optometrist explaining your partial blindness. You must attach a new statement to your tax return every year.

The doctor's statement must be specific, but it doesn't need a lot of detail. The statement must indicate your corrected vision in your better eye or your field of vision.

To know how much additional deduction you can get, count how many additional deductions you qualify for. You get an additional deduction if you are elderly, your spouse is elderly, you are blind, or your spouse is blind. On a joint return, you could have up to four additional standard deductions. Sorry, but you can't get the additional deductions if your dependent is blind or elderly. Only you and your spouse are eligible for these deductions.

Each additional standard deduction is worth the following amount on a 1998 tax return:

Paper Trail

Tip for the partially blind. If your eyesight is never going to improve, you don't have to get a new doctor's statement each year. Have your doctor explain in the tax statement that your condition will never improve. In future years, just attach a copy of the original statement.

Table 3.3   Additional Standard Deductions for the Blind and Elderly

Filing Status	Additional Standard Deduction
Single	$1,050
Married, filing jointly	850
Qualifying widow(er)	850
Head of household	1,050
Married, filing separately	850

Let's do a few examples. Barbara is single and over age 65.

Her 1998 basic standard deduction is $4,250. Her additional deduction for being over age 65 is $1,050. Her total standard deduction is $5,300.

Marjorie is married and files jointly with her husband, who is blind. Marjorie is age 70 and her husband is age 66. Their total standard deduction is:

Basic standard deduction	$7,100
Blindness	850
Elderly (2)	1,700
Total standard deduction	$9,650

Mandy is a head of household because she supports her elderly mother, who is blind. Mandy is age 53 and has good eyesight. Her standard deduction will be limited to her basic deduction of $6,250. She can't claim a deduction for her mother's age or blindness.

Some People Get Less

If you can be claimed as a dependent on another person's tax return, you might not be able to claim the full basic standard deduction on your own tax return. Your 1998 standard deduction is the greater of $700 or your 1998 earned income plus $250. You still get your additional deduction for being blind or elderly if you are someone else's dependent.

The "earned income plus $250" test is new for 1998. For 1997 and earlier years, the deduction was limited to just your earned income. If you are covered by the "earned income plus $250" test, you can't get more standard deduction than the table would allow for your filing status.

What is earned income? Essentially, earned income is the fruit of your labors. Earned income includes payment for your services such as wages, salaries, tips, or self-employment income. Taxable scholarships or fellowship grants can also be included in earned income (just for standard deduction purposes).

Some examples might help.

Red Flag

Watch out for the kiddie tax. If your child is under age 14 and has earned income of $1,400 or more in 1998, the unearned income is taxed at your tax rate.

Arlie, a single child, can be claimed on her parents' tax return. She had $350 of earned income in 1998. Her standard deduction is $700 when she files her own return.

Ian, a single child, can be claimed on his parents' tax return as a dependent. He had a summer job and earned $850. His standard deduction is $1,100 ($850 earned income plus $250).

Rachael is single, age 22, and can be claimed on her parents' tax return. She earns $4,100 in wages. Her standard deduction is $4,250. Her earned income plus $250 would be $4,350, but her deduction is limited to the basic standard deduction amount of $4,250 for single taxpayers.

Dorothy is single, age 72, and can be claimed on her daughter's tax return. She has a part-time job and earned $2,800 in 1998. Her standard deduction is:

Earned income plus $250	$3,050
Elderly deduction	1,050
Total standard deduction	$4,100

Some Get None

If you are in any of the following situations, you get no standard deduction:

➤ You are married, file separately from your spouse, and your spouse itemizes deductions.

➤ You have changed your annual accounting period and are filing a return for a "year" that has less than 12 months.

➤ You are a nonresident or dual-status alien. A dual-status alien is someone who is both a nonresident and a resident alien during the year.

These individuals will be forced to itemize their deductions. They are not eligible for the basic standard deduction or the additional deduction for the elderly or blind.

The short tax year rule applies to people who have chosen to use a tax year that ends at some date other than December 31. We call these "fiscal year" taxpayers. It is unusual to be a fiscal year taxpayer. The IRS doesn't even have a reliable way to manage fiscal year tax returns.

The short tax year rule does not apply to people who are born in 1998 or die in 1998. Although their tax year clearly covers less than 12 months, these taxpayers can still take their standard deduction.

Tax returns for aliens can be tricky. Get IRS Publication 519, U.S. Tax Guide for Aliens, if you need help. By the way, we haven't lost our marbles talking about Martians here! An alien is a person who is not a U.S. citizen.

Red Flag

If you file separately from your spouse because of being estranged, you might not know if your spouse itemized deductions or not. This can put you at a real disadvantage. There might be a solution for you, though. Check to see if you qualify to be treated as unmarried (see Chapter 1).

The Least You Need to Know

➤ A standard deduction is taken instead of itemizing your deductions.

➤ By combining the standard deduction and the personal exemption, some people don't have to file a tax return at all.

➤ You can get extra deductions if you are age 65 or older or blind.

➤ Your standard deduction is limited if you can be claimed as someone else's dependent.

➤ Some taxpayers can't claim a standard deduction at all.

Chapter 4

Even Better Than Deductions— Tax Credits

In This Chapter

➤ Defining a tax credit

➤ Determining which credits are available to you

➤ Discovering the new child credit and education credits

➤ Finding how credits are limited

A tax credit will reduce your taxes dollar for dollar. A credit is worth a lot more than a deduction, particularly if you are in a low tax bracket. For example, a $100 deduction will save you only $15 of tax if you are in the 15% tax bracket. That same $100 deduction would save $39.60 if you were in the 39.6% bracket. A $100 credit will save you a full $100. A credit is worth the same amount no matter what tax bracket you are in.

A lot of credits are not available to high-income people. This is Congress's way of raising money and assuring reelection. It is politically popular to give credits to low- and middle-income taxpayers, but it is not popular to give breaks to people with deep pockets.

Why do we have credits? For the most part, credits are in our tax system for social and economic reasons. The low-income housing credit, for example, creates an incentive for investors to spend their money to build housing for low-income people. If enough people take the government up on this credit, our government's responsibility to house low-income individuals will be lightened.

Refunding Credits

A credit can be either nonrefundable or refundable. Most credits are nonrefundable, meaning they can only offset your income tax. If the credit is more than your income taxes, you can't use all of your credit.

Some nonrefundable credits have a carry back or carryover feature. This lets you use the credit to get a refund of tax paid in an old tax year or use the credit to reduce taxes in a future tax year if the credit is more than this year's income tax. The foreign tax credit, for example, can be carried over to future years if you can't use it all in 1998. Other credits, such as the credit for child and dependent care expenses can't be carried back or over. If the credit is more than your income tax, you get no tax benefit from the excess amount.

Nonrefundable credits include the following:

➤ Child Tax Credit

➤ Education Tax Credits

➤ Child and Dependent Care Credit

➤ Adoption Credit

➤ Credit for the Elderly or Disabled

➤ Foreign Tax Credit

➤ Credit for Prior Year Minimum Tax

➤ Qualified Electric Vehicle Credit

➤ Rehabilitation Credit

➤ Disabled Access Credit

➤ Low-Income Housing Credit

➤ Business Energy Credits

➤ Work Opportunity Credit

➤ Welfare-to-Work Credit

➤ Research Activities Credit

A refundable credit can be more than your actual income tax. There aren't very many refundable credits, as you might suspect. Refundable credits include the following:

➤ Earned Income Credit

➤ Credit for Taxes Withheld

➤ Excess FICA Credit

➤ Credit for Estimated Tax Payments

Only one of the refundable credits, the earned income credit, is given to taxpayers as a tax benefit. The other refundable credits are merely giving credit for tax payments that have been made by you.

Personal Tax Credits

There are some credits that give you a tax break because of personal or family situations. There are other credits that relate to business activities. The personal tax credits can make a big dent in your tax return. You won't want to miss out on any of the credits that you can claim. Remember that credits save you taxes dollar-for-dollar. A dollar of credit saves you a dollar of tax.

The Child Tax Credit

Finally, after all of the political debate, parents can take a tax credit for each of their children. This political hot potato of a credit can be taken in 1998 for the first time. The credit is intended to give relief to low- and middle-income parents raising children.

The 1998 credit is $400 per child. In 1999, the credit will be $500 per child. You can take one credit for each child who meets all of the following criteria:

➤ Under age 17 at the end of the year

➤ A U.S. citizen

➤ Claimed as a dependent on your tax return

If your income is more than $110,000 on a joint return or more than $75,000 if you are single, the credit is reduced. The credit is phased out by $50 for each $1,000 of income above the threshold. The credit can't be more than your income tax, but the child credit can transform itself into a refundable credit. This presto-chango trick transforms the child tax credit into a supplemental credit, which is an add-on to the earned income credit.

Education Tax Credits

1998 is the first year for the new education credits. These credits will help taxpayers pay for higher-education expenses for themselves or their children. There are two different education credits: the HOPE scholarship credit and the lifetime learning credit. Each credit is a percent of expenses for education past high school. Tuition and fees qualify for the credit, but room, board, and books don't qualify.

You can take the education credits if you, your spouse, or your dependent is in school. If you are married, you have to file a joint return to claim an education credit.

You take the education credits in the year that you pay for your education. You can even prepay tuition and take the credit early. If you prepay, the course must start before April 1 of the following year. For example, if the new semester starts in January of 1999 and you pay the tuition in 1998, you get a credit on your 1998 tax return. If you borrow the money to pay for your education, you can take the credit when you pay for your education. You don't have to wait until you pay the loan back to get the credit.

The HOPE credit is for the first two years of education after high school. This could be the first two years of college or a vocational program. This doesn't mean that you have to go right into college after high school to get the credit. There can be a gap of years between high school and your higher education and you will still qualify for the HOPE credit.

The HOPE credit can be up to $1,500 a year. The credit is 100% of the first $1,000 of expenses plus 50% of the next $1,000 of expenses. For example, if education expenses are $1,200, your credit is $1,100 ($1,000 plus 50% of $200). If you have more than one person who qualifies for the HOPE credit, you get a credit for each person.

To claim the HOPE credit you must be enrolled for at least half of a full-time course load for one academic term during the year. Your school can tell you what a full-time course load would be.

The lifetime learning credit is 20% of education expenses up to $5,000 per year. The credit can be up to $1,000 per year. The expenses must be incurred after June 30, 1998. Starting in the year 2003, the credit can be taken on the first $10,000 of expenses. The limit is the same amount no matter how many people are enrolled in school. In other words, if you and your spouse are both in college, your credit is still limited to 20% of the first $5,000 of expenses.

This credit will help college students after their first two years of school. The lifetime learning credit will also help people who want to take classes but are not enrolled in a degree program. For example, if you want to take a class to improve your job skills, you can take the lifetime learning credit. You can't take this credit under any of the following circumstances:

➤ You take the HOPE credit on the same expenses

➤ You take a tax deduction for the education expenses (for example, if expenses are job-related)

➤ Your employer reimburses you for the education expenses

➤ You use an education IRA to pay for the expenses

➤ You cashed in U.S. Government bonds to pay for the education and you exclude the interest income from your tax return using the special exclusion for education savings bonds

To claim the lifetime learning credit, you have to take courses from an eligible institution such as a college, university, or vocational institution. If you are taking classes that lead to a degree or certificate, any of your classes will be eligible for the credit. If you are not working on a degree or certificate program, the classes must be taken to acquire or improve your job skills. Classes that relate to your hobby, for example, won't qualify.

You can't use the education credits if your adjusted gross income (AGI) is more than $50,000 on a single or head of household return or more that $100,000 on a joint return. Also, you get a reduced credit if your AGI is between $40,000 and $50,000 on a single or head of household return or between $80,000 and $100,000 on a joint return. The education credits can't be more than your income tax (nonrefundable) and any excess credit is lost. There is no carry back or carryover.

The "Daycare" Fix—Child and Dependent Care Credit

A lot of Americans would like for our government to fix the daycare system. Daycare is a big problem for many working parents. Availability and cost are difficult issues.

Our government is not likely to fix the daycare situation. But to help parents out, the government provides a tax credit for parents with kids in daycare. You can even get a credit if you pay to have a disabled adult cared for while you work.

To take the child and dependent care credit, you must have earned income. If you are married, both you and your spouse must work and you must file a joint tax return. Finally, you must "maintain a household" for a dependent under age 13 or a dependent or spouse who is either physically or mentally incapacitated.

Red Flag

If you qualify for the child credit and the education credit, be wary of the alternative minimum tax (AMT). It can sneak up on you since these credits don't work on AMT. Complete Form 6251 to know for sure.

If you are divorced, you might have custody of your kids but don't claim your kids as dependents. This can happen if you waive your right to the exemption so their noncustodial parent can claim them. You can still take the child care credit.

You can take the credit for daycare in your home, in the caretaker's home, or in a daycare center. The daycare provider can even be your relative, unless the sitter is your dependent child under age 19. Be aware that you have to tell the IRS the name, address, and identification number of your care provider. If the provider is a not-for-profit organization, you don't need the number. Only not-for-profits get the break. You can use Form W-10 to get your care provider's ID number. What if your sitter won't give you his or her number? You can't take the credit. It's that simple.

The child care credit ranges from 20% to 30% of the expenses that you pay. The credit is a percent of the lowest of the following items:

Paper Trail

Your mom watches your kids in her house. Should you pay her? You get a tax credit, but Mom might have to pay income tax. If she is low–income, income taxes might not be a concern, but self-employment tax has to be anticipated. Do some math to see if you can save some tax dollars.

➤ Your earned income
➤ Your spouse's earned income
➤ The care expenses that you paid

For example, your spouse earns $40,000 a year and you make $3,000 working part-time. Your child care expenses are $3,100 a year. Only the first $3,000 qualifies for the credit.

If one spouse is disabled or a full-time student, you can count $200 a month as a fictional earned income. For example, your spouse earns $40,000 a year and you have gone back to school. You pay a sitter to watch your child while you are at school. The first $2,400 of daycare expenses qualify for the credit ($200 per month). If you have more than one child, up to $400 a month is deemed as earned income for taking the credit.

But let's say you want to take the child care credit because you pay a sitter while you do volunteer work. The earned income limit will nix your plans if you don't work outside the home. You can't even take a charitable contribution deduction for the sitting expenses.

School expenses count for the credit if your child is not yet in the first grade. If your child is in nursery school or kindergarten, the entire cost of the program qualifies for the child care credit. If a child is in the first grade or higher, your school expenses might cover both the school day and time before and/or after school. The extra fees you pay for before-school or after-school daycare qualifies for the credit. Your school should be able to help you with the allocation.

How much child and dependent care credit can you take? You can take the credit on up to $2,400 of daycare expenses if you have one person that you pay daycare expenses for. You can take the credit on $4,800 of daycare expenses if you have more than one qualifying person. Form 2441 (Child and Dependent Care Expenses) will walk you through the calculations and limits.

You can't take the credit on expenses that are reimbursed under a child and dependent care plan offered by your employer. Even if the payments are funded by your own contributions through a cafeteria plan, you can't take the credit. It might be worthwhile to give up the credit to use a cafeteria plan to pay for child care. The cafeteria plan saves income tax, FICA tax, Medicare tax, and maybe even state taxes. The taxes you save might be more than the credit you give up.

The credit rate depends on your income. Table 4.1 gives the credit rates.

Table 4.1   Child and Dependent Care Credit Rate

AGI Over	But Not Over	Rate of Credit
$0	$10,000	30%
10,000	12,000	29%
12,000	14,000	28%
14,000	16,000	27%
16,000	18,000	26%
18,000	20,000	25%
20,000	22,000	24%
22,000	24,000	23%
24,000	26,000	22%
26,000	28,000	21%
28,000	No limit	20%

For example, Mark is a single parent with a child under age 13 in daycare. Mark earns $22,000 a year and has no income other than his wages. His child care credit is 24% of his daycare expenses. Mark's maximum credit is $576 (24% of $2,400) since he has one child.

The child and dependent care credit can't be more than your income tax. There is no carryover or carry back. If the credit is more than your income tax, you lose the excess.

Adoption Credit

If you adopt a child, Congress wants to give you a tax break. The adoption credit, which was new in 1997, helps cover adoption costs. The credit is pretty easy. If you qualify, you get a full credit for your adoption expenses. The credit is dollar for dollar. In other words, if you spend $2,000 on adoption expenses, you get a $2,000 credit. To take the credit, the adopted child must be under age 18 or physically or mentally unable to care for himself or herself.

The adoption credit can be up to $5,000. If you adopt a "special needs" child, the credit can be up to $6,000. You can use legal fees, agency fees, traveling expenses, and court costs for the credit. You can't take the credit for any of the following items:

Your Decoder Ring

What is a **cafeteria plan**? It has nothing to do with lunch lines. It is a program that your employer offers to give you a choice of benefits. The benefits might be health insurance, medical reimbursement, or child care reimbursement. Your employer might pay for the benefits or you can use your own money. Any money put in the plan is tax-free. It's a good deal for everyone except the IRS!

➤ Surrogate parenting programs

➤ Adopting your spouse's child

➤ Expenses that are reimbursed by your employer

➤ Expenses that are reimbursed by a government program

➤ Expenses for illegal adoption programs

This credit is phased out if your income (modified adjusted gross income) is more than $75,000. At $115,000, the credit is fully phased out. The credit is nonrefundable, so it can't be more than your income taxes. If you can't use all of the credit, you can carry it over for five years. To claim the adoption credit, use Form 8839.

Credit for the Elderly or Disabled

Some retirees and disabled people don't get a lot of Social Security benefits. The credit for the elderly or disabled was created to help them out. Because of that, you only get the credit if you meet the following criteria:

➤ You are age 65 or older or you are under age 65 and are retired with a total and permanent disability

➤ Your income is less than certain amounts

➤ You are a U.S. citizen or resident

The credit can be as much as $1,125, which is 15% of $7,500 of qualifying income. Schedule R Credit for the Elderly or the Disabled is used to calculate the credit. The credit is nonrefundable, so it can't be more than your income tax. Any credit amount larger than your tax is wasted. The unused credit cannot be carried back or carried forward.

Foreign Tax Credit

If you earn money outside the United States, you might have to pay income tax to another country. For example, if you own stock in a Swedish company, Swedish income tax will be withheld from your dividend payments.

To avoid paying tax to two countries on the same income, a foreign tax credit can be taken. The credit is taken on your U.S. tax return and is the lesser of the foreign tax you paid or the U.S. tax you paid on the foreign income. The foreign tax credit is calculated on Form 1116. The credit can't be more than your income tax, but the extra amount can be carried over for five years.

Credit for Prior Year Minimum Tax

The alternative minimum tax (AMT) is designed to prevent us from using tax breaks to reduce our taxes too much. The AMT is Congress's response to our cries for not letting high-income people get so many tax benefits that they pay no income tax. Guess what's happened? The days of tax shelters for high-income people are gone, but the AMT applies to more people every year. The AMT is acting as a flat tax would.

There are some obvious situations that cause you to be subject to AMT, for example, if you have large deductions for accelerated depreciation. There are more subtle situations that can sneak up on people, though. Look into AMT if you have any of the following tax deductions or credits:

➤ Child tax credit

➤ Education credits

➤ Employee business expenses (or other significant miscellaneous itemized deductions)

➤ State income taxes paid in a high tax rate state

You start with your regular taxable income and start taking away certain deductions. For example, home mortgage interest for buying your home is deductible for AMT, but home equity loan interest is not deductible for AMT. After the adjustments are all done, you apply an AMT rate. If the AMT is higher than your regular income tax, you pay the AMT. If regular tax is higher, you pay only your regular income tax.

Some AMT adjustments don't deny deductions altogether, but they are slowed down. When this happens, you can pay AMT one year and regular tax after that. You might never get the benefit of your deduction. This just isn't fair, so we now get a credit. If you have to pay AMT because of a timing difference between regular tax and AMT, you can take a credit in future years. If you think the credit might apply to you, get Form 8801, Credit for Prior Year Minimum Tax. The form will take you through the calculations.

A Credit for Working Men and Women— The Earned Income Credit

Most of our tax system is "progressive." In other words, high-income people pay higher taxes than low-income people. The progressive tax system is popular. Most Americans support the notion that people who work, but don't make big salaries,

Red Flag

Do you think that AMT might apply to you? If so, it's probably time for you to get some professional tax help. AMT is not for the tax novice.

shouldn't pay income taxes. The earned income credit helps these people by slicing their tax bill.

If our system is progressive, why do we need a credit for people who don't have a high income? The fact is that our income tax system is progressive, but our payroll taxes are not progressive. FICA tax applies to the first dollar of wages and stops at earnings of $68,400 in 1998. Since the tax is heavier on lower-income people, it is a regressive tax, which most people don't like.

How to fix this problem? A tax credit to the rescue! The earned income credit started out as a fix to the regressive FICA tax system. Since it was enacted, the earned income credit has swelled to huge proportions. Some people consider it a federal entitlement program.

The EIC—Who Is It for?

You can take the earned income credit if you meet all of the following requirements:

➤ You have earned income (no surprise)

➤ Your investment income is not more than $2,250

➤ Either you meet an age requirement or you have qualifying children

Earned income is either wages or self-employment income. It is the payment for your work. Earned income is not pension income, unemployment compensation, or Social Security benefits.

People without children at home can take the earned income credit only if they are age 25 to 64 and can't be claimed as someone else's dependent. If you have kids at home, your age doesn't matter. Your credit is also much larger with kids at home, but your kids must meet the following tests:

➤ **Relationship test.** The child must be your son, daughter, grandchild, stepchild, or foster child. A legally adopted child qualifies as your child.

➤ **Residency test.** Your child must live in your home for more than half of the year, and your home must be in the United States. If your child is temporarily away from home for school or illness, he or she is still treated as living with you. A foster child has to live in your home for the whole year to pass this test.

➤ **Age test.** Your child must be under age 19 at the end of the year. If the child is a full-time student, he or she must be under age 24 at the end of the year. If your child is totally and permanently disabled, he or she can be any age and qualify.

If you are married, you have to file jointly with your husband or wife to get the earned income credit. Filing separately disqualifies you from taking the credit.

EIC Math—How Do You Do It?

The earned income credit is a percentage of your earned income. The credit rate depends on the amount of your earned income and whether you have children or not, as illustrated in Table 4.2.

Table 4.2   1998 Earned Income Credit Rate

Number of Qualifying Children	EIC Rate	Max Earned Income	Max Credit
None	7.65%	$4,460	$341
One	34%	$6,680	$2,271
More than one	40%	$9,390	$3,756

For example, David has two children and 1998 earned income of $9,000. His credit is 40% of his earnings, or $3,600. In no event will the credit be more than $3,756. If David's income is more than $12,260 in 1998, his earned income credit will be cut back, and will be completely eliminated if he earns as much as $26,473. This is because the EIC is phased out as his income increases. If either your earned income or your modified adjusted gross income is in the phase-out range, your earned income credit is reduced, as indicated in Table 4.3.

Red Flag

You can lose your earned income credit for not having Social Security numbers for you, your spouse, or your children. Head of household filing status and child care credit can also be denied if you don't put your family's correct Social Security numbers on your tax return.

Table 4.3   EIC Phase-Out

Number of Qualifying Children	Phase-Out Begins	Phase-Out Percent	Phase-Out Ends
None	$5,570	7.65%	$10,030
One	$12,260	15.98%	$26,473
More than one	$12,260	21.06%	$30,095

If David, in our example above, had $15,000 of modified adjusted gross income, his credit would be calculated as follows:

Earnings	$15,000
Phase-out income	$12,260
Difference	$2,740
Phase-out percent	21.06%
Reduction	$577
Maximum credit	$3,756
Reduction	$577
Actual credit	$3,179

Your Decoder Ring

Phase-outs. What are they? It's the way that deductions or credits are taken away from taxpayers as their income increases. Our tax system is full of phase-outs. Why do we have them? Phase-outs increase tax revenues and protect our legislators from being accused of favoring the wealthy taxpayers.

Paper Trail

To get the earned income credit, you have to file an income tax return. You might not otherwise need to file a return, but if you don't file a tax return, you don't get the credit.

To get your modified adjusted gross income, start with your adjusted gross income on your tax return and add tax-exempt interest, nontaxable retirement, or annuity plan distributions, and 75% of your business losses. Is there an easier way to do this? Yes! There is a table in Form 1040 instructions to help you calculate your earned income credit.

Taking What You Can Get

You can get an "advanced" earned income credit. Your employer will actually increase your paycheck for your anticipated credit. You have to file a Form W-5 Earned Income Credit Advance Payment Certificate with your employer. The advanced EIC that you get will count back against your refund on your tax return. You won't get more credit, but you'll get to enjoy the money earlier.

The unique feature of the earned income credit is that the credit can be more than your income tax. It is refundable. You may have no income tax, have had no tax withheld, and still get a tax refund.

General Business Credits

There are many credits that are grouped together and called general business credits. The credits are grouped together so that a person can't combine credits to get huge tax savings. You can earn business credits if you have business activity in any of the following:

➤ A sole proprietorship
➤ An S corporation
➤ A partnership

If you own your own business and it is not a corporation or a partnership, you are a sole proprietor. You will calculate your business credits based on the activity in your business. If you are a shareholder in an S corporation or a partner in a partnership, your share of the business credits will be reported to you each year on a Schedule K-1.

Business Credits Are Limited, of Course!

Your general business credits are limited to your income tax (nonrefundable). Actually, it's not quite that easy. The general business credits can't be more than your income tax reduced by the greater of your tentative alternative minimum tax or 25% of your regular tax that exceeds $25,000.

If your 1998 general business credits are limited, you can carry back the unused credits to 1997. This is a one-year carry back period. Before 1998, there was a three-year carry back period. If your 1998 credits are not all used up in 1997, you can carry the unused credits forward for 20 years. Prior to 1998, the carryover period was 15 years.

Your Decoder Ring

An **S corporation** is one type of a corporation. An S corporation doesn't pay income tax. Instead, each shareholder picks up a share of the corporation's income and reports it on his or her tax return. Credits are "passed through" in this same method.

You don't have a choice about the carry back period. You can't choose to carry your credits forward instead of carrying them back. Use Form 1045, Application for Tentative Refund, to carry your credits back. If you wait past December 31, 1999 to carry your 1998 credits back, you will have to use a Form 1040X, Amended U.S. Individual Income Tax Return. The oldest credits are used first. By doing this, you will have less chance of having credits expire unused.

Let's look at an example. You have $5,000 credit carryover from 1996 and $2,000 from 1997. In 1998, you have $3,000 of business credits. You can use $7,000 of your general business credits in 1998. Your credits will be used as follows:

1996 credit used	$5,000
1997 credit used	$2,000
Total used in 1998	$7,000
Credit to carryover to 1999	
Remaining 1997 credit	$500
1998 credits	$3,000
Total carryover	$3,500

Red Flag

The limit on general business credits is not quite as easy as we have made it seem here. No need to fret. To calculate your limit, use Form 3800. The form will guide you through the calculation.

Rehabilitation Credit

The credit for rehabilitation expenditures was put in place to encourage people to renovate and restore old buildings. The tax incentive is intended to encourage businesses to stay in older buildings instead of abandoning them for new construction. By having businesses in old buildings, inner-city business communities are preserved and historic buildings are maintained.

The credit is not available for renovating your home. Check with your state or county, though. Some state and local governments have programs that give tax credits if you rehabilitate an old home. Some states also have tax credits for rehabilitating old commercial or industrial buildings. Your state might require that you obtain approval before renovation begins. Your local economic development office or historical society is a good place to start looking for information.

To claim the rehabilitation credit, you must "substantially rehabilitate" a qualifying building. There are two parts to this test: substantial rehabilitation and qualifying property. You have substantially rehabilitated a building if your expenses to improve the property in a 24-month period are more than the adjusted basis of the property before the rehabilitation expenses or $5,000, whichever is larger. You cannot count the cost of buying the building as a rehabilitation expense. You also cannot count the cost of adding a parking lot or enlarging the building.

For example, Nina owns an old building in which she runs her gardening shop. The building needs significant improvements. Nina paid $50,000 for the building and has taken $10,000 of depreciation. Her adjusted basis is $40,000. If her improvements are more than $40,000 and the building qualifies, she will be able to take the rehabilitation credit.

A building qualifies for the credit if the building was originally placed in service before 1936 or if it is a certified historic structure. If the building is a certified historic structure, the credit is 20% of the rehabilitation expenses. Other qualifying buildings get a 10% credit.

When you calculate depreciation on your renovated building, you have to reduce the cost basis of your building by the amount of the credit that you have taken. No double dips by taking a credit and taking depreciation, too.

Disabled Access Credit

The Americans with Disabilities Act placed responsibility on businesses to accommodate employees with disabilities. A small business might find it financially difficult to make improvements that help employees or customers who are disabled.

To help these small businesses make their facilities handicap accessible, the disabled access credit was enacted. The credit is 50% of qualified expenditures. The expenditures must be more than $250 to count. The credit is limited to $5,000.

To qualify for the credit, your business must have had gross receipts of $1 million or less in the previous year or not more than 30 employees in the previous year. If your building was placed in service after November 5, 1990, you don't qualify for the credit. Eligible expenses might include the following:

Red Flag

If you rehabilitate a building and take the rehab credit, you have to use the property for business purposes for five years. If you sell the property or convert it to personal use before five years is up, you will have to pay back part of the credit that you took.

➤ Installing ramps

➤ Lowering elevator buttons

➤ Widening doorways

➤ Adding Braille signs

➤ Installing handicap-accessible restroom fixtures

➤ Converting equipment to accommodate handicapped individuals

Low-Income Housing Credit

The low-income housing credit is an incentive to people to build affordable housing for people with low incomes. The credit is a percent of the amount invested in low-income housing. The credit can be taken for 10 years if you continue to own the property and the property continues to meet the credit requirements.

Red Flag

Be wary of products that "pay for themselves" with tax benefits. A salesman might show you the tax savings from the disabled access credit and from depreciation. The result is free equipment! It's not that easy. Your basis for depreciation is reduced by the credit. No double dips.

The credit percent changes every month and is lower for housing that is federally subsidized. The rate in January of 1998 for unsubsidized housing was 8.41%. If you invested $50,000 in a project in that month, your credit is $4,205 for 1998 and each of the nine following years.

Most people get low-income housing credits by investing in large partnerships. While many of these investments are legitimate, it is smart to exercise caution when buying limited partnership units to get tax benefits.

The units can be difficult to resell and there is no guarantee of the property's financial performance.

Paper Trail

When you invest in a limited partnership, you report a share of the partnership income, loss, and credits on your tax return. You get a Schedule K-1 from the partnership that tells you what to report. The K-1 is due on April 15. You might have to file your return at the last minute. If this bothers you, don't buy limited partnership units.

Business Energy Credits

Energy credits have been used to inspire businesses to be creative in developing and using alternative energy sources. As years have passed, most of the old energy credits have expired. We now have a 10% credit for solar and geothermal energy property.

Your state might have credits for the development or use of alternative fuel sources. These days, the state credits and subsidies are often of more value than the federal tax credits.

Work Opportunity Credit

To create an incentive for hiring disadvantaged persons, we have the work opportunity credit. A business will get this credit if it hired a target individual before June 30, 1998. A credit can be taken if you hired any of the following:

➤ Qualified ex-felon

➤ High-risk youth

➤ Food stamp recipient

➤ Veteran

➤ Summer youth employee

➤ Person who was receiving certain welfare benefits

The credit is 40% of the first $6,000 of wages paid to each eligible employee in the first year of employment. You can only take the credit on $3,000 of wages of each summer youth employee. The employee must be age 16 or 17 on the hire date and must live in an empowerment zone or an enterprise community.

Welfare-to-Work Credit

Remember President Clinton's campaign promise to "end welfare as we know it today"? No surprise the tax system is being used to promote this social and economic goal. A new nonrefundable tax credit is given to a business that hires someone who has received family assistance welfare benefits for at least 18 months.

You can't take both the work opportunity credit and the welfare-to-work credit on the same employee. The welfare-to-work credit is available for the first time in 1998 and can be used for employees hired before April 30, 1999. The credit is 35% of the first $10,000 of first year wages and 50% of the first $10,000 of second year wages.

For example, The Goody Shoppe hired an employee on June 30, 1998 and qualifies for the welfare-to-work credit. The employee makes $1,000 a month. In 1998, the credit is 35% of the $6,000 wages paid in 1998, or $2,100. In 1999, the credit is $4,400, which is calculated as follows:

➤ 35% of $4,000 (the remaining eligible first year wages), plus

➤ 50% of $6,000 (qualifying second year wages)

Paper Trail

To claim the work opportunity credit, a local agency must certify that the employee was qualified for the credit. The person must work 400 hours for you or your credit will be reduced.

For this employee, the first year wages are actually $12,000, but you can only use $10,000 for the credit. The first year wages were paid from July 1998 through June 1999. Since you used $6,000 of the first year wages in 1998, you can only use $4,000 of the remaining first year wages in 1999.

Credit for Taxes Paid

The IRS wants our money as soon as they can get it. In fact, they insist that we follow some sort of pay-as-you-go program. You might have taxes withheld from your pay. You might pay estimated taxes. When you file your tax return, you will take credit for any of these payments that you made through the year.

Withholding

Most employees have income taxes withheld from their pay. The IRS leaves us little room for choice on the matter. When you file your tax return, you get full credit for the taxes that were withheld. You must attach your Form W-2 to support the tax withholding amount.

You might also have taxes withheld from dividend or interest payments. If the company that pays dividends or interest to you doesn't have your correct Social Security number they will be required to withhold taxes. Your withholding will be shown on your Form 1099. Credit can, of course, be taken on your tax return for the taxes withheld.

Excess FICA Credit

Your Social Security taxes have two parts: FICA taxes are 6.2% of your wages and Medicare taxes are 1.45% of your wages. Although you have to pay Medicare tax on all of your wages, you only have to pay FICA taxes on the first $68,400 of wages or self-employment income in 1998.

If you changed jobs during 1998 or if you worked for more than one company, you could have had too much FICA withheld. Your FICA tax responsibility ends once you have had $4,240.80 withheld from your pay. Each of your employers doesn't have any choice but to withhold the full FICA amount. You will get the excess withholding amount back on your tax return, though.

Estimated Tax Payments

Some people have to pay their taxes by making quarterly payments to the IRS. These are known as estimated tax payments. There are penalties if you pay too little in estimated taxes. There are some exceptions to the penalties, though. Thumb through the Form 2210 instructions for more information.

If you have made estimated tax payments, you get a credit for the taxes paid on your tax return. If you paid too much, you'll get a refund, but the IRS won't pay you any interest. Not fair? It's the way it is.

The Least You Need to Know

➤ A credit reduces your taxes dollar for dollar.

➤ There is a laundry list of credits that you might be able to use.

➤ There are new credits in 1998: the Child Tax Credit and Education Tax Credits.

➤ Most credits have limits, and some can't be used at all by those with higher incomes.

➤ Most credits can't be more than your actual taxes, but some can be used to reduce other years' taxes.

Chapter 5

Pay Yourself First and Lower Your Taxes

In This Chapter

➤ Using 401(k) plans to defer taxes

➤ Working through a cafeteria plan

➤ Discovering how medical and child care reimbursement plans work

➤ Exploring IRA payroll deduction plans

Your paycheck is chopped down every payday by taxes and benefits. Taxes have to be withheld from each pay check—no options here. You can, however, change the amount of your tax withholdings by filing a new Form W-4, Employee's Withholding Allowance Certificate.

If you hate to owe money with your tax return, you should be sure that enough tax is withheld to avoid having a balance due. If you want to avoid a big refund, you might need to reduce your withholding. Use the Form W-4 to figure out how many withholding allowances you should claim. The more allowances you claim, the smaller your tax withholding will be.

You can have money withheld from your pay voluntarily to cover expenses other than taxes. Some of these withholdings can save income taxes. Even though your paycheck is already sliced and diced by withholdings, it's worth considering these tax-saving payroll deductions.

It's a scientifically proven fact (well, maybe not scientifically proven, but well-known) that we don't miss that which we never have. Taxes are a much softer blow when they are held out in small installments from each paycheck. The same is true with other payroll deductions.

The Retirement Plan for the '90s— The 401(k) Plan

Although they have been around for decades, 401(k) plans came to full maturity in the '90s. What used to be a benefit available to employees of large corporations is now available to employees of even the smallest companies.

The allure of 401(k) plans is striking. Employers like them because they encourage employees to save for their own retirement. Employees like the tax savings, and they love the chance to choose how their retirement funds are invested.

What Is a 401(k) Plan?

Simply put, a 401(k) plan is one type of retirement plan. The tax code refers to these plans as "cash or deferred" accounts. This means that employees can choose between getting cash now or putting the funds in a separate account that they can't touch for many years. Ordinarily, if you can get your hands on money, but say "no thanks, I'll take it later," you have to pay tax on the money anyway. This is called constructive receipt.

Your Decoder Ring

What does **401(k)** stand for? The Internal Revenue Code holds our federal tax laws. The Code has sections that are numbered and subsections that are lettered. So, 401(k) is subsection k of section 401 of the Internal Revenue Code. There is order to the Internal Revenue Code, even though there might not always be logic.

For example, let's say that you are due a paycheck in late December of 1998. Your employer writes the check and tells you that you can pick it up, but you decide to wait until January of 1999 to pick up the check. Ordinarily, you pay tax on wages in the year that you receive the pay, so you might have thought you were clever and pushed the taxes back to another year. Not so quick! Since you could have gotten your paycheck in 1998, but chose to wait until 1999, the IRS will still make you pay tax on the wages in 1998.

Section 401(k) makes an exception to the constructive receipt rule if you take your pay and put it in a certain type of retirement account. The money you put away is still yours, but you have chosen to defer (temporarily divert) it into a retirement account that you can't reach for possibly many years.

Your funds are invested, and you get another tax benefit. Your account earnings are tax-deferred. This means that you don't have to pay income taxes now on your retirement fund's interest, dividends, or capital gains. When you withdraw your funds, you'll pay income taxes on your contributions and all the earnings that have built up in your account. So, with a 401(k) plan, you can accomplish the following:

➤ Take part of your pay and set it aside into a retirement fund.

➤ Defer paying income taxes on the money going into the account.

➤ Defer paying taxes on the account's earnings.

Paper Trail

When can you get funds out of your 401(k) plan? On death, disability, or retirement you can get your funds. If you leave the company, you can get your funds out of the plan. Some plans allow loans or hardship withdrawals. If you take a distribution before age 59$^{1}/_{2}$, you could pay a penalty. Taking funds out of your plan takes some planning.

In exchange for these tax benefits, your employer has to run through a fairly elaborate set of hoops. There are a lot of rules and regulations that have to be followed. In the last couple of years, the rules were simplified to help out small businesses.

The following are three different ways that money can be added to your 401(k) fund:

➤ You put funds in—called elective deferrals.

➤ Your employer matches your contributions to the account.

➤ Your employer can put an additional voluntary contribution in the account— often called a profit sharing contribution.

Now you have money flowing into your account on a regular basis. The funds need to be invested. This is the feature of 401(k) plans that many employees love.

Your plan might allow you to direct your account's investments. Usually, you can choose from a group of mutual funds. Some plans will let you change your investment selection once a year. Some can change once a quarter, and others will let you change your investment options at will.

With the advances in technology, some 401(k) participants can call a phone number to check their account value any time of day and make any changes in the investment mix that they wish to make. This system gives a real sense of control to the participant.

The bottom line is that most people like to have a say in how their retirement funds are invested. The 401(k) plan is most likely going to give that option to you.

What Can You Save?

You will get information each year from your employer telling you what your 401(k) deferral options are. You can instruct your employer to defer a percent of your pay or a fixed dollar amount into the plan. This election has to be done before the new year begins.

For example, your plan might allow you to defer up to 10% of your pay. If you make $40,000 a year, you could defer up to $4,000. You could fill out your forms telling your

employer to defer $4,000 into the plan. Instead, you
might tell your employer to defer 10% of your pay. At
the first glance, it seems like the same instruction, but
it might not be. If you get a bonus or get a raise, you
would be able to defer 10% of the increased pay if
you asked to have 10% deferred into the plan rather
than setting a fixed dollar amount.

There is a limit to how much you can defer. Your
elective deferrals can't be more than $10,000 in 1998.
This limit is increased by a cost-of-living factor each
year. If you are an owner in your business, or if you
are one of the high-income employees, you can run
into other limitations. Essentially, the plan can't
allow you to make large deferrals into your plan if
your employees choose not to participate. That's why many employers use a matching
contribution. It gives employees an incentive to make contributions to the plan, so the
employer gets high plan participation. With high participation, everyone can enjoy
the 401(k) benefits.

How much will your 401(k) contribution save you? It depends on your tax rate. You
will save federal income tax, but not payroll taxes. You might also save state and local
income taxes. Let's do an example.

Cindy is in the 28% tax bracket. She defers $5,000 into her 401(k) plan. Her state and
local income taxes are 5%. Cindy's tax savings from her $5,000 401(k) contribution is:

Federal tax ($5,000 @ 28%)	$1,400
State and local tax ($5,000 @ 5%)	250
Total tax savings	$1,650

So, Cindy has saved $1,650 of taxes and still has her $5,000 in her retirement account.
If Cindy is in the 39.6% tax bracket, her savings would be:

Federal ($5,000 @ 39.6%)	$1,980
State and local ($5,000 @ 5%)	250
Total tax savings	$2,230

Once Cindy starts her 401(k) deferrals, her paycheck will be reduced by her contribution. If she is paid weekly, her $5,000 contribution would cause a $96.15 weekly
payroll deduction. Her paycheck will not go down by the whole $96.15, though. How
can that be? Her federal and state tax withholding will be reduced because of her
401(k) contribution. If her federal and state taxes are 33% combined, her withholding
could go down by $31.73. Her net paycheck would be reduced by $64.42.

Should You Use 401(k)?

If you are trying to decide whether you will make a 401(k) contribution or not, you should consider several factors, such as the following:

➤ Will your employer match your contribution?

➤ Do you need a retirement fund?

➤ Can you afford to have your pay reduced?

Will your employer match contributions to your 401(k)? If so, you have a strong case for making your own contribution. If your employer match is 50%, you could turn a $1,000 deferral into $1,500 immediately. That's an impressive rate of return. Some employer matches sound complicated. The match might be "50% of employee deferrals up to 6%." What does this mean? It means that your employer will add 50¢ to your account for every dollar that you contribute. The employer will stop its matching contribution once your contributions are 6% of your pay. So, the maximum employer match in this example is 3%.

Cindy is deferring $5,000 a year to her plan. Her salary is $100,000 a year, so she is contributing 5%. Her employer matches 50% up to 6%. Her employer will match her contribution with $2,500. Instead of having $5,000 going into her account, she now has $7,500 added to her account.

If Cindy had contributed just $1,000 more each year, she would have gotten the maximum employer match of 3%. By not making the other $1,000 deferral, she missed out on a $500 match. Your employer's match could be different than Cindy's, but the concept is the same. Passing up on an employer match is a terrible waste of an employee benefit.

Do you need retirement savings? Who doesn't? I guess there are some lucky people who truly don't need retirement funds, but the rest of us should be saving for our own retirement. Most of us don't really know how much retirement savings we will need. It is safe to say, though, that Social Security should not be relied on as the complete source

Paper Trail

Your future tax rate can have an impact on your 401(k) decision. If you think that your retirement tax rate will be less than your tax rate is now, using a 401(k) plan is that much more compelling. Even if retirement is a short time away, you will save taxes by moving the income to a lower tax rate.

Paper Trail

The IRS has approved a new 401(k) system that makes an employee deferral automatic. Your employer can take up to 3% of your pay as a 401(k) deferral unless you say that you don't want the deferral. Since the IRS has approved these plans, we'll probably be seeing more of them. If you don't want the automatic deferral, you can elect out.

of your retirement income. The 401(k) plan offers a less painful way to start your savings program.

Remember that the younger you are when you start saving for retirement, the easier it will be. You are never too young to save for retirement. When you save at a young age, you have many years of tax-deferred earnings to make your savings grow. If you are close to retirement, you won't get as much growth in your account, but just get started. Even a late start is better than no start at all.

Can you afford it? It may seem like a pinch when you start your 401(k) contributions. In time, you will adjust and won't even miss the funds coming out of your pay. Passing up an opportunity for an employer match and for big tax savings would be a real financial mistake. You should contribute to your 401(k) as much as you possibly can. Contribute until it hurts. You will thank yourself at retirement time.

Your Investment Choices—What to Do?

You now have to make investment decisions because you have a 401(k) fund. What do you do? Where do you start? The first thing you should do is learn your investment options. Complete the following steps to learn your options:

➤ Read any material your employer has on your investment choices.

➤ Meet with your human resources representative and ask for an explanation of your investment options.

➤ Meet with the investment advisor that your employer uses for your retirement fund.

You should also brush up on investing in general. To do this, you can do the following:

➤ Attend investment seminars (remember, most seminars are designed to sell investment products, so attend more than one seminar and exercise healthy skepticism).

➤ Read—brochures, investment magazines, and books.

➤ Check out Internet web sites—most mutual fund companies have them.

➤ Hire a personal financial planner.

After you have done some homework, you will feel more confident in making your investment choices. You don't have time for this? You really can't afford to sell this decision short. How much time did you spend when you bought your last car? What about buying a bathing suit—did it take some time to get just the right one? Make some time for this important decision. After you have done your homework, follow a simple rule and diversify. This is the good old adage "don't put all of your eggs in one basket."

If you are really interested in learning more about investments, there is a good source of information you might check out. *The Complete Idiot's Guide to Making Money on*

Wall Street (Alpha Books, 1997) has lots of good information.

Who Clues the IRS in?

You know that virtually everything that happens in our tax system has to be reported. The IRS needs to know our every tax move. Your employer will take care of this for you. On your Form W-2, Wage and Tax Statement, there is a box that reports your total taxable wages. Your employer will subtract your 401(k) contribution from your taxable wages when your W-2 is completed. There is nothing special that you need to do.

You don't take a deduction for your 401(k) contribution because your W-2 wages are already reported net of your contribution.

You will notice on your W-2 that your Social Security wages will be greater than your taxable wages. Why is this? You have to pay Social Security tax on the money you put in the 401(k) plan.

Your Decoder Ring

What does **diversification** really mean? It means balancing your investments so that you won't suffer a big loss if one investment should fail. When you diversify, you get a balance between stocks and bonds and you don't concentrate your investments in one industry or one company.

401(k) Versus the New Kid on the Block, the Roth IRA

The Roth IRAs are new for 1998. These accounts are not tax-deferred, but are actually tax-free. This is a tax opportunity that we have never had before.

When you make a contribution to a Roth IRA, you can't take a tax deduction for your contribution. A distribution of your contributions will always be tax-free. Your earnings can be distributed tax-free if you held the fund in the Roth IRA for five years and you meet one of the following four criteria:

➤ You are age $59\frac{1}{2}$.

➤ Your Roth IRA is paid out after your death.

➤ You are disabled.

➤ The distribution covers "qualified first-time homebuyer expenses."

Paper Trail

If your employer makes a mistake on your W-2, you can get it corrected. A Form W-2c, Statement of Corrected Wage and Tax Amounts, can be filed by your employer. You will need to attach the Form W-2c to your tax return.

Roth IRA's can't be used by everyone. There are income limits that prevent high-income people from participating. We'll cover Roth IRA's in more detail in Chapter 23, "IRAs: Saving for Your Own Retirement."

Because of the many Roth IRA advantages, some people have questioned if they should continue to contribute for their 401(k), or if they should contribute to a Roth instead.

The good news is that you can do both. You might not be able to afford both, so you might need to choose. The following are some things to consider when making this decision:

➤ Don't pass up an employer match in a 401(k) plan.

➤ If you are really close to retirement, the 401(k) will most likely be better.

➤ If you have a long time until retirement, check out the Roth IRA.

You might decide to split your retirement funds between the 401(k) and the Roth IRA. Whatever you do, keep saving for your retirement, and don't give up your employer match. The immediate return on your investment is too valuable to leave on the table.

IRAs—They Are Not All Created Equal

IRAs are back! After slumbering in the background for many years, the new IRA options have born a renewal of interest in IRAs. Your employer might sponsor IRA programs. Some of these programs can save you tax dollars.

403(b) Contributions

Here we go with another Code section. So what is 403(b)? It is the cousin of the 401(k) that can be used by employees of not-for-profit companies. They are often called Tax Sheltered Annuities, or TSAs. Like the 401(k), you set money aside in a retirement account. You don't pay income tax on the money that you set aside, and your account grows tax-deferred.

The actual account that you have for a TSA is different than a 401(k) plan, though. A TSA account is in your name. The 401(k) funds are held by the trustee of your plan for you. A TSA is more like an IRA, but you can contribute more to it—up to $10,000 a year.

The investment vehicle for a TSA is usually an annuity product. You might have investment options in your TSA. You might be able to choose among annuity products that resemble mutual fund choices. There could be equity (stock), fixed income (bonds), and balanced (stocks and bond) investment options. Your employer should give you booklets explaining each of your investment options. Check them out and make the best selection for you.

Cafeteria Plans

Cafeteria plans are popular employee benefit programs. A cafeteria plan is nothing more than a combination of employee benefits. Each benefit could be offered as a separate employee benefit plan. Combining the benefits under the umbrella of the cafeteria plan gives the employee the opportunity to choose which benefits they want. Hence, the name cafeteria plan.

The Cafeteria Plan Recipe

To participate in your company's cafeteria plan, follow these simple steps:

1. Assemble your ingredients. Visit your human resources representative. He or she can explain your plan to you and give you the forms you need. One of the documents you will want is a Summary Plan Description.

2. Measure your needs. If you need medical reimbursement, estimate your annual out of pocket medical expenses. If you need child care, estimate what your expenses are for the year.

3. Mix it up. Fill out your election forms.

4. Start cooking. You are now saving taxes!

Your tax savings are impressive. You can save income taxes, FICA taxes, Medicare taxes, and maybe even state and local taxes on each dollar you put in your cafeteria plan.

Let's look at a simple example. Carmen can participate in her employer's cafeteria plan to pay for her family health insurance coverage and her out-of-pocket medical expenses. Combined, these benefits cost $440 a month. Carmen is in the 28% tax bracket. Her state and local taxes are 5%. Her tax savings with the cafeteria plan each month is as follows:

Red Flag

You can't participate in a cafeteria plan if you are self-employed, are a partner in your business partnership, or are an employee of an S corporation and own more than 2% of the S corporation stock.

Federal (28%)	$123.20
FICA (6.2%)	27.28
Medicare (1.45%)	6.38
State and local (5%)	22.00
Total tax savings	$178.86

The tax savings is an impressive 40.65% of the benefits chosen. For one year, the savings would be $2,146.32. Carmen would have been spending her money on health insurance and medical expenses without the cafeteria plan, but she would have been using after-tax dollars to pay her expenses. The cafeteria plan lets her change an after-tax expense to a pre-tax expense. Pretty good trick!

So far, we've only talked about the benefits to you. There is a savings for your employer, too. Every dollar of FICA or Medicare tax you pay is matched by your employer. If you use a cafeteria plan, your FICA and Medicare taxes are lowered. Your employer's match is lowered, too. The tax savings to the employer are often enough money to pay for the administration of the plan.

Paper Trail

Your employer might also put money into the cafeteria plan for you to use to buy benefits. This is not the typical way that cafeteria plans work, but it is one of the design options.

Your Decoder Ring

Does **dental insurance** figure into the cafeteria plan? Yes, dental insurance is treated just like medical insurance for cafeteria plans.

Health Insurance Premiums

Health insurance premiums are the number one benefit offered by most cafeteria plans. Some plans only offer health insurance premium payment in their cafeteria plans. In other plans, health insurance premiums are just one of the options you can choose. If your employer doesn't pay for all of your health insurance premiums (as is usually the case), the part that you have to pay can be done through the cafeteria plan. Any portion that your employer pays is usually not part of the plan.

Although medical insurance premiums are tax-deductible, your medical expenses have to be more than 7.5% of your adjusted gross income before any of them are deductible. For this reason, most working people can't deduct their medical expenses. By paying your health insurance premiums through the cafeteria plan, you can pay for every dollar of your medical premiums with pre-tax dollars. This is a good deal. I can't think of a reason why you would not want to take advantage of this employee benefit.

Disability Insurance Premiums

You might be able to buy disability insurance through your cafeteria plan. It works pretty much the same way that health insurance premiums work:

1. Your employer sponsors a group disability plan.
2. You decide to participate.
3. Your premiums are deducted from your pay.
4. Your premiums are paid with pre-tax dollars.

This isn't the end of the story for disability benefits, though. Disability plans can take one of the two following paths:

➤ If your premiums are paid with after-tax dollars, any disability benefits are tax-free.

➤ If your premiums are paid with untaxed dollars, your benefits will be taxable.

This is a real dilemma. Of course, most people don't think that they will ever really become disabled. Truth is, though, that a disability can be one of the most financially damaging experiences you and your family could ever experience.

If you are faced with a disability, you probably won't want to pay income taxes on your benefits. Carefully consider if you should use your cafeteria plan for disability insurance. However, you almost always will use a cafeteria plan for disability premiums if it is the only way that you can afford the premiums or if your employer puts the money into your cafeteria plan for you and you don't need any other benefits.

Red Flag

To pay for medical insurance through a cafeteria plan, the insurance has to be a group policy sponsored by your employer. If you have your own separate policy, you can't pay for it through the cafeteria plan. You also can't pay for a policy sponsored by your spouse's employer.

Medical Reimbursement

Medical reimbursement in a cafeteria plan is sometimes called a flex plan or a flexible spending account. The process is pretty easy, as shown in the following steps:

1. You estimate what your out-of-pocket medical bills will be for the year.
2. Divide your annual medical expenses by the number of pay periods in the year.
3. You have your employer hold that much out of your pay and put it in a reimbursement account for you.
4. As you have medical bills, you pay your doctor or dentist the part that is not covered by your insurance.
5. You submit your medical bills to your cafeteria plan for reimbursement.
6. You get a check from your medical reimbursement account for the medical expenses.

You might have noticed that it's your own money that you get back. So what are you gaining? It all comes back to you tax-free. Does this sound a bit too good to be true? Perhaps, but there are some pretty stiff rules to follow for you to get this benefit. The most demanding rule is the "use it or lose it" stipulation. This means that you will lose any money left in your account that is not used to reimburse yourself for medical expenses.

Let's say that Diane puts $100 a month into her medical reimbursement account. At the end of the year, her out-of-pocket medical expenses were only $1,000. She put $1,200 in her account and got $1,000 back. Unless she can come up with $200 more in medical bills that she overlooked, she is going to lose the $200 she put into her medical reimbursement account.

This is a pretty dramatic loss, but you can limit your potential losses by taking the following actions:

➤ Carefully project what you think your expenses will be. Don't estimate on the high side.

➤ Watch your medical spending. As you approach the end of the year and funds are not spent, accelerate a dental appointment or reschedule your doctor visit to get the expense into this year.

➤ If your circumstances have changed, you might be able to change your deferral part way through the year. This is known as a change in family status.

Under the change in family status rules, your change in your cafeteria plan contributions must be consistent with your change in status. If, for example, you adopt a child, you might need to increase your medical reimbursement and add child care reimbursement. The following are some examples of change in family status:

➤ Marriage

➤ Divorce

➤ Birth or adoption of a child

➤ Death of a family member

➤ Job change for spouse

Most medical reimbursement plans will limit how much you can defer for medical reimbursement. For example, the plan might allow each participant to defer up to $2,500 per year. The dollar limit is set by the employer sponsoring the plan.

If you can use a medical reimbursement plan, it makes a lot of sense to participate. Be careful in your estimate of next year's expenses, though.

Child and Dependent Care Reimbursement

The child and dependent care reimbursement plan works like the medical reimbursement plan. You defer money to the plan and claim it back for your child care or dependent care expenses. There is a $5,000 maximum per year limit on child care reimbursement. This limit applies to each married couple. You can't both get $5,000; you have to share it.

If you use a reimbursement plan for child care, you can't take the child or dependent care credit. You will probably get more tax savings from using the reimbursement plan instead of using the credit. Even if you are in the 15% bracket, the reimbursement plan will save more money than a 20% child care credit because you save FICA and Medicare taxes, and you might even save state and local income taxes.

Traditional IRA Payroll Deduction Plans

An employer might withhold funds from an employee's paycheck and automatically make deposits into an IRA. These programs are merely a convenience to the employee. The employee will deduct the IRA contribution on the income tax return if he or she is eligible to make a deductible contribution.

SIMPLE IRAs—Does the Name Tell the Story?

SIMPLE plans are pretty new. 1997 was the first year that they could be used. A SIMPLE plan acts somewhat like a 401(k) plan. There are elective deferrals, and matching contributions. The employer might also make other contributions to your account. Your contribution is withheld from your pay on a pre-tax basis. Your contributions can not be more than $6,000 per year to the SIMPLE IRA.

The SIMPLE plan has fewer rules than a 401(k). So the name is accurate. The trade-off is that there are also fewer plan design options. Some employers will still want a 401(k) plan so that they can fine-tune their plan rules to fit their workforce. The SIMPLE IRA contributions are all put into your own IRA. You control the investments directly with the IRA trustee. If you change jobs, the account is still yours.

Deducting Other Contributions

Your employer might help out a local charity by offering to withhold contributions from your paycheck. It's a pretty easy way to make charitable contributions, so a lot of employees participate.

If you have charitable contributions held out of your pay, you won't find the contribution on your Form W-2. This payroll deduction isn't

Paper Trail

When you open an IRA or 401(k) account, you need to complete a beneficiary designation form to say who gets your benefits when you die. If it's been a while since you set up your account, you might need to update your beneficiary designation. If you are divorced, check your beneficiary designations NOW. Your ex might be in line to get your retirement funds!

Your Decoder Ring

Have you ever heard the term **portable retirement account**? What does it mean? It is an account that is easy to take with you if you change jobs. If an account is in your name, instead of being part of a larger retirement fund, it is portable. A SIMPLE IRA meets this definition well.

reported to the IRS. If you participate, don't forget to take your charitable contribution deduction. It is easily overlooked since there is no cancelled check.

If you are a member of a labor union, you probably have union dues withheld from your paycheck. Your dues are deductible as a miscellaneous itemized deduction. You won't find your union dues on your W-2, so don't miss this deduction.

The Least You Need to Know

➤ Using payroll deductions can be a painless and tax-saving way to pay into your retirement savings account and pay for other employee benefits.

➤ A 401(k) plan contribution can be withheld from your pay to save money for your retirement and save taxes now.

➤ IRA contributions can be made with payroll deductions.

➤ A cafeteria plan is used to offer a variety of employee benefits to employees.

➤ Employee contributions to cafeteria plans are made with pre-tax dollars, turning benefits into tax savings.

Part 2
Itemized Deductions

If you can itemize your deductions, tax savings are just one tax form away. Okay, I'll admit that claiming itemized deductions isn't always a cakewalk. If you can save money by itemizing, though, do it right. To itemize, you'll move up to the long form. It's really not that big of a deal. The tax savings are worth it.

Homeowners can almost always itemize. The mortgage interest deduction opens up the opportunity to claim all kinds of itemized deductions. You won't want to miss out on deductions just because you didn't know what you could take.

Keeping records is a big deal if you can itemize. Don't let this stop you, though. Hang on to your tax records and let the savings begin.

Chapter 6

When You Need More Than an Apple a Day

In This Chapter

➤ Deducting your medical bills

➤ Determining if you can deduct others' medical bills

➤ Discovering how health insurance impacts your medical deduction

➤ Knowing which medical expenses you can deduct

➤ Knowing which medical expenses you can't deduct

Medical expenses can be deducted as part of your itemized deductions. If you don't itemize, you won't be able to deduct your medical bills. Use Schedule A for your itemized deductions, including medical expenses.

Our tax code says that we can deduct medical expenses that are for the "diagnosis, cure, mitigation, treatment, or prevention of disease, or for the purpose of affecting any structure or function of the body." This definition is pretty broad. There is a lot left to personal interpretation. And the government should know that if it gives the taxpayers room to interpret, they definitely will!

Our tax system is democracy in its full glory. Each person who challenges the system has a hand in shaping our tax rules. This process has been alive and well with medical expenses and has shaped the medical deduction into what it is today.

There are some expenses that we know for sure are deductible. There are other expenses that are not deductible, no matter how well you argue your case. And of course, there are always expenses that have not been tested yet. Since medical procedures are constantly changing, it's difficult for the tax rules to keep up. The process of keeping the tax rules in sync with the latest medical breakthroughs is terribly expensive for both taxpayers and the IRS. To slow things down, and to cut back on tax deductions, Congress has limited the deduction for medical expenses.

The limit on medical deductions has slashed the number of people who can get tax benefit from medical expenses. While in some respects, this cap simplifies our tax system, it probably isn't what taxpayers have in mind when they call for simplification. As the saying goes, though, "be careful what you ask for because you just might get it!"

If you have large medical bills, this deduction can make a huge difference on your tax return. Read on to see if it's worth your while to keep track of your medical expenses.

How Much Can I Deduct?

Before we go through which medical bills you can deduct, let's see how much of your medical expenses you really can deduct. There's no need to spend hours adding up bills that might not be deductible.

Don't give up too early, though. There might be some expenses that you didn't realize were deductible. We'll get to them later.

The Medical Floor—Do You Get Off Here?

Check out the Schedule A in Appendix A, "IRS Forms." The first set of lines on the form is for medical expenses. You enter your medical expenses and reduce them by 7.5% of your adjusted gross income (AGI).

Let's try an example. Brenda has an AGI of $55,000. She had some pretty big medical bills this year. Her out-of-pocket medical expenses are $3,500. 7.5% of her AGI is $4,125. Since her medical bills are not more than the 7.5% floor, she can't deduct any of her medical bills.

Renee has an AGI of $48,000. She also had some pretty big medical bills in 1998. Her total medical expenses were $4,200. She can only deduct $600 of her medical bills. Her deduction is calculated as follows:

Medical expenses	$4,200
7.5% of AGI	−3,600
Medical deduction	$600

When to Deduct Your Medical Expenses

You deduct a medical expense in the year that you pay the bill. This is called the cash basis. For example, Jerry has to get a hearing aid. He orders the hearing aid in November of

1998. He doesn't have to pay for the hearing aid until it arrives. Due to manufacturing delays, he doesn't get the hearing aid until January of 1999. He pays the bill in 1999. Even though Jerry ordered his hearing aid in 1998, he will take his deduction in 1999, when he pays his bill.

It would be too easy if this were the end of the story, though. We do have a couple of exceptions to this general rule. If you choose to prepay a medical bill, you can't speed up your deduction. If Jerry had voluntarily paid for his hearing aid when he ordered it in 1998, his deduction wouldn't move forward to 1998. He still has to deduct his hearing aid in 1999.

On the other hand, if you must prepay your medical expense, you can take a deduction in the year of payment. For example, if Jerry had to pay half of the cost of his hearing aid when he placed the order, he could deduct the half he paid in 1998 on his 1998 tax return. The remaining half would be deducted in 1999, when he pays the balance of the expense. If Jerry voluntarily paid for the whole bill in 1998, the half that wasn't due until 1999 can't be deducted until 1999.

If you use a credit card to pay for medical expenses, you get the deduction in the year you charge the expense. For example, Randy picks up a prescription for his daughter in December of 1998 and pays for it with his credit card. He gets his credit card statement in January of 1999 and pays his bill then. Even though Randy wrote his check to the credit card company in 1999, he can deduct the prescription as a medical expense in 1998.

Your Decoder Ring

What is a **deduction floor**? The 7.5% of AGI reduction of medical expenses is a good example of a deduction floor. No expenses up to the floor amount are deductible. Only expenses above the floor, which is 7.5% of your AGI, can be deducted. You will find a floor applied to miscellaneous itemized deductions also.

Red Flag

For alternative minimum tax (AMT), you can only deduct medical expenses that are more than 10% of your adjusted gross income. If your medical expenses are really large, work through Form 6251 to see if AMT kicks in.

There is also an exception to the cash basis rule for someone who has died. If your estate pays medical bills within one year of your death, you can deduct those medical bills on your final tax return. Your estate will have to waive its right to claim the medical expense as a deduction. If you don't have a taxable estate, it would be worthwhile to see if an income tax deduction would help.

A Tip for You

If your medical expenses run close to 7.5% of your AGI year after year, you never get the benefit of your medical deductions. If you control the timing of some of your medical bills, you might be able to get some medical deductions where previously there were none. Expenses you can control might include new eyeglasses, dental work, and prescription refills.

By clumping your deductions every other year, you might be able to go over the 7.5% floor every other year. Let's do an example. Alan's medical expenses each year are about $3,000. 7.5% of his adjusted gross income is usually about $3,200. Alan is terribly frustrated because he never gets a penny of medical deductions even though he has big medical bills. About $1,000 of his medical deductions each year are for his family's annual dental visits.

If Alan adjusts the timing of his dental appointments, he can get two visits in one year. His family usually has their dental appointments in January, which they did in 1998. Instead of scheduling the next visit in January of 1999, he could schedule them in December of 1998. They won't go back to the dentist again until January of 2000. Alan now has $4,000 of medical expenses in 1998 instead of his regular $3,000. He has picked up a tax deduction of $800 because his medical bills are $800 more than his $3,200 floor.

Paper Trail

The clumping technique also works for total itemized deductions. If your deductions are close to the standard deduction amount every year, clump your deductions every other year. In the low years, you still get your standard deductions. In the high years, you can itemize. Charitable contributions, real estate taxes, and estimated state income taxes are the easiest deductions to control.

If you have high medical bills, but are unable to deduct your medical expenses, there is one more trick you might try. See if you can improve your tax situation if you and your spouse file separately. If the spouse with the lower income has higher medical bills, you might be able to pick up some deductions by filing separately. To know for sure, try filling out your forms both ways and see which way gives you the best result.

Whose Expenses Can You Deduct?

You can deduct medical expenses for you, your spouse, and your dependents. You must pay the medical expense to get the deduction. You can also deduct medical bills for some people that you can't claim as dependents (Chapter 2, "Personal Exemptions," lists the five tests for claiming a dependent).

For claiming medical expenses, you have to meet the support test, the relationship or member of household test, and the citizenship test. You do not have to meet the gross income test or the joint return test.

For example, Steve's daughter got married in 1998 and filed a tax return with her new husband. Steve supported his daughter during 1998, and he paid all of her medical insurance and medical bills. Even though Steve can't claim his daughter as a dependent on his 1998 tax return, he can deduct her medical expenses. Steve has met the support, relationship, and citizenship tests.

As another example, Pamela pays more than half of the support for her grandfather. Pamela can't claim her grandfather on her tax return, because he has gross income of $3,500. She meets all of the dependency tests other than the gross income test. Pamela can deduct the medical bills that she pays for her grandfather even though she can't claim him as a dependent.

There is another exception to the general rule that you can only deduct medical bills for your dependents. The exception is for divorced parents. The parent who claims the kids as dependents can always deduct medical bills that he or she pays. If you are the noncustodial parent, you can claim the children's medical bills if you meet the following requirements:

➤ Your spouse claims the exemptions for the kids.

➤ You could have claimed the kids if the custodial parent had signed a waiver.

➤ You paid for the medical expenses.

If your child support payments include a factor for medical expenses, that won't give you a medical expense deduction. You will have to actually pay the medical bills yourself.

Paper Trail

Here's a tip if you support your parent and can deduct his or her medical expenses. Chances are good that your parent doesn't need the tax deduction, so you should pay the medical bills. Let your parent pay for nondeductible expenses, such as food and clothing, if he or she wants to pay some of the bills.

If you are a pet owner, you might spend as much for your pet's medical care as you would for another family member. Sorry, but you can't claim medical bills for your pets.

What If I'm Reimbursed?

You can only deduct unreimbursed medical expenses on your tax return. If a bill is paid directly by your health insurance plan, you can't deduct it, and if you pay a bill and are reimbursed in the same year, you can't deduct it. Your reimbursements might come from health insurance, dental insurance, long-term-care insurance, a medical reimbursement plan sponsored by your employer, or a cafeteria plan.

All too often, medical bills and reimbursements span more than one year. At the end of the year, you have submitted bills to the insurance company for reimbursement, but you haven't gotten your check yet. You're not even sure how much the insurance will pay back to you. What to do? In calculating your medical deduction, you don't have to anticipate what your reimbursement might be.

For example, Matt pays $1,200 in medical bills in late 1998. He files a claim with his insurance company, but does not get reimbursed before the end of 1998. He can deduct the $1,200 on his 1998 tax return. If Matt is reimbursed in 1999 for the whole $1,200, he might have to include $1,200 in his 1999 gross income. He would need to determine if he got a tax benefit from the $1,200 expense. To the extent he got a tax benefit, he has to recognize 1999 income. If Matt itemized his deductions in 1998 and was able to deduct only $400 of his medical expenses because of the 7.5% of AGI limit, he would only have to report $400 of his insurance refund as taxable income.

Your Decoder Ring

Under the **tax benefit rule**, if you receive a refund for a prior year's expense, you need to determine if you got a tax benefit in the prior year for that expense. To the extent you benefited from the expense on your tax return, you now have taxable income for the refund. You will find this rule for a lot of tax items, including state income taxes.

Stop or Go: Which Medical Bills You Can Deduct

Now we'll get down to the nitty gritty of medical expense deductions. Each of the following sections discusses deductible and nondeductible medical expenses by category. We're going to use a traffic light scale, which the following explains:

➤ *Green light.* No doubt about it, deduct full steam ahead.

➤ *Yellow light.* It's possible that you could deduct. You might have to meet some special requirements or only part of the expense might be deductible.

➤ *Red light.* No way, no how. You can't deduct.

Insurance

Green Light

Premiums paid on the following insurance policies are deductible:

➤ Medical and hospitalization insurance.

➤ The Medicare premium that is withheld from your Social Security check (check your Form 1099-SSA for the amount that you paid).

➤ If you voluntarily pay for Medicare A coverage, the premiums are deductible.

➤ Dental insurance premiums.

➤ Contact lens insurance.

Yellow Light

If you are self-employed, you might be able to split up your health insurance premiums. 45% can be taken as an adjustment in arriving at AGI. The other 55% can be taken as a medical deduction on Schedule A (itemized deductions).

A portion of your long-term-care insurance is deductible. This is insurance that will provide long-term care of a chronically ill person. The prime example is nursing home insurance. The amount that you can deduct is limited. Your deduction will depend on your age at the end of the year. For 1998, the deduction limits for long-term-care insurance are shown in Table 6.1. Each year, the long-term care insurance deduction limits are adjusted for an inflation factor.

Table 6.1   Long–Term–Care Insurance Limitation

Age	Limit
40 or less	$210
Over 40 up to 50	$380
Over 50 up to 60	$770
Over 60 up to 70	$2,050
Over 70	$2,570

Red Light

The following premiums are not deductible as medical expenses:

➤ Health insurance premiums that your employer pays for you tax-free

➤ Health insurance premiums that you pay through a cafeteria plan (they are already deducted from your wages)

➤ Disability insurance premiums

➤ The portion of your car or home insurance that covers medical expenses of injured persons

➤ Life insurance

Medical Services

Green Light

No questions asked, the following expenses are fully deductible:

➤ Visits to your doctor or dentist (even if preventative)

➤ Orthodontist fees

➤ Chiropractor fees

➤ Hospital fees, inpatient or outpatient

➤ Lab fees

Paper Trail

Shareholders in S corporations who own more than 2% of the company's stock are treated as self-employed persons for health insurance premium purposes. Your health insurance premiums should be included on your Form W-2 as wages. You then deduct your premiums like other self-employed people. You don't have to pay Social Security taxes on your health insurance benefits. If your W-2 indicates that your wages for Social Security purposes were increased, your employer may have made a mistake.

➤ Psychological or psychiatric services

➤ Physical therapy

➤ Surgery other than unnecessary cosmetic surgery

➤ Legal abortion

➤ Vasectomy and other sterilization procedures

➤ In-home nursing care for a medical condition

➤ Payroll taxes that you pay for a nurse who works in your home

➤ Nursing home (including meals and lodging) if you are in the nursing home to receive medical care for a medical condition

➤ Expenses (tuition, lodging, meals) for a special school if the primary reason for attending is to alleviate a mental or physical handicap

➤ Alcohol or drug rehabilitation programs

➤ Acupuncture

➤ Attendant to accompany a blind student to school

➤ Note taker to accompany a deaf student to school

Red Flag

If you hire the nurse to come into your home, you might have to deal with the household employee reporting requirements. If you use a nursing service, you do not have to worry about the household employee rules.

Yellow Light

Cosmetic surgery is deductible only if it is necessary surgery. What does that mean? Surgery is considered necessary if it corrects or relieves any of the following:

➤ A deformity arising from a congenital abnormality

➤ A personal injury

➤ A disfiguring disease

For example, if you are in an automobile accident and have broken your nose, surgery to correct the injury would be deductible. If you have surgery because you don't like the shape of your nose, your surgery is not deductible. If you broke your nose 15 years ago and it still bugs you that it's a bit crooked, you're in the caution zone. If your insurance company won't pay for the surgery, you'll have to do some strong convincing for the IRS to accept it.

Nursing care in your home will only be partially deductible if the caregiver also performs household chores, such as cleaning and laundry. You will need to allocate the nursing costs between medical care and household help to claim your deduction for the medical services provided.

Nursing home costs can be partially deductible if you are in the nursing home for personal care reasons. If you are unable to care for yourself at home or don't have family to care for you, but do not have a medical condition that you are being treated for, your meals and lodging in the nursing home are not deductible. Any medical or nursing care you receive in the nursing home is deductible, though.

For example, Linnie is 92 years old and unable to care for herself at home. She enters a nursing home. The medical staff is unable to identify any disease. Linnie's advanced age has caused her to become frail and unable to handle daily chores at home. Linnie's room and board at the nursing home is not deductible. Any medical care or prescription drug charges will be deductible.

Paper Trail

Be sure that you have documentation from the nursing home that supports your allocation of the nursing home costs. The nursing home will be able to give you detailed statements of all charges incurred.

Tuition for a private school might not be deductible even if attendance is motivated by a medical condition or disability. If the child attends the school to receive medical care, the school expenses are deductible. It's not always easy to tell the difference. It's important to determine if care for the medical condition is being received. Even if a physician recommends the private school, the cost still will not be deductible if care isn't given for the medical condition or handicap.

For example, Chris's daughter uses a wheelchair because of a congenital disease. The public school facilities are old and not wheelchair-accessible. Chris sends her daughter to a private school that is wheelchair-accessible on her doctor's recommendation. The doctor felt that the daughter would progress more quickly in an environment without physical barriers. Chris's daughter receives no special instruction or care because of her handicap. Even though the physician recommended the private school, the cost of the school is not deductible as a medical expense.

A program to help lose weight or stop smoking is not deductible if it is recommended by your doctor to improve your general health. A program recommended by your doctor as treatment of a specific disease is, however, deductible.

For example, if you are fighting a heart condition that is worsened by obesity, a weight-loss program prescribed by your doctor will be deductible. On the other hand, if your family has a history of heart conditions and you are overweight, your doctor might recommend a weight-loss program to prevent heart disease. This program will not be deductible because it does not treat a disease that you have.

Red Light

You cannot deduct any of the following expenses:

➤ Unnecessary cosmetic surgery such as a face lift, tummy tuck, or collagen injections
➤ Marriage counseling fees

➤ Exercise classes for general health
➤ Health club for general well-being
➤ Swimming lessons
➤ Funeral, burial, or cremation expenses
➤ Babysitting expenses while you visit your doctor

Drugs

Green Light

You can deduct any of the following expenses:

➤ Prescription drugs
➤ Birth-control pills
➤ Insulin

Red Light

You can't deduct any of the following expenses:

➤ Nonprescription drugs, even if recommended by your doctor
➤ Illegal drugs, even if prescribed
➤ Health foods
➤ Nonprescription herbal remedies
➤ Bottled water
➤ Cosmetics, even if used to mask scars
➤ Sunscreen, even if recommended by your doctor for skin cancer prevention
➤ Nonprescription contraceptives

Equipment

Green Light

You can deduct any of the following expenses:

➤ Eyeglasses and contact lenses
➤ Hearing aids
➤ Telephone equipment for the hearing impaired
➤ Crutches
➤ Braces
➤ Wheelchair
➤ Artificial limbs

➤ The cost to acquire, train, and maintain a dog or other animal to assist a blind, deaf, or disabled person

➤ Oxygen equipment and oxygen

➤ False teeth

➤ Handicap controls for your car

➤ Disposable diapers used because of disease

➤ Closed caption decoder for your television

Yellow Light

The cost of orthopedic shoes that is in excess of the cost of regular shoes is deductible as a medical expense. For example, John needs orthopedic shoes because his right leg is slightly shorter than his left leg. The shoes that he purchases ordinarily cost $55. With the prescription changes to the shoes, John has to pay $160 for his shoes. $105 of the cost of John's orthopedic shoes is deductible as a medical expense.

Red Light

You can't deduct any of the following expenses:

➤ Maternity clothes

➤ Nonprescription sunglasses

➤ Nonprescription reading glasses

➤ Baby diapers or diaper service

Travel

Green Light

You can deduct any of the following expenses:

➤ Ambulance charges

➤ Ten cents a mile for medical travel

➤ Out-of-pocket expenses to use your car for medical purposes (instead of using mileage)

➤ Air fare, taxi fare, or bus fare to seek medical care

➤ Parking fees and tolls while seeking medical care

➤ Transportation expenses for a parent accompanying a child receiving medical care

➤ Transportation expenses of travel companion for person who cannot travel alone while seeking medical care

Your Decoder Ring

Medical travel includes trips to your doctor or dentist for check-ups or treatment. You don't have to travel out of town for medical treatment to deduct your travel expense.

Yellow Light

Lodging (hotel expense, for example) while away from home to seek medical care might be deductible. The following rules must be met to deduct your lodging expense:

➤ The lodging must be essential to receiving the medical care.

➤ The medical services must be provided in a licensed medical facility or hospital.

➤ The lodging must not be lavish or extravagant.

➤ There must be no significant personal pleasure, recreation, or vacation associated with the travel away from home.

If the lodging expense meets these four tests, it is deductible, but it is limited. Only $50 per night for each person is deductible.

For example, Kim has to take her daughter out of town to a children's hospital for treatment after an injury. Kim and her daughter stay in a hotel for two nights while tests are being run. She can deduct up to $200 of lodging costs for the trip.

Red Light

You can't deduct any of the following expenses:

➤ Meals while traveling to receive medical care

➤ Parking tickets or speeding tickets, even if en route to receive medical care

➤ Transportation expenses of companion who accompanies you for moral support

➤ Travel recommended by your doctor for rest and relaxation

Improvements to Your Home

Green Light

You can deduct any of the following expenses:

➤ Expenses to make your home accessible for a physically handicapped family member. These expenses could include support railings in bathrooms, wheelchair ramps, widening doors and doorways. These expenses are fully deductible in the year paid.

➤ The cost to remove lead-based paint (see IRS Publication 502).

Yellow Light

Home improvements for medical reasons are deductible only to the extent that they don't increase the value of your home. Such costs could include installing a swimming pool, a spa, an elevator, or an air conditioning unit.

Your physician must have recommended the home improvement for alleviation of your medical condition, but that isn't enough. The value before and after the improvements has to be measured to know how much is deductible. An appraiser can help you with this measurement and documentation.

Red Flag

If you deduct home improvements as medical expenses, get ready for the IRS to come calling. Your deduction will be larger than the IRS would expect a medical deduction to be, so you might get pulled for audit. Don't be afraid, just be prepared.

For example, David has suffered a shoulder injury. The most appropriate treatment includes swimming laps twice a day. There is not a swimming pool available to David that offers lap swimming at the times of day he can exercise. David's doctor recommends that he install a lap pool in his back yard. David spends $18,000 for the pool and fencing that is required by local ordinance. In an appraiser's opinion, his home is now worth $10,000 more than it was without the pool. David can deduct $8,000 of the cost of the pool.

Red Light

You can't deduct home improvements or equipment that make things easier for you, but are not needed for treatment of a medical condition. You might, for example, find occasional hot baths soothing to your muscles. Installing a hot tub will not give you a medical expense deduction. You might need to exercise to stay physically fit, but home exercise equipment will not yield a tax deduction for you.

The Least You Need to Know

➤ Medical expenses are deductible as an itemized deduction.

➤ Medical expenses that are less than 7.5% of your adjusted gross income are not deductible.

➤ Insurance premiums, medical services, drugs, equipment, and medical transportation are all deductible if they pass IRS scrutiny.

➤ Document your medical expenses if they are large. You might have to support your deductions if you are audited.

➤ Improvements to your home for medical reasons are deductible to the extent that they don't improve the value of your home.

Chapter 7

Taxes You Can Deduct

In This Chapter

➤ Deducting state and local income taxes

➤ Using property tax deductions

➤ Discovering other taxes that you can deduct

➤ Knowing which taxes that you can't deduct

Everywhere you turn there are taxes! Your paycheck could have four or five different types of taxes withheld. You pay taxes to license your car, to own your home, and to put tags on your dog. You might even pay taxes to leave your money to your family when you die.

All levels of government impose taxes. There are income taxes, excise taxes, luxury taxes, property taxes, franchise taxes, transfer taxes, sales taxes, intangibles tax, and more. In this madness, somebody got smart and realized that it isn't fair for us to pay federal income taxes on money that we use to pay state taxes. As a result, we can deduct state and local taxes on our federal income tax return. Some states even took it on themselves to let you deduct federal income taxes on the state tax return. In these states, you don't pay state income tax on money you use to pay federal income taxes.

This isn't the end of the story. State tax deductions have been limited by regulations and slashed by tax law changes. Some state taxes, like sales tax and fuel tax, were difficult to measure. When Congress needed to increase tax revenues, these difficult-to-measure state tax deductions were eliminated.

Your taxes are deductible as an itemized deduction on Schedule A. If you own your own business, you'll pay state income taxes on your business income. It would be nice to deduct those state taxes on your business (Schedule C), but you can't. All state income taxes that you pay are itemized deductions.

To take a deduction, the tax you pay must be your own tax. You can't deduct someone else's taxes. Even if you are legally bound to pay someone else's taxes, you can't deduct them because they are not your own. If you pay your child's state income taxes, for example, you can't take them as a deduction. Only your child can deduct the taxes.

You will deduct taxes in the year you pay them. In other words, you're on a cash basis for tax deductions.

Soften the Blow: Write Off Your State Income Taxes

It is important to know something about your state's taxes. It will help you out on your income taxes. Why? Your deduction for state taxes will depend on the kind of state taxes you pay. Each state has its own tax laws, and no two states are exactly alike. Wherever you live, you should pretty much know what your state taxes are like. If you move from state to state, it can be a real challenge to keep up. If you have to file as a nonresident in a state where you don't live, you have yet more challenges. You might need help from a tax professional.

Some states don't have income taxes, such as Alaska, Florida, Nevada, South Dakota, Texas, Washington, and Wyoming. Oh, people in these states still pay taxes! They just don't pay state income taxes. If you live in one of these seven states, this section isn't for you. Check out the other parts of the chapter, though.

Any income taxes you pay to your state can be deducted on your federal tax return. You can also deduct local income taxes. Local taxes would include county and city taxes. You might be paying income taxes to a U.S. possession. Those taxes are deductible. If you pay income taxes to an Indian tribal government that is recognized by the Treasury department, you can deduct any taxes you pay to the tribal government also.

Putting the Pieces Together

Do you ever feel like doing your tax return is like working a jigsaw puzzle—except this puzzle doesn't have a picture on a box for you to follow? It doesn't have straight edges to let you know when you've reached the edge, either. Your state income tax deduction can have many pieces. Unfortunately, a lot of taxpayers don't know all of the places they can find all of their state tax deductions.

On your 1998 tax return, you can deduct the balance that you owed on a 1997 state tax return. You can deduct the balance you paid as long as you paid it in 1998, of course. If you filed a tax return in more than one state, you can deduct payments made with each of your state tax returns. If you got a refund from one state, but owed tax to another state, don't offset the refund from one state against your deduction for the other state's taxes.

For example, Sally filed both an Illinois and Missouri tax return for 1997. She owed $325 with her Illinois return, but got a $100 refund from Missouri. What does she deduct? $225? No, she has to do two things. First, she must deduct the $325 she paid to Illinois. Then, she must report $100 from Missouri as a taxable state tax refund, unless she didn't itemize her deductions in 1997. If she didn't itemize in 1997, her refund isn't taxable, and the full $325 paid to Illinois is still fully deductible.

In 1998, you might have paid state taxes for an old tax year. Old years' taxes might need to be paid because of the following reasons:

➤ Filing an amended return

➤ An audit of a prior tax year

➤ Filing a prior year tax return late

Any payment in 1998 for an old tax year can be deducted on your 1998 tax return. You can't deduct any interest or penalties you pay on taxes, even if the interest and penalties were charged through no fault of your own.

You can deduct any state or local taxes that are withheld. You deduct the taxes in the year they are withheld. For example, state taxes withheld in 1998 from your pay are deducted on your 1998 tax return. You could have taxes withheld from several sources, such as the following:

➤ From wages—reported on Form W-2

➤ From pension or retirement plan payments—reported on Form 1099-R

➤ From gambling winnings—reported on Form W-2G

➤ From some partnership income if the partnership does business outside your state

Paper Trail

If you filed an extension for a 1997 state tax return, you might have sent a check with your extension. Don't forget to deduct your extension payment. This deduction is very easy to miss.

Red Flag

If the IRS audits your tax return, it will share the results of your audit with your state. Guess what? The state will come calling next! You might be able to file an amended state return to beat them to the punch. Some states also have arrangements for sharing information between the states.

Estimated State Taxes: Challenges and Opportunities

You might have to make estimated state income tax payments. The estimates are deductible in the year you pay them. That sounds pretty easy, but it can be tricky.

Let's start with an example. Lou lives in Indiana. She makes estimated tax payments because she has investment income that isn't covered by tax withholdings. Indiana's quarterly estimated tax payments are due on the following dates:

➤ April 15

➤ June 15

➤ September 15

➤ January 15 (of the following year)

In 1998, Lou wrote the following checks to the Indiana Department of Revenue for estimated taxes:

➤ January 15, 1998; $300 for fourth quarter of 1997

➤ April 15, 1998; $350 for first quarter of 1998

➤ June 15, 1998; $350 for second quarter of 1998

➤ September 15; 1998, $350 for third quarter of 1998

The fourth quarter Indiana estimated tax payment for 1998 was made in January of 1999. Lou will deduct the four checks that she wrote in 1998. Even though one of the checks was for 1997 income taxes, it was paid in 1998, so it is deducted in 1998. The fourth quarter Indiana estimate for 1998 will be deducted in 1999, when it was paid.

Paper Trail

An easy way to speed up tax deductions is to pay your fourth quarter estimate in December, rather than January, when it is due.

That example was pretty easy. Let's make it a bit more interesting. When Lou files her 1998 Indiana tax return, she is overpaid by $500. In Indiana, if you are overpaid on your tax return, you can either get a refund or you can credit the overpayment to the next year. Lou needed to make a $400 estimate on April 15, 1999. She didn't really want to write a check to Indiana for $400 knowing that they owed her $500, so she had $400 of her overpayment credited to her 1999 estimate. The other $100 was refunded to Lou.

Lou will get a surprise when she gets a form from Indiana saying that they reported a $500 refund to the IRS. Did Indiana make a mistake? No, they did exactly what they were supposed to do. When an overpayment is applied to an estimate, you create a fictional exchange of money. It's as if the state pays you the refund, then you write a check for your estimated tax payment. Since Lou itemized her deductions in 1998, the $500 refund she receives in 1999 is a taxable state tax refund. She will also take a deduction in 1999 for the $400 first quarter estimated tax payment that she paid in 1999.

Tax Planning at Its Best

If you know that you are going to owe money with your state tax return, you have a terrific opportunity to do some tax planning. You have to act before the end of the year, though. You will be able to choose when your state taxes will be paid. By doing this, you control when the state taxes are deducted. Isn't it always best to get a tax deduction as early as you can? In general, yes. There are times, though, that patience pays off.

Let's say you are going to owe $1,000 with your 1998 return. It is now December 1, 1998. You don't actually have to make estimated tax payments because your withholding is enough to help you avoid underpayment penalties. You have the following two choices:

➤ You could pay the $1,000 with your tax return when you file your return in April of 1999.

➤ You could make an early estimated tax payment of $1,000 in 1998.

To decide which path is best, you have to put your pencil to work. Better yet, dust off that tax software package you used last April. If you use an accountant to prepare your tax return, make an appointment. Your task is to determine if you'll get more tax savings by paying the taxes this year than next year, or vice versa.

Tax rates will play a role in your decision. You might be in a higher tax bracket this year than you expect to be in next year. In that case, it might be best to pay the taxes early. On the other hand, you might expect 1999 to be an even bigger year than 1998. If your tax rate in 1999 will be higher than 1998, it might pay to wait.

The wild card that you can't forget about is the alternative minimum tax (AMT). State taxes are not deductible against your AMT. This tax is a real sleeper. It can creep up on you when you least expect it. Don't let it surprise you, antici-pate it.

Paper Trail

When do you have to make esti-mated state tax payments? If you have income that doesn't have state taxes withheld, you might have to pay state estimates. The only way to know for sure if you have to pay state estimates is to check your state estimate rules. Read your state tax return filing instructions or call your tax advisor if you might need to pay estimates.

If you're using the pencil pushing technique, fill out a Form 6251 to see if AMT applies. If you're using software, be sure to activate that part of the program. If your program doesn't calculate AMT, get new software. If you're using an accountant, ask about the AMT impact. If your accountant doesn't calculate AMT, get a new accountant.

Red Flag

If you think that alternative minimum tax (AMT) is just for the very rich, think again. With the combined impact of some new credits (child credit, education credit) and the denial of state tax deductions, middle-income taxpayers can be pushed into AMT.

This planning scenario works well if you are in one of the following situations:

➤ Have larger-than-anticipated gains in the stock market

➤ Haven't paid your state estimates so far this year

➤ Sold a business

➤ Sold property at a gain

➤ Have higher business income this year than last

➤ Got lucky and won the lottery

This prepaying technique for state taxes can be tempting. What if you are in a high tax bracket this year, so you just pay a whole bunch on your state tax estimate in December? You would get a deduction at this year's high tax rate. You'll get the money back in a state tax refund next year. You'll pay tax on the refund next year at a lower tax rate. Sounds pretty good, doesn't it?

Watch out, though! Ever heard the "hog theory"? Pigs get fat, but hogs get slaughtered. If you pay more in your estimate than is reasonable for you to expect to have to pay, the IRS will nix your deduction for the excessive estimated tax payment.

Self-Employment Tax Deduction

Every business has to match the Social Security taxes paid by its employees. Businesses that are corporations have always been able to deduct their Social Security match as a business expense.

People who own their business as a sole proprietorship or partnership have to match their own Social Security taxes. They pay both halves of the tax. This is the self-employment (SE) tax. If you're self-employed, you need no introduction to this tax. You might pay more SE tax than income tax!

For many years, you couldn't deduct any of your SE tax. This just wasn't fair since corporations could deduct their match. You can now deduct half of your SE tax. It is an adjustment taken before AGI. It is not an itemized deduction.

Real Estate Taxes

Real estate taxes can be claimed as an itemized deduction. Most of our real estate taxes are pretty easy to identify. If you own property, it might pay to take a closer look.

To deduct a real estate tax, the tax has to be based on the assessed value of your property. There are as many different formulas for calculating real estate taxes as there are taxing districts—and there are a lot of taxing districts in our country. As long as your tax is in some way based on value, though, you will be paying deductible real estate taxes.

You can even deduct property taxes that you pay to foreign governments. So, you can deduct those pesky taxes you pay on your villa on the Riviera. Aren't you glad to hear that!

Your Home Is Your (Tax) Shelter

You can deduct the real estate taxes that you pay on your home. This is usually an easy step. However, if you move, buy a new house, or live in an area with creative taxes, your real estate taxes might not be quite as easy to sort out.

Your Decoder Ring

Remember the difference between a **business deduction** and an **itemized deduction**? Itemized deductions come after AGI. Deductions are more valuable if we can take them before AGI.

If you own your own home, you might write checks directly to your county treasurer, township assessor, and so on. No problem identifying these taxes. You might not pay your taxes directly. Instead, your taxes might be paid out of *escrow*. Each month, a part of your mortgage payment goes into an escrow account. The taxes are paid out of the escrow account. What do you deduct? Do you deduct what you pay in each month for taxes or what is paid out for taxes?

You deduct your real estate taxes when they are paid out of escrow. You'll get a statement from your bank or mortgage company telling you how much was paid for taxes. Use this statement for your taxes.

If you rent, part of your monthly rent covers your landlord's taxes. As a renter, you can't deduct the taxes. Remember that you can't deduct someone else's taxes. Even if your rent gets increased because real estate taxes went up, your higher rent is still not deductible as real estate taxes. Some renters might pay the real estate taxes on their home directly. This happens more in commercial leases than it does in home rentals. Even if you pay the taxes directly, you still can't deduct the taxes that you pay.

Your Decoder Ring

Ever wonder what an **escrow account** is? It's money that belongs to you but is held by somebody else. The money is held for a specific purpose. With your home, the escrow account is for paying real estate taxes and insurance. This isn't a service to you. The mortgage company is protecting its collateral.

Do you live in a co-op? Co-op owners don't own their own apartments. They actually own shares in a cooperative housing corporation. As a co-op owner, you make monthly payments. A part of your payment is for real estate taxes. You can deduct the portion of your payment that is for taxes. What about that rule that you have to own the property? As a co-op owner, you own a part of the co-op, and the IRS says that's good enough.

Paper Trail

Renters might get state tax breaks. Some states give renters a special deduction or a credit. Check out your state. The best place to start is by reading your state tax booklet. It's not fascinating reading, but it can pay off.

Ministers sometimes receive an allowance to pay for their housing. Because of a special tax treatment, ministers get their housing allowances tax-free. Ordinarily, you can't have your cake and eat it, too. Standard tax logic would conclude that ministers shouldn't be able to deduct the taxes that they pay with their tax-free housing allowance. Believe it or not, ministers get a break. They can deduct their real estate taxes. Members of the military can also get these tax-free housing allowances and still deduct their real estate taxes.

Your property taxes might include charges for services. These charges might be for trash collection or water consumption, for example. Or you might have to pay interest charges if you pay your taxes late. Even though you pay these charges with your real estate taxes, you can't deduct them.

You might also have to pay a special assessment with your taxes. Special assessments are levied for improvements or repairs. If the special assessment is to make improvements to your property, you can't deduct the assessment. For example, the county might plan to add sidewalks in front of your home. This type of assessment is not deductible. You have to add the assessment to the cost basis of your home.

If you pay an assessment for improvements to public facilities like roads or existing sidewalks, you can deduct the assessment.

You might have appealed your real estate tax assessment and won. You'll now get a refund of your real estate taxes. How do you handle the refund? If you get a refund in 1998 of taxes paid in 1998, offset the refund against your 1998 tax deduction. If you get a refund in 1998 of taxes paid in a prior year, your refund might be taxable. To the extent you got a tax benefit when you paid the taxes in the prior year, you now have taxable income. Include the refund on page one of Form 1040 on the line for Other Income.

Real Estate Taxes When You Buy or Sell Property

If you sold your home, you may have paid taxes at the closing. Even though you didn't write a check for the taxes, you can deduct the taxes that can be allocated to you. Check your closing statement to find out how much the taxes were.

In the year that you sell your home, the deduction for real estate tax has to be divided between the you and the buyer. To do the allocation, you have to do the following:

➤ Know your state's "real property year."

➤ Determine how much of the real property year you owned the property. The date of the sale is treated as the buyer's day.

➤ Divide up the taxes based on how much of the real property year you owned the home.

Your purchase agreement might legally bind you to pay a certain amount of the real estate taxes. That doesn't mean that you can deduct them. The allocation formula is the only way to divide the taxes for taking the tax deduction. You need to know how your state assesses taxes. Each state will have a real property year. Your state could use the calendar year as its real property year, but it could be a fiscal year ending in any month.

Your Decoder Ring

What do you mean—**appeal** your real estate taxes? Yes, you can appeal your property tax assessment. There is a lot of judgment that goes into a property tax assessment. There can also be a lot of errors in your assessment. Check it out.

An example might help. Consider the following:

➤ Erin sold her home June 21, 1998.

➤ Erin's state has a real property tax year that ends June 30, 1998.

➤ The real estate taxes are due on September 30, 1998.

➤ The buyer paid the taxes that were due in September, which were $3,500.

Erin owned the home for 355 days of the real property year. $^{355}/_{365}$ of the real estate taxes are allocated to Erin. She can deduct $3,404 of the real estate taxes—$3,500 times $^{355}/_{365}$. Even though Erin didn't pay the taxes, she can deduct them.

Erin isn't done yet. She got a $3,404 tax benefit from the deal. Almost every tax benefit has a cost. Erin has to follow through with a tax fiction. She has to act as if the buyer gave her $3,404 and then she paid the taxes. If the buyer gave her $3,404, there has to be a tax consequence. Erin has to increase the selling price of the property when she reports the sale of her home on her tax return.

The person who bought Erin's house can't deduct $3,404 of the taxes even though he paid them. Remember that you can't deduct someone else's taxes. The $3,404 allocated to Erin is treated as her taxes, not the buyer's taxes. Following through with the fictional payment of cash to Erin to pay the taxes, he has paid $3,404 more for his house because he paid Erin's taxes.

This allocation of real estate taxes has to be done for your home, a vacation home, rent property, or commercial property.

Taxes on Your Second Home

You can deduct property taxes on all of the properties that you own. There is no limit to the number of properties on which you can deduct property taxes. You can even deduct property taxes on property that you own but don't live in. For example, if you

own a home that your daughter lives in, you can deduct the real estate taxes that you pay on the house that she lives in. If she pays the taxes, she can't deduct them. They aren't her taxes.

If you own vacant land, you can also deduct the taxes you pay on the land. You have a choice, though. If the property is unimproved and unproductive (you don't get any income from it), you can chose to either deduct or capitalize the taxes. Why would you pass up a tax deduction? If you don't itemize your deductions, the tax deduction won't help you out at all. By capitalizing the taxes, you are adding them to the cost basis of the land. When you sell the land, your gain will be less because of the capitalized taxes.

Rental Property

You can deduct your real estate taxes on rental property, but not as an itemized deduction. Rental income and rental expenses are reported on Schedule E, Supplemental Income and Loss. The first page of Schedule E includes Part I, which is for rental real estate. Each piece of property is reported separately.

On Schedule E, you calculate your net income or loss from rental property and carry the net income or loss up to page one of your tax return Form 1040. You can't use Form 1040A or 1040EZ if you have rental property. The property taxes that you pay on rental property has to be reported as one of the expenses on your rent schedule. You can't choose to report the taxes as an itemized deduction instead.

There's a tax break if you rent out a home for a short time. If you rent out the home for fewer than 15 days, you don't have to report the rent income. The rent is tax-free. You can use this break on your primary residence or a vacation home. You can't use the break on commercial or industrial property. When you get this tax-free rent, your property taxes are still deducted as an itemized deduction. The following are examples of times you might rent a home out for a short period of time:

➤ There is a popular festival that attracts visitors and you can rent your property for a short time.

➤ You rent a vacation condo or house for 14 days or less.

➤ The Olympics are held in your home town. No joke! You can get high rental rates. If you rent for only 14 days or less, your rent is tax-free.

There has been a lot of political talk about taking away the tax break for renting your house fewer than 15 days. So far, this break is still on the books. This break has been on the chopping block several times, but it has survived so far.

If you rent out an apartment in your home, you'll have to do some allocating. Using a reasonable allocation method, divide the real estate taxes between your living portion and the rental portion. The taxes allocated to your living space are deducted with your itemized deductions. The taxes allocated to the rent space are deducted on your rent schedule.

A duplex is no different than having an apartment in your home. You'll have to divide up your taxes. It might be easier, though, because both units in a duplex are usually identical. If so, half will be allocated to each unit.

What if your renter pays the real estate taxes? This is a typical commercial rent arrangement. The renter is paying your taxes, but you remember the rule about only deducting your own taxes. Any taxes paid by the tenant are treated as additional rent payments. If your tenant is a business, it will deduct the taxes as a business expense. You will report the extra rent income and take a deduction for the taxes. The net effect is zero on your federal tax return.

Some states don't allow you to deduct real estate taxes. By treating the tax payments as rent income, you will pay more state taxes. This isn't an optional method of treating taxes, though; unfortunately, it is mandatory.

Vacation Property

We've already mentioned the opportunity to get tax-free rent from vacation property. If you rent for less than 15 days, the rent is tax-free and you deduct your real estate taxes as itemized deductions. What if you rent more than 14 days? You have entered the world of vacation home allocations and limitations. It's a pretty wild ride, so hold on to your hat. Your home will have to be put into one of the following categories:

➤ Not used as a home. If you fall into this category, the income and expense are all reported on the rent schedule (Schedule E).

➤ Used as a home, but rented for part of the year. If you fall into this category, your expenses will have to be allocated between personal use and your rent schedule. You can't claim a tax loss for the rent part.

What does it mean to be "used as a home"? It means that you use the home for personal purposes more than the greater of 14 days or 10% of the days it is rented to others at fair rental price. For example, Jim owns a vacation condo. He rents it out for 160 days each year. As long as he uses the condo for 16 days or less each year, he is treated as not using the condo as a home. This means that the condo is treated as rental property. He reports the rent income and his condo expenses on his rent schedule. He can even take a rent loss as long as the passive activity loss rules don't kick in. If Jim had used the property for more than 16 days, he would not be able to take a loss on his rent schedule, so he is motivated to control the number of days he personally uses his condo.

There are some minimum requirements for being considered a vacation home. The home has to have the following items:

➤ Sleeping space
➤ A toilet
➤ Cooking facilities

Clearly a house, condominium, or mobile home would meet these requirements. RVs and boats can also be considered vacation homes if they have these facilities.

If your vacation home expenses have to be allocated between the rent schedule and personal use, your real estate taxes will be split up. Since you can't claim a loss on the rent schedule, you will want to allocate as much of your tax expense as possible to your itemized deductions. The IRS and the Tax Court don't really agree on how to do this allocation.

To get the highest deduction, you would use the Tax Court allocation method. We'll illustrate with an example. Let's go back to Jim. He rented his property for 160 days in the year and used it personally for 20 days. His real estate taxes are $3,000 a year. You can divide your real estate taxes two different ways.

The IRS Method		
Rent days	160	
Personal use days	20	
Total days	180	
Taxes allocated to rent	(160/180)	$2,667
Personal portion	(20/180)	$333
The Tax Court Method		
Taxes allocated to rent	(160/365)	$1,315
Personal portion	(205/365)	$1,685

The Tax Court method lets you count unrented days as your personal days. You'll have to decide for yourself which method to use, but the Tax Court method will give you more taxes to deduct with your itemized deductions. These are just the basics of the vacation home rules. We have really just scratched the surface of the rules you have to follow. If you want to know more, read up on vacation home rules in other tax publications.

Before you buy vacation property, think through what you want to do with the property. If you are buying it for personal enjoyment, don't let the tax rules end up depriving you of enjoying the property. Rent losses are often greatly overrated since passive activity loss rules may apply.

Business Use Property

If you own your own business and report your income on Schedule C, your real estate taxes on business property you own will be deducted right on your Schedule C. If your business is a corporation, you should consider owning the real estate outside the corporation. You could own the property personally and rent it to the corporation. You would then claim the real estate taxes on your rent schedule.

The most popular method of holding real estate used in a business is a partnership or partnership-like entity. This would include the following:

Your Decoder Ring

You don't have to be at your **vacation home** for personal use days to be logged. If you let your family use your vacation home, those days are treated as personal use days. If you let a friend stay in your home at less than fair rental, that's a personal use day.

➤ General partnership
➤ Limited partnership
➤ Limited liability company
➤ Limited liability partnership

The real estate taxes would be deducted by these partnership entities.

If you are deciding how to own real estate, take the time to visit with both your attorney and your CPA. There are legal considerations that your attorney needs to address. Your CPA can help you get the best tax result.

Personal Property Taxes

These are the hardest taxes to identify. There aren't very many personal property taxes that are paid by individuals. You have to know your state taxes pretty well to find them.

The most likely personal property tax you pay would be on your car. To deduct the tax, it has to be based on value alone. For example, your car tax might have two parts, one part based on value and another part based on model, horsepower, year, or weight. Only the part based on value is deductible

Some states impose *intangibles taxes*. An intangibles tax is usually calculated as a percent of the value of certain investments. This type of an intangibles tax is deductible as a property tax. Florida and Kentucky are two states that assess intangibles taxes.

Paper Trail

The business real estate entity, if well chosen, can give you income tax advantages, legal liability protection, family financial planning, and estate planning opportunities. Take the time and spend the money to do it right.

Paper Trail

Don't just take the easy route and deduct your foreign taxes. See if you can use the credit. If you can, it might save you more money than the deduction. Use Form 1116 to calculate the credit.

Knowing your state taxes comes in handy. You might be paying personal property taxes and not even know it. Check it out with some tax professionals in your state. They will know what you can deduct.

Other Taxes

You can deduct foreign income taxes. If you invest in a foreign company, you might have noticed foreign tax being withheld from your dividend checks. You have a choice. You can either deduct your foreign taxes or take the foreign tax credit. It's your choice.

You can deduct state unemployment taxes that are imposed on employees. You'll see it on your W-2 if this applies to you. The following are some examples:

➤ Mandatory contributions made to the California, New Jersey, or New York Nonoccupational Disability Benefit Fund

➤ Mandatory contributions made to the Rhode Island Temporary Disability Benefit Fund

➤ Mandatory contributions made to the Washington State Supplemental Workmen's Compensation Fund

Payroll taxes you pay for nursing care in your home aren't deductible as a tax expense. These taxes might be deductible as medical expense, though. If you can deduct the nursing care as a medical expense, you can deduct the payroll taxes that you pay on the care giver's wages.

Taxes You Can't Deduct

Much as you would like to deduct the following taxes, they are just not deductible. Some of these taxes used to be deductible, but you can't claim any of these in 1998.

➤ Federal income taxes

➤ Penalty taxes imposed by the IRS or any state taxing authority

➤ FICA and Medicare taxes withheld from your pay

➤ Payroll taxes you pay on household employees unless they are deductible as medical expenses

➤ Sales tax—even sales taxes on car purchases are not deductible

➤ Estate tax

➤ Gift tax

➤ Inheritance tax

➤ New York renters' tax—it is not considered a property tax

➤ Excise taxes such as taxes on alcohol, fuel, or cigarettes for personal consumption

➤ Customs duties

➤ Taxes assessed by a utility company

Even if they are called taxes, fees are not deductible as taxes. The following are examples of nondeductible fees:

➤ Car inspection fees

➤ Dog tags (if tags are for a seeing eye dog, they are deductible as medical expenses)

➤ Marriage license

➤ Driver's license

➤ City taxes for services like trash pick-up or snow removal

➤ Parking tickets

➤ Traffic violations, such as speeding tickets

Red Flag

Sales taxes are no longer deductible. Even if you pay sales tax when you buy business equipment, you have to include your sales tax in the cost of the item that you depreciate. You can't claim the sales tax as a business expense deduction. Even if your state doesn't have an income tax, but has a high sales tax instead, you still can't deduct sales tax.

The Least You Need to Know

➤ State taxes are an important itemized deduction.

➤ You can do some effective tax planning by controlling the time that you pay your state taxes.

➤ You can deduct income taxes and real estate taxes that you pay to a state, county, or city government.

➤ If you own vacation property, you might have to allocate your real estate taxes between the rent portion and your personal portion.

➤ There has been a cutback in the taxes that are deductible. Some of the taxes we used to be able to deduct are now off-limits.

Chapter 8

Paying Interest

In This Chapter

➤ Deducting interest other than your home mortgage interest

➤ Knowing which interest charges you can't deduct

➤ Learning how to deduct interest on money you borrow to invest in stocks and bonds

➤ Determining who can take the new student loan interest deduction

➤ Discovering how to deduct interest you incur to make business investments

I could be nostalgic about the good old days of deducting interest expense. We used to tally up any interest at all that we paid. It doesn't do any good to take this little trip down memory lane. Interest deductions are very limited, but there are many interest deductions still on the books. We're going to talk about home mortgage interest in the next chapter. Right now, we're going to review other types of interest that you might pay and how your interest expense might impact your tax return.

To deduct interest, it has to be your interest. Actually, to deduct interest, the debt has to be yours. You can't deduct interest on another person's debt. Interest is the cost that you pay to borrow or use someone else's money. Ordinarily, it's easy to identify interest charges, but there are hidden interest charges you could pay without even noticing it. The hidden interest charges that most of us pay are for personal purchases, which won't give you an interest deduction anyway.

For example, you buy a computer with 18-month financing and zero interest charges. Do you really think the store hasn't considered interest when it offers the deal to you? The IRS makes you reduce the price of the computer so that part of what you pay is treated as interest. This is called "imputed interest." Your payments, for example, might be $2,500 with zero interest. You might really (according to the IRS) be paying $2,100 for the computer and the other $400 is for interest.

The IRS requires interest to be imputed on below-market loans. If you are buying the computer for your business, the imputed interest rules will matter. If you are buying the computer for personal use, you can't deduct the interest anyway. There are some limited exceptions to the imputed interest rules for certain loans to family or employees. Check the rules if you're planning a below-market loan.

You can only deduct interest expense when you pay it, but you can't deduct interest that you prepay. This is a type of modified cash basis. If your mortgage payment is due on the first day of the month, you pay last month's interest charges each time you make your mortgage payment. When you make your June payment, for example, you are paying the interest that built up in May. So, if you pay your January 1, 1999 mortgage payment on December 31, 1998 you aren't paying interest in advance. You are paying interest that has built up through December 31, 1998. You can deduct the interest you pay in December on your 1998 tax return.

On the other hand, if you pay both your January and February payments on December 31, you'll have to wait until 1999 to deduct the interest part of the February payment. Why is this? You have paid the interest for January of 1999 in 1998. This is an interest prepayment. You can't deduct prepaid interest. You won't lose the deduction for your prepaid interest, but you will have to wait until 1999 to take your deduction.

Consumer Interest

Consumer interest is not deductible. But what in the world is consumer interest? The definition of consumer interest is a backward definition. You'll find a lot of backward definitions when you work with income taxes. If something is hard to define, Congress explains what it isn't instead of explaining what it is. It's not always easy to follow a backward definition, but it works. Consumer interest is all of your interest except any interest you pay on debt that is for any of the following:

➤ Your trade or business
➤ Making investments
➤ A passive activity, like rental property
➤ Your home (qualified residence interest)
➤ Estate taxes in special circumstances that involve closely held businesses

Examples of consumer interest charges include the following:

➤ Credit card interest

➤ Annual fees paid to credit card companies

➤ Interest on car loans

➤ Interest paid on student loans (other than the new rules covered later)

➤ Interest on loans to buy personal use items like furniture or appliances

➤ Interest paid on installment agreements for personal use items

➤ Consolidation loans if they pay off consumer debt and are not home equity loans

You might borrow money from the cash value in your life insurance policy to pay premiums. These loans will let you use your built up cash value to pay premiums instead of paying your own cash for the premiums. Loans can also be used to buy an additional policy. The interest that you will pay on the loan from your cash surrender value is not deductible.

Have you noticed that you don't get year-end statements telling you how much interest you have paid on consumer loans any more? Well, now you know why. You can't deduct the interest, so they don't bother to send statements. If you need (or want) to know interest you paid to a lender, just call. Most companies will send statements on request.

Red Flag

If you borrow money from one life insurance policy to pay premiums on other new policies, be careful. Some life insurance agents have gotten into big trouble for churning out policies. The agent gets a big commission on each new policy. Check out your options with a reputable life insurance professional.

If you have to pay interest on income taxes, the IRS says that you can't deduct the interest. Sometimes, though, the taxes that are paid late are on income from a trade or business. Taxpayers have fought the IRS because the taxpayers don't think that this interest is consumer interest. Taxpayers want to deduct the interest on past-due taxes on business income as a business expense.

This sounds pretty logical, doesn't it? Well, the IRS doesn't agree, but a district court has allowed this interest expense as a business expense. There is a battle going on between taxpayers and the IRS. If you deduct interest on past-due taxes on business income, you take the interest deduction at your own risk. The IRS still hasn't agreed that the district court is right. You certainly would have some support behind you for taking the deduction, though. The deduction for interest paid on past due taxes will have to be resolved either by a higher court or legislative action. Stay tuned to this issue if it impacts you.

If you own more than two homes that you use as personal residences and you have loans on more than two homes, you will have consumer interest. This could happen if you own your regular home, a vacation condominium, and a home for your mother to live in. Check out the next chapter on home mortgage interest.

Borrowing Money to Make Money: Investment Interest Expense

When you borrow money to make investments, you will pay investment interest expense. This is one of the types of interest that is not consumer interest. So, you can deduct investment interest. Right?

Although you can deduct investment interest, you might not be able to deduct all of your investment interest expense. The investment interest expense deduction is limited to your net investment income.

How You Get Investment Interest

The following are examples of loans that generate investment interest expense:

➤ Margin loans with your brokerage company

➤ Loans taken out to buy stocks

➤ Loans taken out to buy bonds

➤ Loans to buy stock in your employer's company, if it is a C corporation

➤ Loans to lend money to someone else

➤ Loans to buy land for investment purposes

Your Decoder Ring

Interest on debt that you incur to buy tax-free bonds is not investment interest expense. The interest is not deductible at all. The IRS will even disallow interest that you pay on debt that allows you to "carry" investments that give you tax-free income.

You could also have investment interest expense if you have invested in a limited partnership. Partnerships don't pay tax on their own income. Instead, the partnership divides its income and deductions up among all of its partners. Each partner picks up his or her share of partnership income and deductions on his or her tax return. Investment interest expense, since it can be limited, is passed through separately to each partner.

Each partner will get a report of his or her share of partnership income, deductions, or credits. The schedule is called a Schedule K-1. Your share of the investment interest expense will be reported to you on the Schedule K-1. You add this interest expense to your other investment interest to determine if your deduction is limited or not.

Tally Up Your Investment Income

Now we know that your investment interest expense is limited to net investment income. How do you calculate net investment income? Investment income includes the following:

➤ Interest income

➤ Dividend income

➤ Annuity income

➤ Royalties that are not received in your business

➤ Investment income passed through to you from a partnership, S corporation, or trust

What about capital gains? You have a choice to make. You can include capital gains as investment income, but at a price. To count your gains as investment income, you have to give up your special capital gains tax rate (10% or 20%). Most taxpayers don't want to give up their special capital gains rate, but there are some taxpayers who will want to do this.

Let's say, for example, that Ralph borrowed money to buy stock in a growth company. Most growth companies don't pay dividends, but investors are looking for an increase in the stock's value. Ralph doesn't have any other investment income. This venture into buying the growth stock was a step out for Ralph. At the end of two years, Ralph's stock value has increased some. He's nervous that the price might fall, so he sells the stock. He has a small capital gain and he also has investment interest expense. Although he hates to admit it, Ralph has spent more on interest expense than he has in capital gains.

Ralph should do two things:

➤ Consider electing to treat his capital gains as investment income for his investment interest expense limitation

➤ Develop a sound investment approach

Now you know what your investment income is. You get your net investment income by subtracting your deductible investment expenses.

Your investment expenses will likely include miscellaneous itemized deductions. These expenses can only be deducted to the extent they are more than 2% of your adjusted gross income. You only need to count the investment expenses that you can actually deduct after the 2% floor has been applied. Your non-investment expenses are treated as being used up by the 2% floor before you use up investment expenses.

For example, you have $1,000 of non-investment expenses and $400 of investment expenses that are miscellaneous itemized deductions. Your 2% of AGI floor is $1,200, so only $200 of your miscellaneous deductions can be taken. You will only have to use $200 of your investment expenses in calculating your net investment income.

Investment expenses could include the following:

➤ Investment advisor fees

➤ Fees charged to your investment account

➤ Fees for safe-deposit boxes that hold investments

➤ Investment publications

➤ Legal fees related to investments

➤ Property tax paid on investment property

➤ Intangibles tax paid on your investments

➤ Postage and long-distance telephone charges related to your investments

I Can't Deduct It All—What Do I Do?

If you have investment interest that you can't deduct, you don't lose the deduction forever. You can carry the interest expense over to future years. You can deduct it against future investment income until you use it all up. There is no time limit on investment interest expense carryovers.

Paper Trail

Use Form 4952 to calculate your investment interest expense limitation. The instructions to Form 4952 are really pretty good. The IRS also prints Publication 550 dealing with investment interest expense.

Let's look at an example. Betty has the following 1998 income:

➤ Wages of $40,000

➤ Interest and dividend income of $3,000

➤ Capital gains of $2,500

➤ Net rental income of $5,000

Betty's adjusted gross income is $50,500. Betty itemizes her deductions. She has $4,200 of investment interest expense. Included in her deductions are the following miscellaneous itemized deductions:

➤ Tax return preparation fees $450

➤ Employee business expenses of $800

➤ Investment-related expenses of $200

Betty's total miscellaneous itemized deductions are $1,450, of which $1,010 ($50,500 times 2%) is not deductible. The actual deduction for miscellaneous itemized deductions is $440. Since Betty's investment expenses are only $200, all of her investment expenses are used in her investment interest expense limitation. Betty's net investment income is calculated as follows:

Interest and dividends	$3,000
Investment expenses	200
Net investment income	$2,800

Betty can deduct up to $2,800 of investment interest expense. The remaining $1,400 of her investment interest expense will be carried over to 1999. The unused interest will continue to be carried over until Betty is able to use it all up. Betty could also choose to include her capital gains in her investment income. All of her investment interest would then be deductible in 1998. Betty would give up her alternative capital gains tax rate to make this election, so she needs to weigh this option carefully.

Student Loan Interest

Starting in 1998, some people will be able to deduct their student loan interest. When the deduction for consumer interest was taken away, student loan interest was no longer deductible, but the law has finally changed in this regard—to a certain extent. The new interest deduction isn't available to everyone, and there are also limitations on the amount you can deduct.

If your modified adjusted gross income (AGI) is more than $75,000 on a joint return or $55,000 on a single return, you can't take the student loan interest deduction at all. Your deduction is phased out if your modified AGI is between $60,000 and $75,000 on a joint return and between $40,000 and $55,000 on a single return.

You can deduct interest paid on debt that you incurred for your own education, your spouse's education, or your dependent's education. The loan has to be in your name to take a deduction for the interest. Remember that you can't deduct someone else's interest expense.

The student loan must have been used to pay for tuition, fees, or room and board at a school of higher education. The loan proceeds must be used to pay expenses for a student who is enrolled in at least a half-time course load.

If you are someone else's dependent, you can't claim the student loan interest deduction. The loan can be taken out in a year that you were someone else's dependent. If you are still a dependent when the loan is paid back, though, you don't get the deduction.

Your Decoder Ring

If you take out a **student loan** for education related to your work, is the interest a business expense? Sorry, but no. Your only hope of deducting the interest is under the new rules.

The student loan interest is not an itemized deduction. It is an adjustment that you take before your adjusted gross income. This means that you don't have to itemize your deductions to take the student loan interest deduction. The deduction will also reduce your AGI for all of those "percent of AGI" limitations. The student loan interest deduction is much more valuable than an itemized deduction.

The amount of interest that you can deduct is limited to a fixed dollar amount. The amount changes each year until 2001, as shown in Table 8.1.

Table 8.1 Student Loan Interest Deduction Limitation

Year	Deduction Limit
1998	$1,000
1999	$1,500
2000	$2,000
2001	$2,500

You can only deduct interest that is paid in the first 60 months that you have to make payments of interest. If you have a period of time that you don't have to make any payments, you don't have to count that grace period in your 60 months.

For example, Brian finished his college education in May of 1996. He had a one-year time period after graduation that he didn't have to make any interest or principal payments. He started making payments in June of 1997. If he meets the AGI limitations, he will be able to deduct interest paid through May of 2002. His deductions will be limited to the fixed dollar amount that applies each year—$1,000 in 1998, etc.

Paper Trail

If Brian's parents borrow the money for Brian's education, and their AGI is too high for the student loan interest deduction, the student loan interest deduction is wasted. Neither Brian nor his parents can take the deduction. When borrowing for higher education, be sure that the person who might be able to take the deduction is the person who borrows the money.

Interest Paid for Rental Property

If you borrow money to buy or improve rental property, your interest will be deducted on your rent schedule. Rent income and expenses are reported on Schedule E, Supplemental Income and Loss.

Rent income is treated as passive income for most people. Real estate professionals don't have to treat their rent income as passive income. You have to be in the real estate business and meet some other requirements to be a real estate professional. Passive losses can only be used to offset income from other passive activities. Any excess loss is carried over.

There is a break for rental real estate, though, from the passive activity loss rules. You might be able to take a loss from your rental real estate of up to $25,000 each year. You have to be involved in the rental activity by doing things like the following:

➤ Approving new tenants
➤ Deciding on rental terms
➤ Approving capital improvements
➤ Approving repairs

To take the special rent loss deduction, you also have to have modified adjusted gross income under $100,000 ($50,000 if married filing separately). There is a phase-out between $100,000 and $150,000 of modified AGI (between $50,000 and $75,000 if you are married filing separately).

Form 8582 is used to calculate the limitation. Your passive losses have to be accounted for for both regular tax and alternative minimum tax purposes. The instructions to Form 8582 are very thorough and run a full 10 pages long. If you struggle with passive activity losses, it might be time to seek professional tax help.

Red Flag

Did you see it again? The marriage penalty is found in the real estate passive loss rules. A single person can have up to $100,000 of modified AGI and take a rent loss. Married people combined have the same $100,000 limit.

Business Interest Expense

If you borrow money for your business, the interest is deductible against your business income. Your business could take different forms. The form of your business will dictate how your interest will be deducted.

If your business is not incorporated and you are the only owner, you are a sole proprietor. You will use Schedule C to report your business income and expenses. Your business interest expenses will be deducted on Schedule C. This is much better than taking an itemized deduction. You pay self-employment tax on your business income in addition to paying income tax. A business interest deduction will save both income taxes and self-employment taxes.

Your business might not be incorporated, but you might not be the only owner. You would be a partner with your other co-owner. If the partnership borrows money for its business operations, it will deduct the interest on the partnership return Form 1065.

If you borrow money to put the cash into your partnership business or to buy your partnership interest, you can deduct the interest that you pay on the loan. Your share of partnership income is reported on your return through Schedule E. You can also deduct the interest on your partnership-related loan on your Schedule E. The interest expense will also reduce your self-employment income from the partnership.

Your business might be a corporation, but the corporation has elected to be taxed as a Subchapter S corporation. If you borrow money to buy your S corporation stock, your interest will be deductible on Schedule E. You don't pay self-employment tax on S corporation income, so the interest has no impact on self-employment tax.

If you borrow money to lend to your S corporation, your interest expense will be investment interest. The interest expense will then be an itemized deduction and will be limited to your net investment income.

Your Decoder Ring

What is an **S corporation**? It is a corporation that has elected special tax treatment. An S corporation doesn't pay tax on its own income. Each shareholder reports his or her share of the corporation's income on their personal tax return through Schedule E. Each shareholder will get a Schedule K-1 listing his or her share of the corporation's income, deductions, and credits.

The Debt Tracing Rules

How do you know how to treat interest expense? The IRS doesn't leave it to chance. You might think that a loan that is secured by your investments would automatically be investment interest. That isn't the case. The IRS looks at how you actually use the proceeds of the loan to determine how the loan should be categorized. Once the loan is categorized (business, consumer, or investment interest), the interest paid on the loan follows. If the debt is used for a consumer purchase, the interest is consumer interest.

Essentially, the IRS makes you trace the money from the time you borrow it to the time you use it. The interest tracing rules are pretty intricate. You can have some unintended results if you mix up your funds. For example, you might borrow money to make an investment. You put the funds into your personal checking account. You buy some groceries, pay your bills, deposit your paycheck, and eventually make your investment. You could be treated as having used the loan for consumer purchases. Your paycheck could be treated as having been used to make the investment. You thought that you had investment interest, but you end up with consumer interest.

To be safe, keep borrowed money separate from other personal funds if you are borrowing for investment or business purposes. If you are careless about keeping the funds separate, you might unintentionally lose some of your interest expense deductions.

The Least You Need to Know

➤ Personal interest is not deductible.

➤ Interest on money that you borrow to make investments is deductible, but the deduction is limited to your investment income.

➤ Interest on student loans is deductible again in 1998, but not everybody can take the deduction.

➤ Business interest is deductible against your business income.

➤ To keep your interest properly categorized, you have to look at the way the loan proceeds are used.

Chapter 9

Your Home Mortgage Interest

In This Chapter

➤ Meeting the home mortgage interest deduction requirements

➤ Knowing when you can deduct interest on home equity loans

➤ Deducting mortgage points to buy your home or to refinance your mortgage

➤ Answering the IRS if they send you a letter questioning your mortgage interest deduction

---

If you think that nothing is sacred when it comes to income taxes, think again. The mortgage interest deduction has survived many would-be attacks. Most attacks are headed off long before they even reach the floor of Congress.

What is the big deal about mortgage interest? The American dream is at stake when you threaten to mess with mortgage interest. It is a political hands-off issue because the middle-income taxpayer would be greatly harmed if mortgage interest was not deductible.

If you couldn't deduct your mortgage interest, the real cost of owning a home would increase. Your home buying power would be significantly impaired. Home prices could fall. When home prices fall, retirees, low-income, and middle-income homeowners take a hit they probably can't afford.

Just imagine all of the political factions a member of Congress could offend if he or she tried to eliminate home mortgage interest deductions! Retirees, the real estate industry, the banking industry, and labor unions would all weigh in. Television news magazines would immediately feature him or her as the newest demon. Why would you want to harm the working people of America, anyway? You get the picture.

Do We All Need a Revolution?

It would probably take a tax revolution to remove our mortgage interest deduction. A flat tax or a value added tax would be that type of revolution. A lot of people say that they support a flat tax, but don't know what that means. For one thing, it could mean no mortgage interest deduction.

In the days when we could deduct any old interest expense, there was no fuss about what type of interest you paid. If it was your interest and you paid it, you could deduct it. Today, the deduction choices for interest are much more limited. The most generous interest deduction that remains is home mortgage interest. To keep people from taking advantage of this tax generosity, we now have home mortgage interest rules.

The rules we covered for all other interest apply to mortgage interest also:

➤ You can only deduct your own interest. In other words, the mortgage debt has to be your debt.

➤ You can only deduct interest that you pay.

➤ You can't deduct interest that you pay in advance (prepaid interest).

If you are separated or divorced, you might have to pay the whole mortgage payment even though the house is owned jointly by you and your former spouse. You can only deduct half of the mortgage interest you pay as an itemized deduction. The other half (that you are paying for your former spouse) might qualify as an alimony deduction.

As you can see, even with all the rules associated with it, the mortgage interest deduction is a really nice tax deduction for homeowners. It's highly unlikely that anyone would support a revolution that would eliminate this gem from our income taxes!

Reversing Your Mortgage

Reverse mortgage loans are gaining in popularity with elderly or chronically ill taxpayers. Just like your regular mortgage, the debt is secured by your home. In other words, your lender takes your home as collateral.

A reverse mortgage has a reversed payment schedule. Instead of your making monthly payments to the lender, the lender pays you a fixed amount each month. You run up a tab with the lender. The amount you owe to the lender is increased by the monthly payments you receive from the lender and the interest that builds up on your loan.

The plan is to pay back the loan when your home is sold. Your home would be sold after you die or after you have to move out for good. When do you deduct the interest? Remember the rule about only deducting interest that you pay. As the interest builds up and is added to your loan, you can't take a deduction because the interest is not yet paid. The interest is paid when your house is sold and the loan is paid off.

Why do people do reverse mortgages? If you need to tap the equity in your home for living expenses or medical expenses, a reverse mortgage can give you the cash flow that you need. These arrangements enable elderly or ill people to live in their homes and use their equity during their lifetime. When the time comes to sell the house, the loan is paid back.

Home Equity Loans

You might need to borrow money for any number of reasons. You might need to put your child through college, pay medical bills, or make improvements to your home. If you owe less money on your home than it is worth, you might be able to take out a home equity loan.

A home equity loan is nothing more than a loan you take out using your home as collateral. There are some nice tax breaks for home equity loans, and you probably can get a much lower interest rate than a personal loan.

The Goal: Qualified Residence Interest

The generous deduction rules only apply to qualified residence interest. How do you get qualified residence interest? Is it the residence that has to be qualified, or is it the loan? Actually, there are two parts to the qualification process. Both your mortgage loan and your home have to qualify.

A qualified residence mortgage can be either of the following:

➤ Acquisition debt
➤ A home equity loan

A qualified residence is either of the following:

➤ Your principal residence
➤ One second home

So, acquisition debt on either your primary home or your second home is qualified. Home equity debt on either your primary home or second home is also qualified.

> **Red Flag**
>
> If you are interested in a reverse mortgage, shop around and ask a lot of questions. Compare rates. Compare the arrangement to a home equity loan. Be sure that you understand all of the terms of the agreement. You are borrowing against the equity in your home, so only deal with a reputable lender.

When a House Is a Home

Your principal residence has to be owned by you. The home has to be used by you as your primary residence. Your principal residence doesn't have to be a house, though. It could be any of the following:

➤ Cooperative apartment

➤ Condominium

➤ Boat

➤ Trailer

➤ Recreational vehicle (RV)

Your home has to have cooking, sleeping, and toilet facilities to qualify as a residence.

Your Principal Residence

So, what is your *principal residence*? It is the place that you live most of the time. When you are away from home, it's the place you come home to. For most people, it's pretty easy to tell which home is their principal residence.

Your Decoder Ring

Your **principal residence** is the home that could give you a tax-free gain. To exclude the gain (up to $250,000 per person), the home has to be your principal residence for two of the last five years. Be consistent and careful in identifying your principal residence if you own more than one home.

If you're temporarily away from home for medical reasons, don't worry. Your home is still your principal residence even if you have to be away to seek medical treatment.

Your Second Home

You can also deduct the mortgage interest on your *second home*. What is a second home? It is a home that isn't your principal residence, but you still use it as a home. You can have only one second home at a time. Each year, though, you can choose which house is your second home.

For example, Jennifer owns the home that she lives in. She also has a vacation condominium in Florida. Jennifer's grandfather becomes ill, and the old family farm is going to be sold. Jennifer doesn't want the farm to be sold to someone else, so she buys it. Since the farm is in the country, Jennifer's family uses it as a get-away for weekends and holidays. Jennifer can choose whether her condo or her grandfather's home is her second home. It doesn't matter that the farm is the third home that she bought. She is free to choose which home is her second home. She will, of course, want to choose the home with the greatest amount of mortgage interest expense.

You will have to allocate your interest between your personal use and your rent schedule. The part allocated to personal use is treated as qualified residence interest on a second home. In Chapter 7, we discussed the vacation home rules and how the deduction for property taxes is allocated. The mortgage interest deduction is handled the same way as property taxes. Complete the following steps to allocate the interest:

Paper Trail

Your second home can't be a rental home. You can rent the house for less than 15 days, though, and still consider the home a residence.

1. Add up the number of your rent days.
2. Determine what percentage of the year is rent and what percentage is personal.
3. Divide up the interest using those percentages.
4. Report the rent portion on your rent schedule.
5. Report the personal portion as an itemized deduction.

If you own more than two homes that you use as residences, any interest that you pay on the third home is consumer interest. You can't deduct the third home's interest expense. If you really want to deduct mortgage interest for your third house, you could try one of these approaches:

➤ Use some home equity financing to buy the third home. Check out home equity loan rules later in this chapter.

➤ Convert one of your homes to rental property. You would then have two personal residences and one rental home. The rental home's interest would be deducted on your rent schedule.

If you are a member of the clergy or the military and get a tax-free housing allowance, your home mortgage interest is still deductible. You have to meet all of the same rules as everyone else. Your tax-free housing allowance won't foil your mortgage interest deduction.

Paper Trail

Usually, a mortgage must be filed with a local government agency for the loan to be secured by your home. If you use a bank to finance your home, the bank will see that the proper papers are filed. If you finance your home with an individual, such as the seller, make sure that the papers all get filed. Don't take chances. Use your attorney.

To deduct home mortgage interest, the loan has to be secured by your home. This means that the lender takes your home as collateral. If you make your mortgage payment late, you'll probably have to pay a penalty. That penalty is treated as additional interest and can be deducted as mortgage interest.

Acquisition Debt—What Is It?

You can deduct interest that you pay on your mortgage if it is acquisition debt on your primary residence or your second home.

Which loans count as acquisition debt? Acquisition debt is a mortgage loan that you take out to do any of the following:

➤ Buy your home

➤ Build your home

➤ Substantially improve your home

There is a limit to the amount of qualified acquisition debt you can have. Most taxpayers don't have too much trouble with the limit. You can only deduct interest on $1 million or less of acquisition debt. If you are married and file separately, the limit is $500,000. A single person can deduct interest on the full $1 million of acquisition debt.

The $1 million limit applies to all of your acquisition debt combined. If you own two homes, both mortgages have to be added together to see if you meet the $1 million limit. If you go over $1 million, only the interest on $1 million of debt is deductible. As you pay your mortgage down and your debt goes under $1 million, all of your interest becomes deductible.

Paper Trail

If you bought a new home this year, check your closing statement for interest you may have paid at closing. Your lender might include this interest when your mortgage interest is reported to you, but check the amounts to be certain.

If your mortgage was taken out before October 13, 1987, the $1 million limit does not apply. Your mortgage is grandfathered under the old rules that didn't have any dollar limits.

If you are building a house, you will probably have two different loans. You'll have a construction loan, which will be followed by permanent mortgage when your house is completed. The permanent mortgage that replaces the construction loan will qualify as acquisition debt. On the other hand, if you build your home without debt and borrow the money later, the debt will not be acquisition debt.

For example, Mike is a construction contractor. He builds his own home, doing a lot of the work himself. He was able to buy the materials with money he had saved. After the home was built, Mike borrowed money from the bank to replace the personal funds he had spent. The debt is not acquisition debt, but it is home equity debt.

If you refinance your acquisition debt, the new debt is also treated as acquisition debt. The amount that you refinance can't be more than the old debt was at the time of refinancing. The payment period can be longer than your old mortgage, though.

If you refinance an old mortgage that is more than $1 million and it was incurred before October 13, 1987, you will lose your "grandfather" status if you extend the term of your loan. If your old loan had 12 years left, the new loan can't have more than 12 years left and still be grandfathered. If you do extend the term of your loan, the mortgage is still acquisition debt, but it is now subject to the $1 million limit.

Tapping Your Home Equity

You can deduct interest you pay on up to $100,000 of home equity debt. If your home equity loan was taken out before October 13, 1987, the $100,000 limit doesn't apply to you. If you are married filing separately, the limit is $50,000. A home equity loan must be secured by your home. Your lender has to take your home as collateral for the loan.

You can use the money that you borrow for anything. You can buy a car, pay for your daughter's wedding, or use the money to make an investment. The deduction will still be qualified residence interest. The home equity loan is an important exception to the interest tracing rules. It really doesn't matter how the loan is used at all.

There is a second limit for home equity debt. In addition to the $100,000 limit, your home equity debt is limited by your home's value. You can only deduct interest on your home equity loan as long as the home equity loan plus your acquisition debt is not more than the fair market value of your home.

For example, Dick's home is worth $275,000. He wants to make an investment that will cost him $100,000. Dick's acquisition debt on his house is $200,000. He has $75,000 of equity in his home. If the bank lends Dick the entire $100,000 in a home equity loan, only $75,000 of the debt qualifies for the home equity interest deduction. The other $25,000 of the loan might qualify as investment interest.

Your Decoder Ring

Home equity loans can take many forms. They can be traditional bank mortgages or a line of credit. You can even have a credit card that qualifies as home equity debt. The critical feature is that the lender uses your home as collateral for the loan.

Deducting Mortgage Points

Your bank might charge mortgage points when you borrow money to buy, improve, or refinance your home. Points are usually calculated as a percent of the amount that you borrow. Points might be negotiable, but they will impact your mortgage rate. If you pay lower points, you will pay a higher interest rate on your mortgage. If you pay higher points, your mortgage interest rate will be lower. Points might also be referred to as one of the following terms:

➤ Loan origination fees

➤ Discount points

➤ Maximum loan charges

➤ Loan discounts

Ordinarily, you can't deduct mortgage points in the year you pay them. You take the deduction a little bit in each year of the loan. This is called *amortization*.

Points You Can Deduct Now

There is a big tax break when you borrow money for your primary home. You can deduct points paid on a home mortgage in the year you pay them if you use the loan to do any of the following:

➤ Buy your primary home
➤ Build your primary home
➤ Improve your primary home

Your original home mortgage might not be taken out at the time you actually buy or build your home. You might have bought your home under a short-term contract from the seller. You might have used a short-term construction loan during the time your home was under construction. When you replace the contract or the construction loan with your permanent mortgage, you will be able to deduct your mortgage points.

To deduct your mortgage points, you also have to meet the following requirements:

➤ The loan has to be secured by your primary home.
➤ Charging mortgage points must be a common business practice in your area.
➤ The points that you pay are not more than the points that are usually charged in your area.
➤ The points are calculated as a percentage of the amount that you borrow.
➤ The points are clearly shown on your settlement statement.
➤ You have to pay enough cash to cover your points.

The last rule is the payment requirement. There isn't any need to write a separate check for points, but you do have to provide enough cash to cover the points to get the full deduction. To satisfy the payment rule, the funds that you pay on closing or before closing, plus the points that were paid by the seller, have to be at least as much as the points that you were charged. Your down payment or earnest money can be used to satisfy your payment requirement.

For example, Paula is buying a $61,000 home with a $1,000 down payment. She is borrowing $60,000. Paula is charged mortgage points of 2%, or $1,200. Since she has only paid cash of $1,000 on the transaction, Paula can only deduct $1,000 of her points. The other $200 has to be written off over the life of her mortgage.

Deducting Points You Didn't Pay

If you are buying a home and the seller pays your points for you, you might still be able to deduct the points. It's as if the buyer gives you a rebate on the price of your house and you use the rebate to pay the points. The seller has a reduced selling price. You have a lower cost basis in your home and a deduction for the points paid. The deduction for seller-paid points couldn't be taken before 1991, so it's a fairly new development.

Points You Have to Amortize

Only points paid for the purchase, construction, or improvement of your primary residence qualify for the immediate deduction. All other points have to be amortized.

If you are amortizing points on a loan and you end the mortgage early, you can write off your old unamortized points. The mortgage could be paid off early because you sell your home, pay off your mortgage, or refinance your mortgage. For example, Kendra refinanced her home mortgage and is amortizing her points. She paid $1,000 of points and has deducted $250 of her points so far. The interest rate has fallen again, and Kendra is able to refinance, which she does in 1998. If Kendra pays points on her new mortgage, those points will be written off over the life of her loan. In 1998, Kendra can deduct the remaining $750 of her old mortgage points that she has not yet deducted.

Paper Trail

If the person who sold your house to you paid your points and you didn't deduct them, you might be able to amend your tax return. File a Form 1040X to claim a refund. You have up to three years to amend your tax return. You can file an amended 1995 return up to April 15, 1999.

Points that have to be amortized include points paid on a mortgage for the following reasons:

➤ Refinancing your home mortgage

➤ Taking out a home equity loan

➤ Buying a home other than your primary home (including a rental home)

How to Deduct Your Points

Include your points in the interest section of your Schedule A. If you pay points on your home purchase, the lender will probably report the points on a Form 1098. There is not a separate line on the Schedule A for points that are reported on a Form 1098. You simply add

Paper Trail

When you buy a home, sell a home, or refinance your home, you will receive a settlement statement. The statement is sometimes called a closing statement. Keep this statement. It is an important document.

the points to your other mortgage interest expense and deduct them on one line. If you are nervous about clumping the figures together, attach a schedule showing how you got your numbers.

If you are amortizing mortgage points on refinancing or on a second home, there is a separate line for you to use. Include your deduction on the "points not reported to you on Form 1098" line of Schedule A.

Other fees that are charged for your mortgage, such as appraisal fees or legal fees, are not deductible. Add these expenses to the cost basis of your home. They will reduce your gain when you sell your home.

Paying Off Your Home Early?

If you are fortunate enough to be paying off your home mortgage early, you might have yet another fortunate break. If you have to pay a fee for paying your mortgage off early, the prepayment fee is deductible by you as home mortgage interest. This applies if you were able to deduct the mortgage interest on the loan you are paying off.

Red Flag

As you shop for home mortgages, ask about prepayment penalties. You don't want a mortgage with penalties for early payment. If you pay a bit more each month toward your mortgage principal, you can save big bucks over the life of your loan.

Reporting Requirements

Each year, you will get a Form 1098 from your mortgage lender. The Form 1098 will tell you how much mortgage interest you paid and how much you paid in mortgage points. Your lender also sends a copy of your Form 1098 to the IRS. The IRS puts the information in its computer. The IRS can then compare the deductions that you take to the information that's in its computer.

If the IRS can't match up your mortgage interest to its computer records, they will send you a notice. The notice will tell you how much mortgage interest the IRS thinks you should be deducting. The notice will calculate the tax, penalty, and interest that you can pay if you agree that you claimed too much interest deduction.

Don't automatically assume that the IRS notice is correct and that you have to pay the taxes that are calculated. Check your tax return. Check your records. Find out why the IRS records are different than yours. If you think your tax return is correct, write a letter to the IRS. Enclose a copy of the IRS notice and any other information that supports your position. Don't send original documents. Only send copies and keep a copy of everything that you send.

The IRS is usually good at responding to letters about tax notices. If you get no response, you need to follow up, though. There are usually phone numbers on notices that you can call. If you end up in a letter writing campaign with the IRS, a Problems

Resolutions Officer can help you out. You have to make efforts to resolve disputes first, and you have to keep documentation of your attempts.

If you own property with someone else and have one mortgage loan, only one Form 1098 will be filed. The Form 1098 will report all of the mortgage interest with only one of the borrowers' name and Social Security number. If you are not the person who got the Form 1098, the IRS won't be able to match up your mortgage interest deduction. What do you do?

Red Flag

If you have a large tax bill from the IRS, professional help may pay for itself. An experienced tax professional can evaluate your situation and advise you how to proceed.

The IRS suggests that you deduct your part of the interest and write "see attached" next to the line on your tax return. Attach a statement explaining the situation and give the name and address of the person who received the Form 1098. Even if you do this, you need to be prepared for a possible matching notice. This problem can happen if rental property is owned by more than one person. The problem can also be encountered if two unmarried persons are both liable on a mortgage loan.

Your mortgage might not be with a bank or other lending company. For example, you might have borrowed the money from a family member. You might also be buying your house on contract from the seller. As long as the acquisition indebtedness rules are followed, you can deduct your interest even though it isn't paid to a bank. The requirement that private individuals often miss is having the debt actually secured by the home.

Your lender won't file a Form 1098 for the interest you pay if your lender is a private individual. If you pay mortgage interest to someone who doesn't file a Form 1098, you have to report the lender's name, address, and ID number on your tax return. The ID number for an individual is his or her Social Security number. Guess what the IRS does with this information? They make sure your lender is reporting the interest income.

Mortgage Interest Credit

There is a program that can give you a tax credit for part of your mortgage interest. You can only take the credit for interest paid on your primary residence. Second homes and rental homes don't qualify for the credit. To claim the credit, you have to get a mortgage credit certificate, known as an MCC. Your MCC will be issued by a state or local government agency.

The credit can be used on a mortgage taken out to buy, build, or improve your primary home. The credit is a percent of the interest that you pay. There is a dollar limit that your MCC will authorize. If your loan is more than the dollar amount authorized, you'll take your credit on the interest up to the limit.

For example, Steven gets an MCC allowing a credit of 20% on up to $25,000 of his mortgage. Steven's interest rate on his mortgage is 7.25%. If his mortgage balance is more than $25,000, the interest that qualifies for the credit is $1,812.50 (7.25% of $25,000). Steven's credit is $362.50, which is 20% of $1,812.50.

If your MCC rate is more than 20%, your credit can't be more than $2,000. If you claim the mortgage interest credit, you have to reduce your mortgage interest deduction on Schedule A by the amount of the credit. Steven, in the example above, will reduce his mortgage interest deduction by $362.50.

The Least You Need to Know

➤ Your home mortgage interest is deductible as an itemized deduction.

➤ You can deduct interest on your primary residence and on your second home.

➤ Home equity debt interest is deductible even if you use the proceeds for consumer purchases.

➤ Points that you pay on a new mortgage are either all deductible in the year paid or are deducted a bit each year of the mortgage (amortized).

➤ The IRS will have a record of your mortgage interest from the Form 1098 that your lender files.

Chapter 10

Giving to Charity

In This Chapter

➤ Knowing which donations will give you a tax break

➤ Deducting gifts that are not cash

➤ Keeping the right records

➤ Filing the correct forms

Our society relies on charitable organizations. Charities educate our children, feed the hungry, provide arts in our communities, and operate our churches.

We get a tax break for supporting charities. Congress doesn't give us the tax break just because it has a big heart. Congress knows that taxes would have to be raised if charities didn't provide the services we need and use. If a congressman harms charities and increases your taxes at the same time, it makes for a very tough reelection campaign.

Charitable contributions are one of the itemized deductions that we claim on Schedule A attached to our Form 1040. You have to file the long form to deduct any of your charitable contributions. Each of us probably has more charitable deductions than we realize. Knowing the rules and keeping records is your key to saving tax dollars.

What Is a Charity?

We can deduct contributions made to charities. To be more specific, we can deduct contributions to qualifying charitable organizations.

Not-for-Profit Versus Charitable

To borrow a phrase from high school geometry, a square is always a rectangle, but not every rectangle is a square. All charities are not-for-profit organizations, but not every not-for profit is a charity. It would just be too easy if we could take deductions for gifts to any not-for-profit organization. That kind of simplicity is not the style of our tax code.

Your Decoder Ring

To be **not-for-profit**, an organization doesn't have to lose money. Nonprofits must make money to survive. Profits can't go to the pockets of individuals, though. Profits must be used for the organization's purpose.

So, which organizations qualify? The following list identifies all organizations that the IRS considers charities:

➤ U.S. organizations that have a charitable, religious, scientific, literary, or educational purpose

➤ Organizations that prevent cruelty to children or animals

➤ War veterans' organizations

➤ Lodges (but only contributions individuals make to support their charity work are deductible)

➤ Governmental bodies if your contribution is for public purposes (for example, the U.S. Government, any of the 50 states, the District of Columbia, a U.S. possession, a city, a town, a county, or an Indian tribal government)

Confused? Some examples might help. You can deduct contributions made to the following organizations:

➤ Churches, synagogues, temples, or mosques

➤ Religious associations

➤ Salvation Army, Goodwill Industries, Red Cross, United Way, and similar community charities

➤ Nonprofit schools, colleges, and universities

➤ Nonprofit hospitals

➤ Nonprofit museums

➤ Boy Scouts and Girl Scouts

➤ Nonprofit daycare centers

➤ Nonprofit volunteer fire companies

➤ Public parks

➤ Public recreation facilities

➤ Civil defense organizations

➤ Nonprofit arts organizations (orchestras, ballet companies, and so on)

➤ Your state, county, city, and town

You can't deduct contributions made to the following organizations:

➤ Chambers of commerce

➤ Social clubs (dinner clubs or country clubs)

➤ Labor unions

➤ Foreign organizations (except some Canadian and Mexican organizations)

➤ Groups run for personal profit

➤ Organizations that lobby lawmakers

➤ Homeowners' associations

➤ Individuals

➤ Political organizations

➤ Political candidates or campaigns

How Do I Know If an Organization Qualifies?

Many organizations clearly qualify as charities. For example, your church and your state university automatically qualify as charities.

Some charities, though, must get approval from the IRS to qualify as charitable organizations. If approved, the charity will get a letter stating qualification under Code Section 501(c)(3). You can request a copy of the 501(c)(3) letter to have proof of the charity's qualification. A qualified charity should have a copy of its 501(c)(3) letter on file that it can give to you on request.

IRS publication 78 is a listing of organizations that have received qualified charity status. You can find IRS Publication 78 at your local library or at the IRS web site (http://irs.ustreas.gov). You won't find your local church on this list since churches don't have to apply for charity status.

Red Flag

People do not qualify as charities. For example, gifts to your minister cannot be deducted. If you want to help a family whose home has burned, you can't deduct a gift to the family, but you can deduct a gift to the Red Cross.

How Much Can I Deduct?

There are two factors that determine the amount of your charitable contribution deduction:

➤ The value of the property you gave to charity

➤ The limit imposed on charitable deductions by the Tax Code

Measuring Your Gift

If you give cash or write a check, it's easy to know how much you have given to charity. It's not so clear if you give something other than cash. Your deduction for a charitable gift could be either the fair market value of the property you gave away or your cost basis in the property.

Your Decoder Ring

The term **basis** is often used in the Tax Code. What does basis mean? Basis is the running total that you have invested in the property. Basis is increased by both the cost of buying the property (commissions for stocks) and improvements you make to the property (adding a kitchen to your home). Basis can also be decreased (for example, by depreciation deductions).

Red Flag

If you give stock to a private foundation after June 30, 1998, the deduction is limited to your basis in the stock. This rule might be changed but was the law of the land when we went to press.

To know whether you should use your basis or the property's fair market value, you have to ask yourself a question: "If I sold this property, would I have a long-term capital gain or an ordinary gain?" If the answer is capital gain, you can take a charitable deduction for the full fair market value of the property you donated. If the answer is ordinary income, your deduction is limited to your basis in the property.

Let's look at some examples. The following gifts would be valued at fair market value:

➤ Stock in a publicly traded company, unless you are a dealer in marketable securities

➤ Real estate, unless you are a real estate dealer

➤ Art work that you did not produce

➤ Books that you did not write

However, the following gifts would be valued at your basis (cost):

➤ Items from inventory of your business

➤ Items that you created, such as art or manuscripts

➤ Stock that you have held less than 12 months

Limits, of Course!

Congress couldn't let us take a deduction without limiting how much we can claim. Charitable deductions can be limited. Most givers don't struggle with the limits, but generous souls can find this a nasty trap. The maximum amount of your charitable deduction takes your AGI and the type of gift you made into account.

The charitable contribution deduction limit is a percentage of your AGI. Your total gifts cannot be more than 50% of your AGI. Some donations cannot be more than

30%. Yet another type can't be more than 20% of your AGI.

The 50% limit applies to cash gifts (including checks) given to the following types of organizations:

> ➤ Churches and associations of churches
> ➤ Educational organizations
> ➤ Hospitals and medical research organizations
> ➤ Publicly supported charities
> ➤ Private operating foundations
> ➤ Private nonoperating foundations that distribute all contributions to charities no later than two and a half months after the foundation's year ends
> ➤ Certain private foundations that use common funds and donate to public charities

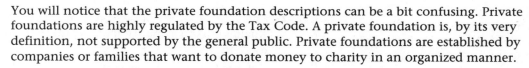

Your Decoder Ring

Remember what **AGI** is? It's the income on your tax return before you subtract personal exemptions and itemized deductions.

You will notice that the private foundation descriptions can be a bit confusing. Private foundations are highly regulated by the Tax Code. A private foundation is, by its very definition, not supported by the general public. Private foundations are established by companies or families that want to donate money to charity in an organized manner.

Thirty percent gifts are limited to 30% of your AGI. These gifts are the following:

> ➤ Capital gain property (such as stock) given to a publicly supported charity
> ➤ Cash gifts to veterans' organizations, fraternal societies, and nonprofit cemeteries
> ➤ Cash gifts to private nonoperating foundations

Twenty percent gifts are the most limited and include gifts of capital gain property to veterans' organizations, fraternal societies, nonprofit cemeteries, and private nonoperating foundations.

If your gifts are more than you can claim, don't despair. You can use the excess gifts as a deduction in the next five years. Of course, you have to apply the percent of AGI limit in those years, too.

For example, Dan made a generous contribution in 1998 to his church's capital campaign. Dan contributed publicly traded stock that is worth $20,000. He paid $5,000 for this stock five years ago. Dan's AGI is $60,000 in 1998. Dan's deduction is limited to 30% of his AGI, or $18,000. On Dan's 1998 return, he will deduct $18,000. In 1999, Dan can add the remaining $2,000 left over from 1998 to his 1999 contributions on his tax return.

The 50% limit applies to gifts of cash to public charities. A public charity is supported by the general public. A private charity, on the other hand, is supported by a limited number of people.

The 30% limit applies to the following:

➤ Gifts of capital gain property to public charities

➤ Gifts of cash to a private foundation

The 20% limit applies to gifts of capital gain property to a private foundation.

Cash Gifts

Cash donations are certainly the easiest gifts to measure. There is no question of the value of the gift. Keeping records, though, can make the difference between getting a deduction or not. Remember the following documentation tips when making cash contributions:

Paper Trail

If you face having your charitable contributions being limited, it may be time to seek help with your tax return. These calculations might be best handled by the pros.

➤ Keep your canceled checks as proof of the gift.

➤ Keep that letter from the charity thanking you.

➤ If a gift is $250 or more, you must have a letter from the charity. Your canceled check is not enough to claim the deduction.

➤ The $250 letter is not needed if you make smaller gifts to a charity that add up to $250 or more for the year.

➤ Get a receipt if you give cash.

If you mail a check to a charity for a donation, you can deduct the contribution in the year that you mail the check. If you charge your donation on a credit card, your donation deduction is taken in the year of the charge.

Paper Trail

For gifts of $250 or more, the letter from the charity must state that you did not get anything in exchange for your gift. This letter must be in your hands before your tax return is filed. Without the letter, your donation is not deductible.

Gifts from Your Closet

Many of us donate our used clothes, toys, or furniture to charities. These donations are deductible, but they are difficult to value. What is the rule? You can deduct the value of the item donated. What is the value? It's probably less than you think.

If you give items to Goodwill Industries or Salvation Army that will be sold in their thrift shops, your deduction is limited to the thrift shop value. It doesn't matter that you paid $100 for a blouse, the charity might only be able to sell it for $1.00. Guess what your deduction is? It's $1.00. Even if the blouse is in great shape, $1.00 is all you can deduct.

It is unrealistic to revisit the shops to find out how your items are priced, so what do you do? My best advice is the following:

➤ Ask the charity if it will value the gift for you.

➤ Be realistic.

➤ Take a picture of the items you give.

➤ Know the appraisal rules if you make a large gift.

If you are audited and you have given clothing and furniture to charity, you can bet the agent will try to adjust your deduction. The agent won't want to increase the value, either. The value is a judgment call. A receipt from the charity with a dollar value can help you tremendously.

If the charity won't give you a value of your donation, ask if they have an average price list for their thrift shop. The price list will give you good ideas of selling prices. If there is no price list to be gotten, you will have to come up with values yourself. Make a list of the items you gave. Try to estimate the original cost of the items given. You can then estimate the resale value. The resale value might be as little as 10% or 5% of the original cost. Make your best effort to come up with a reasonable value.

When You Need an Appraisal

If you make a noncash donation of more than $5,000, you need to obtain a written, signed appraisal by a qualified appraiser. The appraisal rule applies if you give smaller gifts of similar items that add up to more than $5,000 for the year.

For example, Kim gave $2,000 of furniture to a homeless shelter in January. In June, she gave another $4,000 of furniture. Since Kim gave more than $5,000 of used furniture in the year, the appraisal requirement will apply to both gifts.

The appraiser must meet the following requirements:

➤ Be a person who is qualified to make the appraisal

➤ Regularly perform appraisals for the public

➤ Not base the appraisal fee on a percentage of the property's value

➤ Be unrelated to the donor (you)

➤ Not be an employee of the charity

➤ Sign Form 8283, Section B, Part III, declaring that he or she meets all of the requirements

The appraiser can be subject to penalties if the value of the property is inflated. Many appraisers will pause at the statement they will sign on the Form 8283. This pause is exactly the reaction that Congress and the IRS were seeking.

The fee that you pay for an appraisal is not deductible as a charitable contribution. The fee is, however, deductible as a miscellaneous itemized deduction. These deductions are also claimed on Schedule A.

133

If an appraisal is needed for a gift, you must also have the charity sign Part IV of Section B of Form 8283. This is called the Donee Acknowledgment.

Gifts of Stocks

The stock market boom has created an opportunity for exceptionally tax-effective charitable giving. If you give stock that has increased in value to a charity, three big tax benefits result:

➤ You deduct the full value of the stock.

➤ You avoid paying capital gains tax.

➤ The charity can sell the stock without paying any income tax.

If the stock is traded on the stock market, the appraisal rules do not apply. If the stock is privately held, an appraisal is needed if the stock is worth $10,000 or more.

Red Flag

Obtaining a value for an asset that you don't normally sell can be a very difficult task. If you donate this property to charity, choose your appraiser carefully. A well-drafted valuation report can prevent lengthy battles with the IRS. This is no time to deal with amateurs.

Charitable Trusts: A Primer

Charitable trusts can be an effective way to give money to charity. Charitable trusts can be flexible and very tax-smart. For the most part, charitable trusts are for large gifts. Some charities are now sponsoring programs that allow you to make donations in trust without much ado. The emergence of community foundations has opened up the opportunity to give money in trust also.

When you give money in trust, you will be separating two different types of property rights. Every property has two distinct sets of rights:

➤ Income rights
➤ Principal (corpus) rights

For example, a bank certificate of deposit will pay you interest (income). When the certificate matures, you will get your principal (corpus) back. Even your home has income and principal rights. You have a right to enjoy and use your home (income), and you have the rights to the proceeds when you sell the home (principal).

There are two types of charitable trusts:

➤ Charitable remainder trusts

➤ Charitable lead trusts

In a charitable remainder trust, the charity gets the trust property when the trust terminates (the trust remainder). You will get a stream of income from the trust either for a fixed number of years or for your lifetime. Charitable remainder trusts are very effective if you have highly appreciated property, if you would like to make a charitable gift, and if you would like to get a stream of income.

The tax benefits of the charitable remainder trust are pretty impressive:

➤ You get a current charitable contribution deduction for the gift. The deduction is discounted since it is a gift that will be made in the future.

➤ You don't have to recognize capital gain when you give the property to the trust.

➤ The trust can sell the property without paying income tax.

➤ As you take distributions from the trust, you will have income taxes. Your taxable income won't be more than your distributions from the trust, though.

Let's say that Rod has stock that is highly appreciated. The stock is worth $100,000 and he paid $5,000 for the stock. He would like to make a substantial gift to his favorite charity. He can't really afford to give away the entire $100,000 and would still like to get some cash flow.

Rod contributes the stock to a charitable remainder trust. Rod is going to get a 6% distribution each year (approximately $6,000). The trust can sell the stock without paying tax on the capital gain. The trust can reinvest the stock sale proceeds entirely in other securities since it pays no income tax. Each year, Rod will pay income tax on part or all of his distribution from the trust. At the end of the trust term, the remaining trust assets will go to charity.

Rod has converted his appreciated stock to a stream of payments. He has gotten a tax deduction for a portion of the value of the stock. He has also made a significant gift to his favorite charity.

A charitable lead trust is the reverse of a charitable remainder trust. In a charitable lead trust, the charity will get a stream of payments. At the end of the trust term, a person (or persons) will get the remainder of the trust assets. A charitable lead trust can be used if you want to give money to charity during your lifetime, but you want the assets to go to your heirs when you die.

Little-Known Charitable Deductions

Wouldn't you hate to find out that you could have taken a deduction that you just didn't know about? Here is your chance to find out about those deductions that might be hidden in the corners of the tax law.

Paper Trail

If you are interested in charitable trusts, talk to your CPA, your attorney, and your favorite charity. There are a lot of requirements that must be met. Be sure that you understand the arrangement and that you are using qualified professionals to complete the transaction.

Driving Your Car for Charity

Any volunteer knows how many miles can be put on the car when helping a good cause. In 1998, each charitable mile you drive will earn you a 14¢ charitable deduction.

As an alternative to mileage, you can claim your actual gas and oil expenses that are used while driving for charity. You cannot deduct a portion of your car maintenance, insurance, and so on.

Paper Trail

The key to supporting mileage deductions is a well-kept calendar or log book. Write down the date, place, purpose of your travel, and the number of miles. If you travel for business and charity both, the same calendar or log book can be used for both.

Foreign Students

If you host a foreign exchange student in your home, you can deduct $50 for each full month that the student is in your home. A month counts if the student is with you for at least 15 days that month and the student meets the following three requirements:

➤ Lives in your home under a qualified foreign exchange program

➤ Is not your relative or dependent

➤ Attends school full-time in the United States in the 12th grade or lower

Uniforms

If you must wear a uniform when you volunteer, the cost of the uniform and its upkeep is deductible as a charitable contribution. The uniform must be unsuitable for everyday use. For example, a candy striper smock would be deductible, but you can't deduct a logo T-shirt.

Representing an Organization

Your favorite charity might ask you to attend its annual convention. If you attend an event as a representative of your charity, your expenses can be claimed as a tax deduction. Remember, you must be representing your organization. Merely going as a member will not make the trip deductible.

You can deduct your travel, hotel expenses, meals, and convention or meeting expenses. You can't deduct personal expenses such as sightseeing tours or theater tickets. You also can't deduct the expenses of a companion or your family if they travel with you.

For example, Leslie is actively involved as a board member of the local chapter of the Red Cross. She is asked to attend a national convention as a representative of her Red Cross chapter. She will learn information about services that can be rendered. She is expected to bring this information back to her chapter to enhance their services. All of Leslie's expenses to attend the convention will be deductible as a charitable contribution.

Out-of-Pocket Expenses

Many volunteers spend their own funds for charitable events. These expenses are deductible, but can be hard to prove. For example, Beth hosted a lunch in her home to raise funds for her favorite charity, the Humane Society. Beth paid for all of the food herself. These food expenses are deductible as a charitable contribution. In an audit, how could Beth prove that the grocery receipts were for this event? It is a difficult task. Any of the following tips might help:

➤ Have the charity reimburse you for your expenses and write a check back to the charity for your donation.

➤ Keep a copy of the invitation or program for the event with your tax records to prove your participation in the event.

➤ Keep your thank-you note from the charity and make sure they mention that you donated all of the food.

➤ If your donation is $250 or more, remember that you must have a letter from the charity documenting your gift.

Out-of-pocket expenses can include the cost of travel. If the travel is for the charity, your expenses are deductible. For example, if you are a Cub Scout leader, your expenses to lead a camping trip are deductible. The primary purpose of the trip must be related to the charity's purpose. If there is a significant element of personal pleasure, the trip is not deductible. This doesn't mean that you can't have fun, though!

Athletic Boosters

Many colleges and universities have booster clubs. If you donate to the club, you earn the right to buy athletic tickets. If you receive tickets in exchange for your donation, that portion of your donation is not deductible. If you merely earn the right to buy the athletic tickets, 80% of your booster club donation is deductible. The IRS arbitrarily set the deduction at 80%, but it sure is nice to have an easy guideline.

Foster Parents' Expenses

If you are a foster care provider, you may be able to take a charitable deduction for some of your expenses. If you spend more money to support the individuals in your care than you receive as a foster care provider, the excess is deductible.

To claim this deduction, you must not be in the business of providing foster care, and your expenses must be greater than the support you are receiving.

Traps

Even the most generous taxpayers can lose out on deductions if they don't know the rules and follow them. Don't get caught. Know the rules.

Be a Pack Rat

You may be swimming in a sea if paperwork, but don't lose charitable deductions to sloppy records. Always keep the following records for at least seven years:

➤ Cash receipts

➤ Canceled checks

➤ Receipts for property donations

➤ Receipts for out-of-pocket expenses

➤ Thank-you notes

➤ Published lists of donors in programs or newsletters

➤ Letters of acknowledgment (required if gift is $250 or more)

➤ Required appraisal if gift is $5,000 or more

You might not need all of these items, but they could come in handy if you get audited.

What You Can't Deduct

Some gifts are valuable to charity, but they are not deductible on your tax return. You can't deduct any of the following:

➤ Babysitting expenses while you volunteer

➤ The value of your time

➤ Tuition

➤ Blood you donate to a blood bank

➤ The cost of raffle tickets

➤ Bingo games

➤ Lottery tickets

➤ Admission to an event up to the reasonable value of the event, even if called a contribution

➤ Political contributions

➤ Country club or social club dues

Paper Trail

Important documents are worth safeguarding. If you have made a large charitable donation, consider keeping your appraisal in your safe-deposit box. You can't safeguard all of your tax records, but critical items should be protected when possible.

Fundraisers

Do you have a weak spot for those yummy chocolate bars that all the kids sell? Do you own a dozen public radio coffee mugs? Have you rented a tuxedo for enough fundraisers that you could have bought one by now? If so, join the ranks of the loyal supporters of our charitable organizations.

Red Flag

If you send your children to a school that is run by your church, you can't deduct your tuition payments. Just because you write your checks to the church, the tuition is not a tax deduction.

When you give money to a charity and get something in exchange, watch out! Not only will your name go on the list for the next event, but your charitable deduction might be limited. If you receive a small item in exchange for your gift, you will have no problem. If you receive a calendar, bookmark, or logo coffee mug, for example, the premium you receive will not influence your tax deduction. If you receive more than a token gift from the charity, your deduction will be limited.

Some examples might help:

➤ If you buy an item at a charity auction, you can take a deduction only to the extent you pay more than the item is worth.

➤ If you attend a charity lunch or dinner, subtract the value of the meal from the ticket price to determine your donation.

➤ If you buy retail items for a fundraiser at retail price, you get no deduction.

➤ If you receive a calendar and a program guide when you become a member of your local public TV station, your entire gift is deductible.

➤ If you attend a charity golf outing, the portion of your payment that covers the value of the round of golf and your meals is not deductible.

A charity must tell you the value of the goods or services you will receive in exchange for your donation if you make a payment of $75 or more. Keep the ticket or invitation that contains this information. You might need it during an audit.

Forms, Forms, Forms

What forms do you need? Refer to the following to refresh your memory:

➤ Schedule A for claiming your deductions.

➤ Form 8283, Section A, if you make noncash gifts over $500 (but not over $5,000).

➤ Form 8283, Section A, for gifts of marketable securities (even if more than $5,000).

➤ Form 8283, Section B, for noncash gifts of more than $5,000 that require appraisals.

The Least You Need to Know

➤ Donations to qualified charitable organizations are tax deductible. You must keep records to support your deduction.

➤ If you give property to a charity, you might get a deduction for the full value of your gift. Giving stocks that have increased in value can save you a lot of taxes and help the charity.

➤ Your charitable contribution deduction is limited to a percentage of your income.

➤ If you volunteer for a charity, you can't deduct the value of your time, but you can deduct mileage and out-of-pocket expenses.

➤ If you give $250 or more to a charity, you must have a letter from the charity. Without this letter, your gift is not deductible.

Take this too! I need the deduction!

Chapter 11

Casualty and Theft Losses: Save Taxes When Disaster Strikes

> **In This Chapter**
>
> ➤ Deducting losses from casualties or thefts
>
> ➤ Knowing the cutbacks that limit your personal casualty and theft deduction
>
> ➤ Taking a loss if your business or rental property is damaged
>
> ➤ Reporting a gain from a casualty—better yet, how to postpone the gain
>
> ➤ Filing the correct forms with your tax return

If you lose property because of a casualty or a theft, you can take a tax deduction for your loss. Your deduction is an itemized deduction if you lose property that you use personally. If you lose business or rental property, your deduction is a business loss, which is not an itemized deduction.

Each personal casualty and theft loss has to be reduced by $100. All of your losses are then reduced by 10% of your adjusted gross income (AGI). This means that you will only get a write-off if your losses are large or your income is small.

Taking a tax loss for a casualty or theft softens the blow of your misfortune. Ordinarily, you can't take a tax loss for items that you use personally, so the casualty and theft loss rules are worth checking out.

Losses You Can Deduct

There are two types of losses that you can deduct: casualties and thefts. A casualty is the result of an event that is sudden, unexpected, and unusual, such as the following:

➤ Fire
➤ Automobile accident
➤ Flood
➤ Storm (hurricane, tornado, thunderstorm, etc.)
➤ Earthquake
➤ Shipwreck
➤ Sonic boom
➤ Mine cave-in
➤ Volcanic eruption
➤ Vandalism

A theft is when someone illegally takes your money or your property. Thefts include the following:

➤ Blackmail
➤ Burglary
➤ Embezzlement
➤ Extortion
➤ Kidnapping for ransom
➤ Larceny
➤ Robbery

If you lose or misplace your property, you won't get a theft loss. For example, if you lose your wallet, you can't claim a loss on your tax return. On the other hand, if your wallet is blown away in a tornado, you can claim a tax loss.

What if you loan money to someone and they don't pay you back? Is that a theft? No, but it can give you a tax loss. If the loan was not related to your business, you have a nonbusiness bad debt. The bad debt is a short-term capital loss.

Doing the Math: Calculate Your Loss

You have suffered a loss; it qualifies as a casualty or a theft. To claim the loss, you have to come up with a number. You have to measure the amount of your loss. In some cases, it's not easy to measure your loss. In an audit, proving the amount of your loss can be a difficult task, so keep good records.

There are three steps to calculating your loss:

1. Calculate your adjusted basis (cost) in the property before the casualty or theft.
2. Calculate how much the value of your property decreased as a result of the casualty or theft.

3. Determine whether your basis or the decrease in value is less. From the lesser amount, subtract the insurance reimbursement that you got or expect to get.

This calculation is done separately for each item of personal property that you lose. For example, Pam had a small fire in her home. Three items were lost: a set of drapes, a chair, and an antique table. Her loss calculation might look like this.

	Drapes	Chair	Table
Cost	$500	$300	$150
FMV before fire	$100	$200	$550
FMV after fire	-0-	-0-	-0-
FMV decrease	$100	$200	$550
Tax Loss	$100	$200	$150
Total Tax Loss	$450		

Note: FMV=Fair Market Value

If you lost real estate in a casualty, the tax loss is calculated for the entire property as if it were one item. In other words, calculate your loss as if the building, improvements, trees, and landscaping were one piece of property rather than separate items. This makes the calculations much easier and can increase the amount of the loss that you can claim.

If you have to pay appraisal fees to support your casualty loss, you can deduct your appraisal fee. The deduction is not added to your casualty loss. The fee is taken as a miscellaneous itemized deduction. The cost of taking photographs to support your casualty loss or to support your insurance claim is also deductible as a miscellaneous itemized deduction.

Red Flag

Be ready to support your bad debt if you claim a loss on your tax return. The IRS might make you prove that the loan was not really a gift. They might make you prove that you tried to collect the money and were not able to get it back. Be prepared. Document your loan with a signed note, and document your attempts to collect.

Expenses related to a casualty are not deductible. Examples of nondeductible related expenses are the cost of a rental car while your damaged car is repaired, or medical care if you are injured in a casualty.

It would be much easier to just use the cost of repairs as the measure of your casualty loss. You might be able to do that. You can use your repair and clean up costs as the measure of your loss if you meet all of the following conditions:

Your Decoder Ring

Personal property is property that is tangible, meaning you can touch it. It is also not real estate, as you can move it. Many investments are intangible assets, such as stocks and bonds, so they aren't personal property. Furniture, equipment, and cars are all examples of personal property. Personal use property is an item that you don't use in your business.

➤ The repairs are needed to restore the property to its condition before the casualty.

➤ The repair expense is not excessive.

➤ The repairs only take care of the damage caused by the casualty.

➤ Your repairs did not increase the value of the property compared to its value before the casualty.

For example, Melody's yard is seriously damaged by a thunderstorm. She lost trees and shrubs, and her fence was badly damaged. Melody has the fence repaired and restores her landscaping to the condition it was in before the storm. She didn't upgrade any of the materials or add additional plantings. Melody can deduct her repair costs as her casualty loss.

If you rent property that was damaged and you have to pay for the repairs, calculating your casualty loss is easy. Subtract your insurance reimbursement from your repair costs to get your tax loss.

What if you don't file a claim with your insurance company? If your loss is covered by insurance and you don't file an insurance claim, you can't take a tax loss for the amount that would have been reimbursed by your insurance. The part that would not have been covered by your insurance is still deductible.

For example, Shawn had an $800 fire loss. The loss was covered by his insurance, but he has a $500 deductible. If Shawn makes a claim against his insurance, he will lose his premium discount. Shawn decides not to file an insurance claim. In calculating his casualty loss for his tax return, his loss is only $300. Shawn can't deduct any loss that the insurance company would have covered.

If you get payments related to your casualty for any personal physical injury that you suffered, the payments are tax-free. On the other hand, damages received for non-physical injuries are taxable. For example, payments for loss of income or for anxiety are taxable.

How Much Can You Deduct for Your Loss?

Now that you have calculated the amount of your casualty or theft loss, you still have some more math to do. Each casualty or theft of personal use property must be reduced by $100. All of your casualty losses from personal use property have to be combined and reduced by 10% of your adjusted gross income (AGI).

For example, Brad is in an automobile accident. His casualty loss is $8,000. This is the amount of his repairs that were not covered by his insurance company. Brad's AGI is

$65,000. Brad's deductible casualty loss is calculated as follows:

Amount of loss	$8,000
Less $100	–$100
Less 10% of AGI	–$6,500
Deductible loss	$1,400

Poor Brad has a second casualty. A storm damages his home. His storm loss has to be reduced by $100. He would combine his storm loss with his car accident to apply his 10% of AGI floor, though.

Paper Trail

If family members or friends give you cash gifts after a casualty, the gifts won't reduce your casualty loss. Gifts are tax-free income. You can use the money that you receive as gifts to replace your lost property and still deduct your casualty loss.

If your loss is from business or rental property, the $100 and 10% of AGI reductions don't apply. If your loss is partly personal and partly business or rent, you will have to divide your loss to separate the personal losses. The $100 and 10% of AGI reductions will only apply to the personal use portion of the loss.

Proving Your Loss

To support your casualty or theft loss, there are two things that you have to be able to prove:

➤ That you had a loss caused by a casualty or theft.

➤ The amount of the loss that you claim.

The key is to keep good records. Pictures can be invaluable in proving that you actually had a loss. Don't send your pictures to the IRS with your tax return. Keep them in case you get audited. You need to be able to prove when the casualty or theft occurred. Insurance claims or police reports can help with this documentation. It might be difficult to prove your home was burglarized without a police report.

You will need to be able to prove that the loss was a direct result of the casualty. For example, you might claim that your roof was damaged by a hail storm. You will need some proof that a storm caused your damage. The IRS agent might just think you're trying to deduct a repair bill. A contractor's report might help with this documentation. Keeping a copy of newspaper reports of a storm that caused local damage might be helpful in an audit.

When to Deduct Your Loss

The general rule is that casualty losses can only be deducted in the year of the casualty. Even if the repairs are made in a later year, the tax loss is taken when the damage was done.

Paper Trail

The most effective documentation you can have to support your loss is correspondence with your insurance company. Keep a copy of your claim. Keep a copy of any letters or statements sent to you from the insurance company. Keep a copy of your reimbursement check. These papers may come in handy if the IRS calls on you.

Red Flag

If you own your own business, don't think that your trusted employees won't steal from you. Only those employees that you trust will have the opportunity to steal from you. Given enough opportunity and financial stress, otherwise honest people will steal money. Protect yourself and your employees by having good controls over your cash.

For example, Charlotte has serious damage to her home caused by a December ice storm in 1998. She isn't able to get the repairs done until January of 1999. Since the damage was done in 1998, Charlotte's casualty loss will be claimed on her 1998 tax return. What about the rule that you can only deduct something when it is paid? That rule doesn't apply here.

If your loss is from a casualty in a federally declared disaster area, you can report your loss in the year before the casualty. You will get the benefits of the tax loss sooner because you can get a refund of your prior year's taxes. See the "Disaster Losses" section of this chapter.

Theft losses are taken in the year that you discover the loss. This special rule is needed because a theft loss might not be discovered in the year of the loss. In particular, embezzlement losses are often deducted well after the deed was done.

If you lose money because your bank, credit union, or other financial institution failed, you can deduct your loss when you can reasonably estimate the amount of your loss. It can take years to unravel the financial picture of a troubled financial institution. When the smoke clears and your loss can be calculated, you can claim your deduction.

When you calculate your casualty loss, you might be using an estimate of your insurance recovery. What if the actual amount you get from the insurance company ends up being different than what you expected? What do you do?

In the year that the insurance reimbursement is settled, you may need to include additional loss or income on your tax return. If the loss was personal use property, you won't have to apply the $100 floor again. You already did that. Unfortunately, the 10% of AGI reduction will have to be taken again.

If you receive less insurance reimbursement than you anticipated, you will take a loss in the year the insurance is settled. If the reimbursement is more than you expected, you might have to include the increased settlement as income. You only have to include the extra reimbursement in your income to the extent that you got a tax benefit from your loss.

146

Losses You Can't Deduct

If you misplace property, you can't take a loss. You can't deduct a misplaced engagement ring, for example. You also can't take a tax loss for accidentally broken items that are being used under normal conditions. For example, you can't claim a loss for china that is broken while setting the table. The value of the item is not important. If you drop an $8,000 vase while placing it on a shelf, you will not be able to take a tax deduction for your loss. If you set fire to your own property, you can't take a tax loss for the damages. If you paid someone else to set the fire, you will also not be able to claim a tax loss. (But since these acts are generally considered "fraud," not being able to claim a loss will be the least of your worries.)

If your willful act or willful negligence caused an automobile accident, you can't claim a casualty loss deduction. If someone else willfully caused the accident acting on your behalf, you can't claim the loss. You can't deduct the loss because you caused the damages on purpose. That is hardly an unexpected event. Remember the three tests: sudden, unexpected, and unusual.

Slow or progressive damage or deterioration won't cause a casualty loss. Progressive damage isn't a sudden event, so it doesn't meet the definition of a casualty. The following are examples of progressive damage that won't give you a casualty loss:

➤ The steady weakening of a building under normal weather and wind conditions.

➤ Termite or moth damage to your home, trees, or clothing. A sudden infestation by insects, though, could result in a casualty loss.

➤ If your water heater rusts out and finally bursts, you can't take a loss for the water heater. Damage caused to other items in your home, such as flooring, furniture, and drapes by the water coming out of the burst water heater can result in a casualty loss.

If you suffer a loss that is related to a casualty, you don't get a tax deduction. Your loss has to be for damage actually caused by the casualty. Confused? An example might help. A landslide destroys your neighbor's home and your home's value plummets. You can't take a casualty loss. Your home wasn't physically damaged by the landslide.

Casualty or Theft of Business or Rental Property

If your loss involves business property or rental property, your loss won't be an itemized deduction. Instead, you will claim your loss in

Your Decoder Ring

Is **termite damage** sudden enough to give you a casualty loss? The IRS says no, but some courts have allowed it. One court allowed a loss for damage from a 15-month termite infestation. You have to prove extraordinary circumstances and be prepared for the IRS to disagree.

arriving at your adjusted gross income, which is an above-the-line deduction. We like those deductions.

A casualty or theft loss involving business or rental property is not reduced by the $100 floor or the 10% of AGI adjustment. If you suffer a loss related to business or rental property that you have owned for 12 months or less, the loss is an ordinary loss. If you have held the property for more than 12 months, the loss could be either ordinary or capital. You have what is known as a Section 1231 loss. Section 1231 is a fairly unique opportunity where you combine all of your Section 1231 gains and losses. If the result is a loss, you get an ordinary loss. If the result is a gain, you get a capital gain. Through Section 1231, you get the best possible result for a loss and the best possible result for a gain. Form 4797 should sort it all out for you.

Casualty Gains?

Yes, you can have a gain from your casualty or theft. If your insurance reimbursement is more than your cost basis in the property, you have a gain. This is known as a gain from an involuntary conversion. An involuntary conversion can include more than a casualty or theft. Simply put, an involuntary conversion is when property is converted (usually to cash) through an action over which you had no control (involuntary). The following are examples of involuntary conversions:

➤ Your car is totally destroyed in an accident and you get cash from the insurance company.

➤ Your house burns down and you get cash from the insurance company.

➤ A road is being built and the state takes a part of your property in exchange for cash.

If you lose personal use property that you held more than 12 months, your gain is a long-term capital gain. If you lose business or rent property that you have owned more than 12 months, you have a Section 1231 gain (as we described earlier). If you held the property less than 12 months, the gain is an ordinary gain.

If you have a gain from an involuntary conversion, you have a better option than paying income taxes. You can postpone your gain. To take advantage of this opportunity, you must reinvest your insurance proceeds in similar property. For example, if your rental property is destroyed by a storm, you can purchase other rental property with your insurance proceeds and postpone your gain.

You have two years to reinvest in the new property. More accurately, you have until two years after the close of the year in which you have your gain to replace the property. That's a mouthful! An example might help.

Desiree loses her rental home in June of 1998 to fire. She can postpone her gain if she reinvests her insurance proceeds in other rental property by the end of the year 2000.

If your involuntary conversion involves a condemnation, your replacement period is three years instead of two years. If your home is lost in a Presidentially declared disaster, you have four years to reinvest your proceeds.

To defer all of the gain, you must use all of your insurance proceeds to buy your new property. If you don't invest all of your proceeds, a part of your gain will be taxable.

We'll use Desiree's example again. Desiree received $120,000 from the insurance company for her rental house. Her adjusted basis was $100,000, so she has a $20,000 gain. If Desiree buys a new rental home for $115,000, she will have a taxable gain of $5,000. Desiree's basis in her new rental house is $100,000, which is her cost ($115,000) minus the gain she did not recognize ($15,000).

You might not be able to buy your replacement property from a related person and still postpone your gain. Individual taxpayers get a break. If your gain is less than $100,000, you might be able to buy your new property from someone related to you.

Your Decoder Ring

What *is* **similar property**? The definition can be tricky. The new property must be similar or related in service or use to your old property. A grocery store is not similar to a manufacturing plant, but commercial rental property and residential rental property are similar. Seek professional help if you want to defer your gain.

Disaster Losses

Your property might have been damaged by a big event. If the President of the United States determines that your area qualifies for federal disaster assistance, special tax rules apply to you.

You can choose to take your loss in the prior tax year instead of taking it in the year of your loss. For example, a 1998 disaster loss can be deducted on your 1997 tax return. If you don't want to use the loss on your prior year return, you can use it on the current year return. It's your choice.

The way that you make the election depends on the time of the year, as described in the following:

Paper Trail

See IRS Publication 547, Casualties, Disasters, and Thefts (Businesses and Nonbusiness), for how to postpone a gain on an involuntary conversion. We really just touched the surface in our discussion. If you have a gain, you'll want to know more.

➤ If it is not yet April 15th, you can include your loss on the prior year tax return when you file it.

➤ If you filed an extension for your prior year's tax return and you haven't reached the extended due date yet, you can include the loss on your prior year's tax return when you file it.

➤ If you have already filed your prior year's tax return, you'll have to file an amended return to make the election. You have until the original due date of this year's return (next April 15) to file the amended return.

If you elect to report the loss in your prior tax year, but you want to change your mind, you can. You have to act fast, though. You can revoke your election within 90 days of making your election. You revoke the election by returning the refund to the IRS. If you want to revoke and haven't gotten your refund yet, you can. You'll have to return your refund within 30 days of getting the refund.

When you claim a disaster loss, you must give the following information to the IRS:

➤ The date of the disaster

➤ The city or town and county in which your damaged property was located

➤ The state in which your property was located

Paper Trail

Don't forget about your state tax return. If your state allows itemized deductions or casualty losses, amend your state tax return when you amend your federal tax return.

If your state or local government orders you to tear down or move your home because of a disaster, you can write off the value of your home. The order to tear down or move must have been issued within 120 days of the area being declared a disaster area.

If your main home is damaged by a disaster and you have insurance, you might actually have a gain. Your insurance might pay you for the value of your property, which is more than what you paid for the property. This would be a taxable gain, but there are special tax rules for you. You can also use the following special tax rules if you rent your home:

➤ You don't have to pay tax on any gain on your house's contents (unscheduled personal property).

➤ You can treat all of your insurance as one pool of funds to reinvest rather than separate items.

➤ You have up to four years to reinvest your insurance proceeds.

For example, Greg's home is destroyed by flood in a Presidentially declared disaster. He receives insurance proceeds as follows:

Home	$125,000
Art pieces	10,000
Coin collection	15,000
Total insurance	$150,000

Greg paid $100,000 for his home, $20,000 for the art and $10,000 for the coins. He has a gain from the casualty since his insurance proceeds are more than his cost basis in the items lost.

Greg is going to need the entire $150,000 to rebuild his home. He doesn't intend to replace the art or the coin collection. Greg can treat the involuntary conversion as one event rather than three separate events. As long as he uses $150,000 to rebuild or replace his home, he will have no gain on the casualty. He has four years to rebuild or replace his home.

Did Your Bank Fail?

If your bank, credit union, or other financial institution has failed, you may have lost money that you had on deposit. You can take a tax loss for the lost deposits. You can choose from three alternatives:

➤ You can claim a casualty loss.

➤ You can claim an ordinary loss.

➤ You can claim a nonbusiness bad debt.

If you choose to deduct your loss as a casualty loss, you can take the deduction when you are able to reasonably estimate how much you have lost. You don't have to wait until all of the matters are finally resolved to claim your loss. As a casualty loss, your deduction will be an itemized deduction and will be reduced by $100 and 10% of your adjusted gross income.

Red Flag

When you deposit your money in a financial institution, check to see if your funds are covered by federal insurance. Remember also that mutual funds are not federally insured.

If you want to deduct your lost deposits as an ordinary loss, consider these rules and limitations:

➤ Your loss will be a miscellaneous itemized deduction subject to the 2% of the AGI floor.

➤ You can only deduct $20,000 of loss ($10,000 if you are married filing separately).

➤ You can't use the ordinary loss option if your account was federally insured.

➤ You can't take the loss until you can reasonably estimate the amount of your loss.

If you choose to claim a nonbusiness bad debt for your loss, you have to wait until the actual amount of the loss is finally determined. At this time, you can take the nonbusiness bad debt, which is a short-term capital loss.

How do you report the loss? Use the following guidelines:

➤ If you choose casualty loss treatment, use Form 4684 first, which will direct your loss to Schedule A with your other itemized deductions.

➤ If you choose ordinary loss treatment, report directly on Schedule A with your other miscellaneous itemized deductions.

➤ If you choose nonbusiness bad debt treatment, report on Schedule D, Capital Gains and Losses.

Forms, Forms, Forms

To claim a loss you have to complete Form 4684. The form is divided into three sections:

➤ Section A is used for personal use property.

➤ Section B is used for business and income-producing property.

➤ Section C is used to summarize your gains and losses.

If you can take an itemized deduction for your casualty or theft loss, you will carry the loss from Form 4684 to your Schedule A. If you have a capital gain from your casualty or theft, the gain will be carried to your Schedule D to be combined with your other capital gains and losses. If you have a gain related to business property (such as a rental home), your gain will be carried to Form 4797 to be combined with your other business-related gains and losses. Use Schedule D, Capital Gains and Losses, to report your nonbusiness bad debt losses. The loss is reported in the short-term gains and losses section.

In the IRS instructions for each tax form, there is a section for the Paperwork Reduction Act Notice. This is the IRS attempt at informing you of how long it will take you to complete the form. The instructions for Form 4684 to report casualties and thefts include a time estimate of just over three hours. This form might be intimidating, but don't pass up your deductions because of the form. The instructions to the form are very helpful, and the IRS has several publications that can help you.

IRS Publication 584 can help you make a list of damaged goods and calculate your tax loss. The publication includes schedules that help you measure your loss. IRS Publication 547, Casualties, Disasters, and Thefts (Business and Nonbusiness) will give you a lot of information about the tax impact of a casualty or theft. In IRS Publication 525, Taxable and Nontaxable Income, there is a section on recoveries that will help you if you get money back on a loss you took in the past.

The Least You Need to Know

➤ If your property is damaged by fire, storm, or other sudden event, you could qualify for a tax loss.

➤ If your insurance reimbursement is more than the cost of your property, you could have a gain. The gain might qualify to be postponed.

➤ If you lose property in a disaster, special tax rules apply to you.

➤ Your casualty or theft loss is reported on Form 4684.

Chapter 12

The Last Word If You Itemize: Miscellaneous Deductions and the High-Income Cutback

---

In This Chapter

➤ Deducting investment-related expenses

➤ Using deductible expenses that are related to trying to make money

➤ Identifying deductible expenses that are related to calculating your taxes

➤ Understanding the hobby loss rules

➤ Knowing the overall limit on itemized deductions for high-income taxpayers

---

As the phrase "miscellaneous itemized deductions" suggests, this category of deductions is a catch-all. What are miscellaneous itemized deductions? They are all deductions other than medical expenses, taxes, interest expenses, charitable contributions, casualty losses, and theft losses.

The most striking feature of miscellaneous itemized deductions is not their diversity, however, and it's one you won't really care much for. There is a deduction floor for most of your miscellaneous itemized deductions. The floor is 2% of your adjusted gross income (AGI). To apply the floor, add up your miscellaneous itemized deductions and subtract 2% of your AGI. It's that easy. The Schedule A takes you right through the calculation. Most, but not all, of your miscellaneous deductions are subject to the 2% of AGI floor.

The end result is that you can only deduct your miscellaneous deductions that are more than 2% of your AGI. So, why were miscellaneous deductions targeted for this cutback? First, tax revenues needed to be raised. Second, these deductions are ripe for cheating.

For example, you can't deduct personal living expenses, but with a little bit of slight of hand, some living expenses could look like miscellaneous itemized deductions. Rather than cutting out these expenses, Congress decided to just reduce them. The 2% of AGI floor effectively wipes out some people's miscellaneous itemized deductions. If you have high income, the 2% floor can have a big impact. You'll want to have your deductions taken elsewhere. Sometimes good tax planning can accomplish this for you. Business expenses are most easily shifted if your employer cooperates with you (see Chapter 13, "Deductions If You Are an Employee"). Other times, you're just stuck with the limitation.

High-income individuals are also hit with another loss of their itemized deductions. If your AGI is more than $124,500, your deductions will be cut back. It's a pretty mechanical process. We'll cover the limitation at the end of this chapter.

Employee Business Expenses

Your unreimbursed employee business expenses are deductible as a miscellaneous itemized deduction. These expenses could include business travel, dues, and education expenses. In Chapter 13, there is a discussion of which expenses you can deduct.

If you can claim employee business expenses, you might have to complete a Form 2106 or a Form 2106-EZ. You add your expenses up on the Form 2106 and then carry them forward to your Schedule A. The business expenses will be added in with your other miscellaneous itemized deductions so that the 2% of the AGI floor can be applied.

Investment Expenses

If you have investments, you might have some investment expenses. You can deduct your investment expenses with your other miscellaneous itemized deductions. You will have to include your investment expenses in your deductions that are reduced by the 2% of the AGI floor.

What Expenses Can You Deduct?

You can deduct expenses that you incur for managing your investments. Your investment expenses can include fees and publications that relate to your investment activities. If you are heavily involved in your investments, you might have expenses other than the typical fees and publications, though.

You might buy a computer to manage your investments. You can take a depreciation expense deduction for your computer. You must allocate the cost of the computer between personal use and investment use. Computer supplies that relate to managing your investments are also deductible.

If you have a lot of investments, you might hire clerical help to assist you in managing the investments. This is a deductible expense. If you rent office space for managing your investments, your rent and other office expenses will also be deductible. Again, use caution to not mix personal expenses (paying bills, arranging social events) with investment expenses.

In Chapter 11, "Casualty and Theft Losses: Save Taxes When Disaster Strikes," we talked about taking a loss from the failure of your financial institution as a miscellaneous itemized deduction. Check back in Chapter 11 to see if you want to claim your loss in this manner.

If you own land for investment, claim your real estate taxes with your other deductible taxes. Claim your interest with your investment interest expense. If you have other fees or expenses related to the land investment, deduct them as miscellaneous itemized deductions.

Be careful about mixing personal expenses with business expenses. Even if you check your stocks in your local newspaper, good luck trying to deduct your newspaper as an investment expense. Fees you pay for your personal checking account won't be deductible even though the account pays you interest.

You can't deduct the basic cost of your telephone service in your home, even if you only use the phone for investment or business purposes. Additional telephone features or long-distance charges are deductible if they relate to your investment activity, though.

You can't deduct investment-related seminars, conventions, or meetings. You can't even deduct the cost of attending stockholders' meetings. A special provision in the tax code denies these deductions.

You can't deduct commissions or fees that you pay when you buy or sell investments. Fees paid to buy investments are added to your cost basis in the investment itself. Fees paid to sell investments are offset against the selling price of the stock.

For example, Amy bought 100 shares of stock for $2,300. When Amy bought the stock, she paid a $50 commission. Amy's total cost of the stock is $2,350. A couple of years later, she sold the stock for $3,500 and again paid a $50 commission. Her net selling price is $3,450. Amy's capital gain on the sale is $3,450 minus $2,350, or $1,100.

Your brokerage company will file a Form 1099-B with the IRS reporting the amount of your stock sale proceeds. What if Amy's stock was reported as being sold for $3,500 instead of $3,450? Does she lose her commission expenses from her sale? No. Amy should add the selling expenses to her basis in the stock so that the 1099-B matches the selling price on her Schedule D where she reports capital gains and the amount of her gain is correct.

Deductions from an Estate or Trust

If you are the beneficiary of an estate or a trust, you might have a special deduction available to you. The deduction is called *excess deductions on termination*. What does that mean?

An estate or trust can work either as a tax-paying entity or as a pass-through entity. It depends on whether it makes distributions to the beneficiaries that year. If distributions aren't made, the estate or trust will pay income tax on its income. If distributions are made, the taxable income follows the distributions out to the beneficiaries.

Often, in the final year of an estate or a trust, the expenses are more than the income. This can happen because final fees are paid when the estate or trust closes. These excess expenses are called excess deductions on termination. These expenses are passed through on the estate or trust's final tax return to the beneficiaries. There is a separate line on the Schedule K-1 for excess deductions on termination. Each beneficiary includes his or her share of the excess deductions as a miscellaneous itemized deduction on Schedule A.

Tax-Free Investments and Their Expenses

You can't deduct expenses you pay to earn tax-free income. If you own tax-exempt securities, you can't deduct expenses related to purchasing or carrying the securities. What does this mean? Some examples may help.

➤ If you borrow money to buy tax-free municipal bonds, the interest you pay on your loan isn't deductible.

➤ If you have an investment account that invests in tax-free bonds, the portion of the account fee related to your tax-free bonds is not deductible.

➤ If you are physically injured and receive tax-free personal injury damages, your legal fees related to the damages are not deductible.

Your Decoder Ring

Tax-free damages can only be received if you suffer a physical injury. Wrongful death claims are for physical personal injury. Damages received for nonphysical injuries are taxable. Job-related damages, such as gender or age discrimination, are taxable since they do not cause physical injury.

These expenses are directly related to the tax-free income. They are pretty easy to spot. It's the expenses for "carrying" tax-free securities that are hard to get a handle on. Unfortunately, there isn't a lot of really good guidance. If you have these kinds of expenses, use an allocation that makes some logical sense. You are more likely to win an IRS challenge if you have thought through your approach and have tried to comply.

Expenses for Production of Income

I'm sure that you've heard the old adage that you have to "spend money to make money." Well, someone in Congress heard the adage, too. You can deduct expenses that you pay for collecting or producing taxable income.

We're not talking about your business expenses or rental expenses here. You deduct those expenses on your business schedule or your rent schedule. We're talking about anything else, though. Legal and accounting fees can be deductible if they relate to collecting or producing income. If you are an employee, legal and accounting fees paid to protect your wages or salary are deductible. Your activity as an employee counts as an income-producing activity. Here are some examples of fees and expenses you can deduct:

➤ Legal and accounting fees related to collecting a taxable damage award

➤ Legal fees to collect taxable alimony

➤ Legal fees to petition for an increase in taxable alimony

➤ Legal and accounting fees for estate and tax planning

For example, Ede suffers a loss related to life insurance products that she was sold. Ede's attorney agreed to represent her in a suit against the life insurance company and its agent. The case was settled out of court. Ede's attorney received a third of her damages. Ede was awarded damages of $9,000. She got a check for $6,000, because her attorney's fees were deducted from her damage award.

Ede will have to report $9,000 of income from the damage award. She can then take a miscellaneous itemized deduction for her $3,000 of legal fees. What if her miscellaneous itemized deductions are less than 2% of Ede's AGI? She won't get any tax benefit from her legal fees. There is no remedy for Ede in this situation. The full $9,000 of damages is still taxable.

You can't deduct any of the following items:

➤ Legal fees to prepare your will

➤ Legal fees to draft trust documents

➤ Legal fees related to child support payments

➤ Fees related to a breach of promise to marry suit

➤ Legal fees related to civil or criminal charges resulting from a personal relationship

Red Flag

Miscellaneous itemized deductions are not allowed for calculating alternative minimum tax (AMT). If you have large miscellaneous itemized deductions, AMT might be triggered. This can happen if you have a taxable damage award accompanied by legal fees.

In a strange irony, you can deduct expenses that relate to an illegal activity. All income, whether legal or illegal has to be reported. Even though your income-generating activity is illegal, your expenses to generate that income are still deductible. There is an exception for people who illegally traffic in drugs. Drug dealers can't deduct their income-producing expenses.

You can't deduct illegal payments such as bribes to public officials and illegal kickbacks. You also can't deduct fines for breaking the law. Parking tickets and speeding tickets can't be deducted even if related to an income-producing activity.

Tax-Related Expenses

Any expenses that you pay related to your income taxes are deductible. It seems only fair, doesn't it? The tax rules are complicated. You have to spend money to comply with the rules. You should be able to deduct your expenses.

Paper Trail

To get more mileage out of your tax return preparation fee, try to split it up. If you own your own business (Schedule C), own rental property (Schedule E), or own a Farm (Schedule F), take part of your tax preparation fee on your business, rent, or farm schedule. Only take the part of your fee that relates to non-business income as an itemized deduction.

The most obvious tax-related expense that you can deduct is your tax return preparation fees. You can also deduct any fees you pay to file your tax return electronically. You will deduct your tax return preparation fees in the year you pay them. For example, the fee for your 1998 tax return will be paid and deducted in 1999. You can also deduct these tax-related expenses:

➤ Tax-preparation software
➤ Tax-planning software
➤ Tax publications and books
➤ Fees for tax advice
➤ Appraisal fees for items donated to charity
➤ Appraisal fees to determine your casualty loss deduction

If you have a tax dispute, you can also deduct any fees and expenses to defend your position with the IRS. If the dispute involves a business, rent, or farm schedule, deduct the fees on your Schedule C, E, or F instead of taking a miscellaneous itemized deduction. Fees related to a dispute could include any of the following:

➤ Legal fees or accounting fees
➤ Fees to respond to a tax notice
➤ Fees and expenses for representation in a tax audit
➤ Fees and expenses related to tax litigation
➤ Bank charges to reprint bank statements for a tax audit
➤ Professional fees paid to appeal a property tax assessment

If you are going through a divorce, a part of your legal and accounting fees can be deductible if they are properly billed. Any expenses billed as tax-related services or advice can be deducted. Fees related to your property settlement, the custody of your children, or child support payments are not deductible.

If you have to seek counseling because the tax rules caused you mental distress, your fees are medical expenses. Sorry, but these fees don't qualify as tax-related. If you need marriage counseling because you fight about taxes, this isn't deductible at all!

Hobby Expenses

It's everybody's dream to get paid for doing what you love. It's the IRS's dream to find everybody who tries to take a tax loss for chasing that ideal. The IRS is very skeptical of any business that might be a hobby in disguise. What's the difference? You can only deduct business losses that are related to an activity that is entered into with the intention of making a profit.

It is quite clear that many businesses are entered into with the goal of making a profit. There are other businesses, though, that make a person pause. There are a few people who make very good money racing cars. There are, however, a lot of people who love car racing for the sport and never make a cent for their endeavors. Small farms and racing horses are also good examples of activities that could be purely profit-motivated, but many people dabble in it for pure pleasure.

How can you tell the difference between a professional farmer and the recreational farmer? They both plant crops. They both sell crops. Either one of them could lose money or make money in a given year. The difference is their intention. Did the farmer enter into the activity with the purpose of making a profit?

Intentions are very difficult to measure. How can you know someone's intentions? How can you prove someone's intentions if challenged? This is a very difficult standard to enforce or support. There can be a lot at stake.

If your activity is a business, your expenses are deducted in arriving at your adjusted gross income (AGI). For example, the expenses would be deducted on your Schedule C, Profit or Loss From Business, or your Schedule F, Profit or Loss From Farming. If your expenses are more than your income, you have a business loss.

If your activity is a hobby, the tax result is quite different. You must use the following guidelines when preparing your taxes:

➤ All of your income is taxable.

➤ Your expenses are deductible only to the extent of your income (you can't take a loss).

➤ Your expenses are a miscellaneous itemized deduction, subject to the 2% of the AGI floor.

There can be some pretty nasty outcomes:

➤ If your expenses are more than your income in one year, you can't carry the excess over to another year. You simply lose your excess deductions.

➤ If you don't itemize your deductions, but use the standard deduction instead, you

Red Flag

Do business losses really cause audits? The IRS formula for selecting returns for audit is a well-kept secret. The IRS, however, makes no secret of the fact that losses increase your odds of getting audited. Obviously, not every loss is audited. Only about 1% of all tax returns are audited. If you take a loss, be prepared by keeping good records—just in case you need them.

get no tax benefit from your hobby expenses. All of your hobby income is still taxable, though.

➤ If your miscellaneous itemized deductions are less than 2% of your AGI, you can't deduct any of your hobby expenses. Your hobby income is still taxable. To make matters worse, the hobby income you had to include in your AGI increases your 2% of AGI floor, taking away yet more of your hobby deductions.

Simply put, the hobby loss rules are terrible. What can you do? One thing that you can do is to try to prove that you are not involved in a hobby. You will have to prove that you are engaged in a business for profit. The IRS Regulations can help you. The Regulations provide a list of nine factors that should be considered in separating a business from a hobby:

➤ Running the activity in a businesslike manner

➤ Your expertise or the expertise of your advisors

➤ The time and effort you spent on the activity

➤ Whether you expect the assets used in the activity to increase in value

➤ Your prior success in similar ventures

➤ The history of income or losses from the activity

➤ The relationship of profits to losses

➤ Your financial status—if you don't need the income from the activity, it might indicate you didn't intend to make money in the activity

➤ The degree of personal pleasure or recreation that you can enjoy in the activity

This isn't a test that you can pass or fail. You don't add up the number of yes and no answers. Instead, the factors are to be considered all together to make a judgment call on whether the activity was a business or a hobby.

This is a difficult task, especially when you consider that the burden of proof falls on you. You have to prove your case that the activity was entered into for profit. There is a great deal of room for interpretation. In an audit, how do you prove your position? You can only try to convince the agent of your intentions of entering into the activity for profit. Supporting your case by using the nine factors is critical, but the factors can be interpreted differently by different people.

To help taxpayers out, Congress gave us an easier way to support your activity as a business. If your activity shows a profit in at least three years of any five prior consecutive years, your activity is presumed to be a business. You can claim your losses without having to prove that your activity is not a hobby. If your activity involves horses, you only need profits in two of seven consecutive years.

For example, Bud has been an antique collector for years. He decided to turn his activities into a business, so he opened an antique shop. In 1998, Bud's shop shows a loss. The IRS questions the loss under the hobby loss rules. Bud's shop has the following history of profits and losses:

1997	$2,500 loss
1996	$1,200 profit
1995	$100 profit
1994	$890 loss
1993	$1,300 profit

Since the shop has profits in three of the five prior years, Bud's shop is presumed to be a business in 1998.

The IRS can still challenge your loss as being a hobby loss if you meet the three of five years (or two in seven) test. The burden of proof shifts to the IRS, though, to prove that your activity is a hobby. If you fail the hobby test, it doesn't mean that you can't take a business loss. It means that you have to rely on the nine factors to prove your case.

Expenses Saved from the 2% Floor

Some miscellaneous itemized deductions don't have to be reduced by the 2% of AGI floor. These expenses don't impact most taxpayers. If you have these deductions, though, don't let them slip into the deductions that have to be reduced by the floor.

Paper Trail

If a couple has one person with low AGI and high miscellaneous itemized deductions, they should test separate returns. You don't know if it pays to file separately unless you try it out.

Impairment-related work expenses of a disabled person can be deducted without applying the 2% of AGI floor. If you are disabled, there are expenses that you incur because of your disability. You know best what these expenses are, but they could include any of the following and more:

➤ One-handed keyboard

➤ Telephone amplification equipment if you are hearing-impaired

➤ Tools or accessories that enable you to perform job duties that would be difficult due to your disability

➤ Attendant care services at work

➤ Tape player and accessories if you are blind

If you have income from gambling, you have to include it in your adjusted gross income. This could include casino gambling, race track winnings, and lottery winnings, to name just a few. People who have gambling income usually also have gambling losses. Unless you are a professional gambler, your losses are deductible only to the extent of your gambling winnings. Your gambling losses are miscellaneous itemized deductions, but are not subject to the 2% of AGI floor.

You can deduct the federal estate tax that was paid on income in respect of a decedent. That's a mouthful! Does it apply to regular people? Yes, it can.

Your Decoder Ring

Who pays **estate** or **gift tax** anyway? If you get a gift or an inheritance, do you pay the taxes? The estate pays the federal estate taxes. The person giving you the gift pays any gift taxes. Some state inheritance taxes are levied on the heirs, though.

If you die with an estate worth $625,000 or more in 1998, you will have to pay estate tax. Some items in the estate will also be taxable when they are paid to the heirs. The best example is a retirement plan account. It is included in the taxable estate, and it will also create taxable income when it is paid to you as the beneficiary.

Estate taxes can be as much as 55%. Income taxes can be up to 39.6%. Your state income taxes might be another 5%. That adds up to a 99.6% tax rate. This isn't fiction. It can be very real! To help relieve this situation, you can take an income tax deduction for the estate taxes that were paid. Let's do an example.

Milli's grandmother died and named Milli the beneficiary of her $20,000 IRA. Milli's grandmother's estate was taxable. Estate taxes were paid on the IRA at the rate of 41%, so $8,200 of estate taxes were paid on the IRA. When the IRA is paid to Milli, $20,000 will be included on Milli's tax return as taxable income. Milli can then claim an $8,200 deduction for the federal estate taxes that were paid.

The following are examples of assets that create income in respect of a decedent:

➤ Retirement plan benefits

➤ IRAs

➤ Annuities

➤ Installment sales contracts

➤ Interest income earned up to the date of death but paid after death

Another deduction you can take without applying the 2% of AGI floor relates to annuities. When you receive payments from an annuity, a portion of your payment is taxable: The portion that is for the return of your investment is not taxable. An annuity might stop before your investment is recovered. Usually, the event that stops the payments is death. On the final tax return, the unrecovered investment in the annuity contract can be deducted.

High-Incomers Beware

Congress decided to trim the itemized deductions of high-income people. Why? To raise income taxes without impacting most taxpayers (voters). If you file a joint return with your spouse and your AGI is more than $124,500, some of your itemized deductions will be cut back. The AGI limit for single persons is also $124,500. If you are married and file a separate return, your cutback starts with an AGI of $62,250.

The cutback can trim your deduction for the following:

- ➤ Taxes
- ➤ Home mortgage interest and mortgage points
- ➤ Charitable contributions
- ➤ Miscellaneous itemized deductions that are subject to the 2% of AGI floor

The cutback will not reduce your deduction for any of the following:

- ➤ Medical expenses
- ➤ Investment interest expense
- ➤ Casualty and theft loss
- ➤ Gambling losses

Your Decoder Ring

What does **high income** really mean? There are a lot of tax benefits that are trimmed for high-income people. Each limitation uses a different AGI number. There is no single standard used in the tax code. In case you're interested, in 1994 (the most current info we have), only 5% of all taxpayers had an AGI of $91,226 or more.

The cutback works like this:

1. See how much your AGI is over $124,500. If you are married and file a separate return, see how much your AGI is over $62,250.
2. Take the amount you calculated in step #1 and multiply it by 3%.
3. Add up your deductions that are affected by the limit from the list above.
4. Multiply your affected deductions by 80%.
5. Determine if the 3% calculation or the 80% calculation gives you the lower number.
6. Reduce your itemized deduction by the smaller of the 3% or 80% calculation.

Let's use Patty as an example. Her adjusted gross income is $162,000. She is single. Patty has the following itemized deductions:

- ➤ Medical expenses of $3,500 which she can't deduct because they are less than 7.5% of her AGI
- ➤ Home mortgage interest of $15,000
- ➤ Investment interest expense of $2,800
- ➤ Taxes of $12,500
- ➤ Charitable contributions of $14,000
- ➤ Theft loss of $10,000 which she can't deduct because it is less than 10% of her AGI
- ➤ Miscellaneous itemized deductions of $7,200 less 2% of her AGI for a deduction of $3,960

Patty's itemized deductions before the cutback are as follows:

Paper Trail

If your deductions are limited and you think that making that extra charitable contribution won't reduce your taxes, think again. The reduction of your deductions is a percent of your AGI. As your income goes up, your deductions go down. As your deductions go up, your deductions will still go up.

Medical	-0-
Mortgage interest	$15,000
Investment interest	2,800
Taxes	12,500
Charitable contributions	14,000
Miscellaneous	3,960
Total	$48,260

Patty's deduction cutback is calculated as follows:

1. Her excess AGI is $37,500 ($162,000 minus $124,500)
2. Excess times 3% is $1,125 ($37,500 times 3%)
3. Add up affected deductions:

Taxes	$12,500
Mortgage interest	15,000
Charitable	14,000
Miscellaneous	3,960
Total	$45,460

4. Multiply affected deductions of $45,460 by 80% to get $36,368.
5. Determine if 3% or 80% is less. For Patty, the 3% calculation of $1,125 is less.
6. Reduce Patty's itemized deduction of $48,260 by $1,125. Patty can deduct $47,135 of her itemized deductions.

The Least You Need to Know

➤ Miscellaneous itemized deductions include your employee business expenses.

➤ Investment-related expenses are deductible.

➤ Expenses related to calculating or defending your taxes are deductible.

➤ Most miscellaneous itemized deductions have to be reduced by 2% of your adjusted gross income.

➤ If your income is over $124,500, your itemized deductions will be cut back.

Part 3
Business Expenses

You have to spend money to make money. Whether you work for someone else or you have your own business, the adage still applies.

We can deduct business expenses. It is really only fair since our business income is taxable. Things get sticky, though, when expenses might be business-related or they might be personal. How do you draw the line?

Using your car, your home, your phone, or your computer for business should give you a tax deduction. Should you be able to deduct the whole cost when you also use these things in your personal life? Clearly, Congress says no.

Keeping these expenses straight can make a real difference. There are tax dollars to be saved for those who do it right.

Chapter 13

Deductions If You Are an Employee

In This Chapter

➤ Determining what type of employer reimbursement plan you have and why it makes a difference

➤ Deducting telephone and computer expenses

➤ Which dues you can deduct

➤ Which uniforms and work clothes you can deduct

➤ Deducting job hunting expenses

As an employee, you can deduct business expenses that are not reimbursed by your employer. Your employee business expenses are miscellaneous itemized deductions.

To deduct business expenses, you must report expenses on your Form 2106 or Form 2106-EZ. The deduction will flow from the Form 2106 to your Schedule A and will be combined with your other miscellaneous itemized deductions.

As an employee, you might be able to deduct the following expenses:

➤ Telephone use
➤ Computer equipment and supplies
➤ Dues
➤ Uniforms
➤ Job hunting expenses

➤ Business gifts

➤ Car expenses (see Chapter 15)

➤ Home office (see Chapter 16)

➤ Travel and meals (see Chapter 17)

➤ Education (see Chapter 18)

Employee business expenses don't give you the best tax deduction for the following reasons:

➤ They are reduced by 2% of your adjusted gross income (with your other miscellaneous itemized deductions).

➤ They don't reduce your adjusted gross income. Instead, they are below-the-line deductions.

➤ They aren't deductible for alternative minimum tax (AMT).

Your Decoder Ring

Alternative minimum tax (AMT) was intended to ensure that high-income people couldn't use too many loopholes, but it has changed. The AMT is a second tax calculation that you make. In AMT, some deductions and credits aren't allowed, but the tax rate is lower. (Sounds like a flat tax, doesn't it?) If your AMT is higher than your regular income tax, you pay AMT instead.

With some planning and cooperation from your employer, you can have a better tax arrangement.

Not All Employer Reimbursements Are Created Equal

Many employers reimburse their employees for business expenses. When this happens, the financial burden for the expense moves from the employee to the employer. Clearly, this is good for the employee. The boss is paying you back for your business expenses.

Reimbursement plans fall into two different categories:

➤ Accountable reimbursement plans

➤ Nonaccountable reimbursement plan

An accountable plan will give you a much better tax result than a nonaccountable plan. It can make the difference between having a tax-free reimbursement of your expenses or a taxable reimbursement of your expenses.

Being Accountable

When you receive a reimbursement from your employer, it seems that you should have nothing to report on your tax return. You have been made whole by the reimbursement, so you're not ahead or behind financially. You will only get this clean result if the reimbursement is made under an accountable plan.

When you are reimbursed under an accountable plan, you (as the employee) don't have to report anything to the IRS. You don't deduct the business expenses. You don't report the expense reimbursement as income. It is a simple result for you. There is no tax consequence whatsoever from the expense reimbursement.

In a nonaccountable plan, though, you have to do the following two things:

1. Report the expense reimbursement as taxable income
2. Claim a tax deduction for the business expenses

On the surface, these two options might seem to have the same tax consequences. They don't.

If you are reimbursed in a nonaccountable plan, your business expenses are deducted as a miscellaneous itemized deduction. The negative tax consequences of the arrangement can include the following:

➤ Including the reimbursement in your income increases your adjusted gross income (AGI).

➤ When your AGI is increased, your medical expenses are decreased. Remember that medical expenses are reduced by 7.5% of your AGI.

➤ When your AGI is increased, your miscellaneous itemized deductions are decreased (because of the 2% of AGI floor).

➤ An increased AGI could cause more of your Social Security benefits to be taxable.

➤ An increased AGI might cause you to lose the tax benefit of many deductions and credits, such as personal exemptions, education credits, the child tax credit, and IRA deductions.

➤ Your business expenses are itemized deductions, so you can't claim them if you don't itemize. Your reimbursement is still taxable, though.

➤ Your business expenses are miscellaneous itemized deductions that have to be reduced by 2% of your AGI.

➤ If your state does not allow you to claim itemized deductions, your business expenses are not deductible on your state tax return. The reimbursement might still be taxable, though.

You're probably convinced by now that you should have an accountable reimbursement plan. How do you get one? All of the following requirements must be met:

➤ You have to report all of your expenses to your employer within a reasonable amount of time.

➤ Your employer has to give you full reimbursement for your expenses.

➤ You have to be required to return any excess reimbursements to your employer. You also have to follow through on this requirement and return any excess reimbursement you get.

169

When you report your expenses to your employer, you have to include in your expense report all of these details:

➤ The amount of the expense

➤ The time and place of travel or entertainment

➤ The business purpose of the trip

➤ The business relationship of the person that you entertained or bought a meal for

Paper Trail

If your expenses were paid under an accountable reimbursement plan, your reimbursement should not be reported as wages on your Form W-2. If you employer includes the reimbursement in your wages on your W-2 by mistake, a corrected W-2 needs to be filed. Get in touch with your employer right away. It might take time to get the corrected W-2 completed.

As if this weren't enough, you also have to give your employer some receipts. If you are being reimbursed for lodging expenses (hotel, motel), you have to give your employer your receipt for the lodging. You only need a receipt for other expenses (meals, entertainment) if the expense is $75 or more.

For example, Marilyn takes clients to lunch on a regular basis. She submits an expense report to her employer for reimbursement. Marilyn is required to give her employer complete information about her expenses (who, what, when, where, how much) and provide receipts for each meal of $75 or more. If the expense report is complete, Marilyn's employer will fully reimburse her for the lunches.

This is an accountable plan. Marilyn will report nothing on her tax return. Marilyn's employer will claim the tax deduction for the business meal. Business meals are only 50% deductible, but Marilyn won't have to worry about this. Her employer will deduct 50% of the meal expense on its tax return.

Let's say, on the other hand, Marilyn gets a meal allowance for client entertainment. She gets a $300 allowance each month. Marilyn doesn't have to report back to her employer how she has spent her expense allowance. Marilyn actually spends $300 a month on meals. Marilyn will report $3,600 for the allowance paid during the year ($300 for 12 months). On her tax return, Marilyn will deduct her meals. Meals are only 50% deductible, so she will claim an $1,800 business expense. Marilyn's miscellaneous itemized deductions don't add up to more than 2% of her AGI.

The result is that Marilyn has to pay income tax on her $3,600 allowance. Even though she spent every dime of her allowance on business expenses, she gets no tax benefit from her expenses. Clearly, Marilyn needs to talk to her employer. If Marilyn can convince her employer to switch to an accountable plan, Marilyn will save the income taxes on her $3,600 allowance.

Reimbursed Personal Expenses

If your employer reimburses you for personal (as opposed to business) expenses, the reimbursement is taxable to you. The reimbursement should be included on your Form W-2 as wages.

For example, you are transferred to a different town. To entice you to accept the new position, your employer will pay your first three months of living expenses in your new location. These living expenses are personal expenses that are not deductible by you. When your employer pays these personal expenses or reimburses you for the expenses, you have to pay tax on the reimbursement.

Personal expenses that are reimbursed could include these items:

Red Flag

What if your employer would have reimbursed you for an expense, but you didn't ask for reimbursement? Maybe you didn't get around to filling out the forms. Maybe you would rather pay the expense yourself. You can't deduct the expense. If your employer would have paid for the expense, you can't claim it.

➤ Dry cleaning for your business suits

➤ A housing allowance to live in a high-cost location

➤ Travel expenses for your spouse or family to accompany you on a business trip

➤ Clothing allowance in an office where regular business attire is worn

Per Diems

Instead of reimbursing you for actual meals or lodging expenses, your employer might pay you a *per diem*. A per diem is a fixed daily rate. The IRS approves daily rates each year for per diem allowances.

There are per diem rates to cover just meals and incidental expenses. There are also per diem rates to cover lodging, meals, and incidental expenses.

The IRS has two different types of per diems that it recognizes:

➤ The highest amount that the federal government will pay to its employees for a particular location

➤ The high-low simplified per diem rate

The federal government's reimbursement rate can be difficult for an employer to use. It requires checking the government's list of reimbursement rates for each location to which you travel.

The high-low system is much easier because there are only two rates (high and low). Certain destinations are identified as high-cost areas. For these places, a high-rate per diem is set. For all other areas, a low-rate per diem is set. The high-low per diems for 1998 are as follows:

➤ High rate for lodging, meals, and incidentals is $180.

➤ Low rate for lodging, meals, and incidentals is $113.

➤ High rate for meals and incidentals is $40.

➤ Low rate for meals and incidentals is $32.

Paper Trail

For the most current list of IRS per diem rates, see IRS Publication 1542. The publication will give the rates in the continental United States for the current year. The locations that are eligible for the high-rate per diem (under the high-low rate method) are also listed.

Using a per diem can be easy for an employer. If you need meal money for one day, the amount you will be paid is fixed. There is no need to deal with receipts or employees who spend more money than you want them to spend. You will need to have records to support why the per diem was paid, for example, the date and destination of an employee's travels and the business purpose.

Per diems are easy for employees, too. If you are paid an IRS-approved per diem rate for meals or lodging, you don't have to include the per diem on your tax return, and you don't have to claim any business deductions. Even if your expenses are less than the per diem that you are paid, the per diem is tax-free.

You might spend more on your meals or lodging than your per diem. The rates aren't very generous, so they often don't cover all of your costs. You might want to keep track of your actual expenses. If your expenses are more than your per diem reimbursement, the excess is deductible.

For example, you are paid a per diem of $113 for a business trip. Your actual expenses are $153. You can deduct the extra $40 on your tax return as an employee business expense.

If your employer pays a per diem rate that is more than the IRS approved rate, a part of your reimbursement has to be included on your W-2. The payment up to the IRS rate is not included in your wages, but the excess over the IRS rate is reported as taxable wages to you. If your actual expenses are higher than the IRS rate, you can deduct the excess on your Form 2106.

For example, Vickie is paid $200 a day for a business trip. The IRS approved rate for this location is $180 a day. Vickie's W-2 will include $20 for each day as taxable wages ($200 minus $180). If Vickie's actual expenses were $280 a day, she can deduct $100 on her tax return as an employee business expense for each day. This is the amount by which Vickie's expenses exceed the federal per diem amount. The result is that Vickie is out of pocket $80 a day. She reports $20 as taxable wages and deducts $100 of expenses, which net out to $80 a day for her expenses.

Deducting Your Phone and Computer

You might have to use your telephone or computer for work. The IRS knows that phones and computers are usually used partly for personal purposes even if you use them for business. You have to split your expenses between your personal and business use to take a deduction.

For your home telephone, you can never deduct the cost of your basic telephone service. Even if your office is in your home, your basic service into your home is not deductible.

You can deduct the cost of:

Red Flag

If you are related to your employer, you can't use standard per diem rates for your business expense reimbursements. You will still have to account for your actual business expenses.

> ➤ Long-distance charges for business calls
> ➤ Additional lines that are needed to service your business needs
> ➤ Additional features that are added for business purposes

For example, Rhonda works out of an office in her home. She has to have a telephone for work. Rhonda also needs to operate a fax machine and have complete Internet access. To accommodate her business needs, Rhonda adds an extra phone line into her home. The cost of her basic phone service is not deductible. The second line and any business-related long-distance charges are deductible.

If you use a cell phone in your business, the portion of your cell phone usage that is for business calls is deductible. Knowing the business use can be challenging unless you get detailed records from the cell phone company and actually calculate the business use and personal use. Most taxpayers try to make their best estimate of business use percentage.

If you have to use your own computer for your job, you can deduct your computer expenses. It's not enough that it's helpful to have your own computer to give you a tax deduction. The computer must be required for your job.

A teacher, for example, might be required to keep student records in a computerized data base program. If the teacher has adequate access to computers on the job during planning periods, he or she won't be able to deduct using a personally owned computer. If the teacher doesn't have access to a computer at the school to keep the required records, having a computer at home is the only option. The computer expenses would be deductible.

The actual cost of the computer will have to be depreciated. In Chapter 14, "Deductions If You Are Self-Employed," we discuss depreciation and how it is calculated. Your computer supplies, such as paper, printer cartridges, and diskettes will be deductible.

What Else Is There?

Essentially, any other business-related expense that you have to incur for your job is deductible. The expense has to be something that is "ordinary and necessary." This means that the expense is typical for someone in your business (ordinary) and that it is helpful to you in your business activity (necessary).

If your employer would pay for an expense, you can't deduct it. For example, if your employer provides ink pens, you can't deduct the cost of buying ink pens. If you prefer a different type of pen than your employer provides, that is a matter of personal choice. The different ink pens might be ordinary for your business, but they are not necessary. You can't deduct them.

Dues That You Pay

Union dues and initiation fees that you pay are deductible. Assessments for benefit payments for unemployed union members are also deductible.

You can't deduct the part of your union dues that are for:

➤ Accident or death benefits

➤ Pension fund contributions

➤ Lobbying and political activities

Club dues, such as country clubs or hotel/airline clubs, are not deductible. Even if you use the club 100% for business, you can't deduct the initiation fee or your membership fees. You can deduct dues paid to the following:

➤ Business leagues

➤ Boards of trade

➤ Civic or public service organizations

➤ Trade associations

➤ Professional associations

➤ Real estate boards

➤ Chambers of commerce

These organizations are not considered social clubs, so their dues are deductible if the organization is related to your business. If part of your dues covers lobbying or political activities, you can't deduct that part of your dues. The organization should report to you the amount of the dues that you can't deduct.

Uniforms and Other Work Clothes

There are a lot of jobs that require special clothing. Some people can deduct their work clothes. You can deduct the cost and upkeep of your work clothes if both of these statements are true:

➤ You have to wear the clothes as a condition of your employment.

➤ The work clothes are not suitable for everyday wear.

Unsuitable for everyday wear is not a matter of personal taste. For example, Carrie is 18 years old. She takes a job in a restaurant. Carrie has to wear black trousers, a white shirt, and a tie. In her everyday life, Carrie doesn't wear any of these clothes. In spite of Carrie's personal clothing choices, her work uniform is everyday clothing. Her work uniform is not deductible.

Your Decoder Ring

It's not always easy to tell which **clothes** are not suitable for everyday wear. The IRS takes a very narrow view. It isn't enough that work clothes are distinctive. They have to be a type of clothing that is not considered street wear. A business suit, for example, is street wear even if it is green and yellow.

The following workers might be able to deduct their uniforms:

➤ Health care workers (uniforms and lab smocks, for example)

➤ Delivery workers (uniforms or jumpsuits)

➤ Firefighters

➤ Police officers

➤ Letter carriers

➤ Professional athletes

➤ Transportation workers

Work clothes that are not deductible include:

➤ Slacks or shirts (even if a distinctive color or pattern)

➤ Jackets

➤ Bib overalls

➤ Regular work shoes or street shoes worn for work

➤ Business suits (even if you don't wear them in your everyday life)

➤ Blue jeans (even if they take a beating on the job)

➤ Reading glasses or sunglasses

Protective clothing required for your job is deductible. Protective clothing could include safety shoes, hard hats, protective eyewear, and gloves.

If you are on full-time active duty in the armed forces, you can't deduct the cost of your uniforms. Your uniforms become your everyday clothes. Reservists, on the other hand, can deduct the cost of uniforms if they can't wear their uniforms when off duty. If you are a civilian faculty or staff member in a military school, the cost of your uniforms is deductible.

Job Hunting

You can deduct expenses of looking for a new job in your present occupation. Even if you don't get a new job, your expenses are still deductible.

You can't deduct job hunting expenses if these statements are true:

➤ You are looking for your first job

➤ You are looking for a job in a new occupation

➤ You had a substantial break in time since your last job

Job hunting expenses can include the following:

➤ Resume preparation (typing, printing)

➤ Postage to send letters of introduction and resumes to prospective employers

➤ Employment agency fees

➤ Travel related to your job search

Business Gifts

You can deduct gifts that are related to your business, but the deduction is very limited. Your deduction is limited to $25 for each business gift that you give. Business gifts might include:

➤ Flowers sent to a client

➤ Food baskets sent to customers or suppliers

➤ Retirement gifts

➤ Gifts to acknowledge the promotion of a business associate, customer, or supplier

Twenty-five dollars doesn't go a long way when giving gifts. That's the government's plan. There is not a lot to gain by stretching the rules. Even if you have receipts, cancelled checks, and an ironclad business purpose for the gift, $25 is all you can deduct for each gift.

And So On

Tools that you use on your job are deductible if they won't last more than a year. If the tools will last more than a year, you can take a depreciation deduction for the tools. See Chapter 14 for a discussion of depreciation deductions.

Licenses and regulatory fees that you have to pay for your existing job are deductible. Professional accreditation fees aren't deductible since they qualify you for a new profession. Examples of nondeductible fees are the following:

Red Flag

Remember that business gifts have to be related to your business. Don't try to mix personal gifts. For example, a birthday present for a customer's child won't fly. A holiday gift to a customer will work.

➤ Examination and fees to become a licensed realtor

➤ Accounting certificate fees paid for your initial right to practice accounting

➤ Bar examination fees and expenses to gain admission to the bar

➤ Medical and dental license fees paid to get your initial license

If you are studying for the CPA exam, for example, the cost of study courses and the cost of taking the exam are not deductible. These expenses qualify you for a new profession, so you can't deduct them.

If you are a college professor, you can deduct research expenses. The research must be expected of you as one of your duties as a professor. You can deduct expenses related to research such as:

➤ Travel

➤ Writing

➤ Publishing

➤ Teaching

➤ Lecturing

If you pay premiums for business liability insurance, you can deduct the cost of your premiums. Personal liability coverage is not deductible, though. To deduct the premiums, the insurance must protect you against liability for wrongful acts on the job.

If you pay damages to a former employer for a breach of an employment contract, you can deduct the damages that you pay.

Special Rules

Some employees have special rules for their business expenses. These employees include government officials who are paid on a fee basis, performing artists, and disabled employees.

Government Officials

Some government officials are paid on a fee basis. These officials can deduct their business expenses whether or not they itemize their deductions.

This break is available to an official who works for a state or local government and is paid entirely or partly on a fee basis. To claim your business expenses, complete Form 2106. Carry your expenses to the adjustments section on page one of your Form 1040. Write "FBO" next to the line that includes your deduction.

Performing Artists

Some performing artists can deduct their business expenses even if they don't itemize their deductions. To take advantage of this deduction, you have to meet all of the following requirements:

➤ During the year, you worked for at least two employers. You performed services in the performing arts for at least two employers.

➤ You made at least $200 each from two or more employers.

➤ Your business expenses are more than 10% of your income from the performing-arts business.

➤ Your adjusted gross income is not more than $16,000 before claiming your business expenses.

To claim your business expenses, complete Form 2106. Carry your expenses to the "adjustments" section on page one of your Form 1040. Write "QPA" next to the line that includes your deduction.

Disabled Employees

If you have a physical or mental disability, you might have business expenses related to your disability. These expenses are deductible without applying the 2% of AGI floor. The expenses are still itemized deductions.

Your impairment-related work expenses might include these items:

➤ One-handed keyboard

➤ Amplification equipment for the hearing impaired

➤ Tools or accessories that enable you to perform job duties that would be difficult due to your disability

➤ Attendant care services at work

➤ Tape player and accessories if you are blind

You know first-hand what your impairment-related expenses are. Remember that under the Americans With Disabilities Act your employer might have to pay some of these costs. Talk to your employer.

Employee or Independent Contractor

When a business hires you to perform services, a relationship is formed. The business is engaging you either as an employee or as an independent contractor. There is a big difference.

It is more expensive for a business to hire an employee than it is to engage an independent contractor. An employer has these payroll costs to contend with:

➤ Income tax withholding (federal and state)

➤ Social Security tax withholding

➤ Social Security tax match (FICA and Medicare)

➤ Unemployment taxes (federal and state)

➤ Workers compensation insurance

When an employee is hired, the employer might have to pay for fringe benefits. The employee might qualify for coverage under the company's health insurance and retirement plans.

A worker who doesn't have business expenses might save money by being an employee instead of an independent contractor. The worker saves money on payroll taxes. As an employee, your employer will pay part of the Social Security taxes for you.

You might, however, have to pay a lot of your own business expenses. If you are an independent contractor, you will deduct your expenses against your business income on Schedule C. This might be a better result for you than claiming an itemized deduction for employee business expenses.

The IRS has battled with businesses for years over categorizing workers as independent contractors instead of employees. There is a lot at stake. If the IRS asserts that a worker was misclassified, it can collect FICA tax, Medicare tax, and the employer match. The IRS can also collect income tax withholdings, interest, and penalties for not paying the payroll taxes.

Which Are You?

Clearly, the classification of workers should not be taken lightly. How should a worker be treated, though? Through the years, the IRS has used different methods to determine if an employer-employee relationship exists. The central issue boils down to control. If the business that hires you can tell you what you need to do, when you will do the job, and how to do the job, there might be an employer-employee relationship. With an independent contractor, the business will specify the end result that is required, but does not control how the worker completes the task.

For example, Rebecca is hired to transcribe medical records for a group medical practice. The medical practice controls the software that will be used, owns the equipment that Rebecca uses, directs Rebecca's business hours, and requires Rebecca to work in their business office. Rebecca is an employee.

There are certain factors that indicate an employer-employee relationship might exist:

➤ Furnishing of tools or a place to work

➤ Payment based on time rather than based on output

➤ Right to discharge the worker

The flip side might indicate that an independent contractor relationship exists:

➤ The worker provides his or her own tools or place to work

➤ The worker is paid for the task performed rather than for the time spent

➤ The worker has the right to substitute other workers in his or her place to complete the work to be performed

None of these factors can be taken as absolute tests. All of the facts and circumstances of the situation are weighed to make the distinction between employee or independent contractor. There is a lot of judgment involved.

Let's change the facts for Rebecca to see the result. Rebecca could negotiate a contract whereby she is paid a fixed dollar amount per page of transcription. Rebecca will be bound to a minimum level of production, but the medical practice will have no control over the number of hours that Rebecca works. Rebecca will perform the transcription work using her own equipment at the location of her choice. The medical practice will stipulate the format and content of the reports that are to be produced. In this new scenario, Rebecca is more likely to be an independent contractor.

There is now an additional tax benefit for Rebecca. As an independent contractor, she can subtract her business expenses from her business income before calculating her self-employment tax. An employee has to pay payroll taxes on gross wages no matter how high his or her business expenses are. If you have a lot of business expenses, it can really make a difference.

If a worker performs services for more than one business, this will tip the scales to an independent contractor status. If Rebecca does transcription for several medical practices, for example, the IRS is more likely to accept her status as an independent contractor.

Your Business Expenses

Your classification as an employee or independent contractor controls how you report your business expenses.

If you are an employee, your business expenses are miscellaneous itemized deductions (subject to the 2% of AGI floor). You should get as much of your expenses reimbursed under an accountable plan as possible. Even if you have to take a lower wage to get the reimbursement, you might come out ahead.

If you are an independent contractor, your income and business expenses will be reported on Schedule C, Profit or Loss From Business. In Chapter 14, we talk about all of the expenses that a self-employed person can claim. Instead of reporting your income on a Form W-2, your income will be reported to the IRS and to you on a Form 1099-Misc if you are an independent contractor. If you are paid less than $600 in a year, a 1099-Misc is not needed.

Your Payroll Taxes

It might seem that you would want to be an independent contractor whenever possible. Don't be hasty, though. There is a price to pay. When you are self-employed, you have to pay your own FICA and Medicare match. You pay both the employee and the employer portion of these Social Security taxes.

As an independent contractor, you also don't have income taxes withheld from your pay. You will need to make quarterly estimated tax payments using Form 1040-ES. Your quarterly payments need to include your income tax and your self-employment (Social Security) tax.

Statutory Employees—A Hybrid

There are some employees who are called *statutory employees*. These employees have payroll taxes withheld from their pay. They will receive a Form W-2 for their wages received.

Paper Trail

If you hold yourself out to the public to perform services, act the part. Use business letterhead and have business cards printed. List your business in the business section of the local telephone directory. It might influence how the IRS views your business.

Paper Trail

Some people think that the $600 rule for filing a Form 1099–Misc means that you don't have to pay tax on income if it's kept under $600 for the year. That isn't true. Even though a 1099 doesn't have to be filed, you still have to report the income on your tax return.

In a strange mix, though, a statutory employee uses a Schedule C to report income and expenses from the business. It's like having the best of both worlds. Your employer pays your payroll taxes, but you can deduct your business expenses against your business income. Statutory employees include the following people:

➤ A full-time salesperson who solicits orders from businesses on behalf of his or her employer. The merchandise sold must be for resale (inventory sold to a retail store, for example) or for supplies used in the buyer's business.

➤ A full-time life insurance agent whose principal business is selling life insurance or annuity contracts for one life insurance company.

➤ An agent-driver or commission-driver engaged in distributing meat, vegetables, bakery goods, beverages other than milk, laundry, or dry cleaning services.

➤ A home worker performing work on material or goods furnished by the employer.

If you are a statutory employee, there will be an indication on your Form W-2 to that effect. If you think you qualify, talk to your employer.

The Least You Need to Know

➤ If your employer reimburses you for business expenses under an accountable plan, you don't have to report the reimbursement or your expenses on your tax return.

➤ You can deduct unreimbursed employee business expenses (as a miscellaneous itemized deduction).

➤ Club dues are not deductible. Dues to certain business or professional organizations can be deducted.

➤ Work clothes and uniforms are deductible only if they are required by your employer and they are not suitable for everyday wear.

➤ You can't simply choose if you will be treated as an employee or an independent contractor. There are tax standards to be considered.

Deductions If You Are Self-Employed

In This Chapter

➤ Writing off the cost of products you sell

➤ Depreciating your business assets

➤ Handling the tax responsibilities of having employees

➤ Hiring your children to work for you

➤ Deducting expenses if you do business in a partnership

If you are self-employed, you call your own shots, pay your own bills, and pay your own taxes. Self-employment is the dream of many Americans. Once they discover the world of self-employment taxes and estimated tax payments, however, they can become disillusioned.

You are self-employed if you own your own business by yourself and it is not a corporation. You are a sole proprietor. You report your business income and business expenses on Schedule C, Profit or Loss From Business, with your Form 1040.

You are also self-employed if you are in partnership with someone else. The business income and deductions are reported on a partnership tax return (Form 1065). Your share of the partnership profits or losses is reported on your Schedule E, Supplemental Income and Loss, with your Form 1040.

When you are an employee, your income taxes are withheld from your pay. Many employees never write a check to the IRS. They have enough taxes withheld that they get a refund each year. It's the American way. Self-employed people, on the other hand, have to pay their own taxes. There is no employer to hold out the taxes. The taxes are paid by quarterly estimated tax payments (Form 1040-ES).

Red Flag

If you don't pay enough in esti-mated taxes, you might owe a penalty for underpayment. There are ways to avoid the penalty. Form 2210 is used to calculate the penalty and the exceptions that will get you out of the penalty.

When you are employed, your employer will with-hold your Social Security taxes (FICA and Medicare taxes). The employer also *matches* your Social Security taxes. For every dollar withheld from your pay, the employer pays another dollar in Social Security taxes. The greatest shock to first-time self-employed people is that they have to pay both halves of the Social Security tax, called self-employment tax. Your self-employment tax is calculated on Schedule SE.

The self-employed person has the most to gain by claiming business deductions. By the time you add up the federal income tax, self-employment tax, and state income tax (if you have a state income tax) savings from a deduction, you have a pretty impres-sive tax rate.

Even in the lowest tax bracket, your savings can be:

Federal income tax	15%
Self-employment tax	15.3%
Total savings	30.3%

If you are subject to state income taxes, the savings are even more.

Business deductions for a self-employed person can include the same items that employees can deduct:

➤ Automobile use
➤ Telephone and computer expenses
➤ Travel
➤ Meals
➤ Entertainment

For the self-employed person, though, the expenses are usually broader. Often the self-employed person has to pay all of the business expenses. These expenses could include:

➤ Wages
➤ Property taxes
➤ Advertising
➤ Insurance

184

➤ Office supplies
➤ Professional fees
➤ Rent
➤ Repairs

The list can go on and on.

Most self-employed people deduct their business expenses on Schedule C, Net Profit From Business. Some self-employed people are partners in partnerships. Their expenses are deducted on their Schedule E, Supplemental Income and Loss. Farmers report their deductions on Schedule F, Profit or Loss From Farming.

In this chapter, we'll cover the deductions that might be encountered by a self-employed person. Employees could have some of these deductions, too. Read on to see if you can take any of these deductions.

Selling Your Wares

If you sell products in your business, you can deduct the cost of the goods that you sell. Not surprisingly, this is called your *cost of goods sold*.

Businesses that sell products usually have products on hand. This is their *inventory*. You can't take a tax deduction for items that are in your inventory. The deduction is taken when the items leave your inventory. That happens when the products are sold.

You will have to keep track of inventories if you are:

➤ A retailer
➤ A wholesaler
➤ A manufacturer

You don't have to keep track of inventories if you are in a service business. Examples of these service businesses are:

➤ Painter
➤ Carpenter
➤ Consultant
➤ Doctor
➤ Lawyer

Even someone in a service business can sell products, though. For example, an optometrist will sell eyeglasses and contact lenses. If you sell products in your service business, like an optometrist does, you will have to keep track of inventory for the products that you sell.

Throughout this chapter, we'll use Nina as our sample entrepreneur. Nina owns a medical supply company. She sells bandages, latex gloves, braces, splints, and other items that would be used by a physician in his or her office. Nina's customer will place an order by fax. Nina fills the order and delivers it to the physician's office within 24 hours.

Nina has to have inventory on her shelves. Her customers expect immediate delivery, so she has to be prepared with inventory on hand. How does Nina handle this on her tax return?

When you sell products, you can write off your cost of the products sold. You write off the products as they are sold, not as they are bought. You have to calculate how much inventory was actually sold during the year to take your deduction for cost of goods sold.

On the Schedule C, there is a section called "Cost of Goods Sold." This section walks you through a method you use to calculate your cost of goods sold. The formula works like this:

1. Start with inventory on hand at the beginning of the year.

2. Add in the items that you purchased during the year. These items could be finished goods or raw materials.

3. Add in the cost of labor to manufacture your products (if you are a manufacturer).

4. Add in the cost of materials and supplies that are used in the processing or manufacturing process, if any.

5. Subtract out your ending inventory.

The result of this formula is the cost of the items that you actually sold during the year. Let's make this calculation for Nina. She doesn't manufacture or process any products.

1.	Beginning inventory	$10,000
2.	Purchases	$80,000
3.	Total available for sale	$90,000
4.	Ending inventory	$15,000
5.	Cost of goods sold	$75,000

In Nina's case, she spent $80,000 during the year to buy products. $5,000 of the amount that Nina spent for products was still on her shelves at the end of the year. She can't deduct the $5,000 that hit her shelves until it moves off her shelves and out to her customers.

Your Decoder Ring

When you buy merchandise to resell in your business, you might pay shipping or freight charges. These charges are part of the cost of your inventory. You can't deduct these charges separately as a business expense. As the inventory is sold, the freight charges are deducted as part of your cost of goods sold.

If you use any of your inventory personally, you have to take this out of your cost of goods sold calculation. For example, if Nina's son has knee surgery and needs a pair of crutches, Nina can't deduct the cost of the crutches used by her son in her cost of goods sold. It is a personal medical expense that can be claimed as part of Nina's medical deductions, though.

You also can't take a cost of goods sold deduction for products that you donate to charity. You can take a charitable contribution deduction (an itemized deduction) for the inventory donated. The contribution deduction is limited to your cost of the inventory donated (what you paid for it).

For example, Nina decides to donate medical supplies to a free clinic. The supplies have a market value of $5,000, but she paid $2,500 for them. Nina will not take a business deduction for the donated supplies. Instead, she will take a $2,500 charitable contribution deduction (on Schedule A).

If Nina gives free samples of her products to nonprofit clinics that are customers or poten-
tial customers, the result is quite different. The cost of the samples would be a business deduction. This practice is a type of advertising or business development expense.

Red Flag

Some promoters imply that you can write off items that you use person-ally if you are selling their products. Don't fall for it. Items that you use personally are not deductible as business expenses, even if you call them samples or demonstration products.

To calculate your cost of goods sold, you have to take inventory at the end of each year. It might be a good idea to take inventory more frequently for business reasons. For your income taxes, though, once a year is all you need.

When you take inventory, each item on hand is counted. Multiplying the item count by each item's cost will give you the total cost of your inventory on hand. To do this, you have to determine how to price your products.

You have some choices here. In general, inven-tory has to be valued at your cost. If the value of your inventory drops below your cost, you can use a method that allows you to use the value rather than the cost. This is called the *lower of cost or market* method. Original title, huh?

If the price of a product is increasing, which price do you use? Do you assume that your

Paper Trail

Taking inventory counts can be a good business practice. It gives you a chance to spot theft. Inventories can also be a theft deterrent. If your employees know that you regularly count merchandise, it might make them think twice before taking items from your shelves.

newest products moved out first? Do you assume that your oldest products moved out first? It can make a difference.

The standard approach is known as FIFO. This stands for *first in, first out*. The FIFO system treats your inventory as if the most recent purchases are still on your shelves. It assumes that your products moved out in the same order that they moved in.

You can elect another method, known as LIFO. You guessed it, *last in, first out*. You would want to use LIFO if your product prices increase regularly. You have to apply to the IRS to allow use of the LIFO method. There are different pricing methods available under LIFO inventory methods. LIFO isn't for amateurs. Once you have elected LIFO, you can't change out of it without getting the IRS's permission. If you want to use LIFO, check with a business tax professional.

Depreciation—What Is It, Anyway?

Depreciation might be one of the great accounting mysteries. Many business owners know that they can take depreciation, but don't really understand what it is.

Simply put, depreciation is a deduction that you take for an item that lasts more than a year. Instead of taking a deduction in one year, you spread out the deduction over a period of years.

The tax code tells us how many years to spread out the deductions (the *depreciable life*). It isn't important how long the item will last. Check out the "Depreciation Lives" section in this chapter for more details.

Let's say, as an example, that Nina buys a computer. The computer should last more than one year, but probably less than three years. The depreciation life for computer equipment set by the IRS is five years. Nina will write off her computer over five years by taking a depreciation deduction each year. If the computer is scrapped before the five years is up, the remaining cost of the computer that Nina has not written off as depreciation can be deducted.

You will start taking depreciation deductions when you place an asset in service. This is when you start to use the asset in your business. It doesn't matter when you pay for the asset.

For example, Nina's computer cost $2,500 plus $125 of sales tax for a total of $2,625. She bought it in December of 1998 on a payment program. In 1998, she only paid $500 toward the cost of the computer. When Nina calculates her depreciation on the computer, she will use the full $2,625 cost in making her calculations. Even though she hasn't yet paid the other $2,125, she includes the full purchase price on her depreciation schedule.

There are three different types of write-offs for business assets. The type of write-off depends on what kind of asset you have purchased:

➤ Depreciation is taken for tangible assets (things you can touch and feel)

➤ Amortization is taken for intangible assets

➤ Depletion is taken for natural resources (such as oil, gas, or coal)

Depreciation Lives

There are pre-assigned lives that must be used for assets that go on your depreciation schedule. The condition of the property will not influence the depreciation life. Your estimate of how long the asset will last is also not relevant.

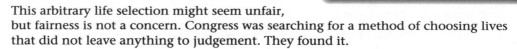

Red Flag

When you buy some types of business property, you might have to pay sales tax on the purchase. You can't separately deduct the sales tax. You have to add the sales tax to the cost of the property that you depreciate.

This arbitrary life selection might seem unfair, but fairness is not a concern. Congress was searching for a method of choosing lives that did not leave anything to judgement. They found it.

For personal property (that is everything except real estate), there are six asset classes:

➤ Three-year

➤ Five-year

➤ Seven-year

➤ Ten-year

➤ Fifteen-year

➤ Twenty-year

In Appendix B, "Depreciation Class Lives," there is a reference chart that you can use to select asset classes.

Depreciation Method

Once you know the life over which you will depreciate an asset, you have half of the formula done. The other half is determining the method of depreciation that you will use.

The straight-line method takes an even deduction each year for the life of an asset. If you are depreciating an asset over 10 years, straight-line depreciation would be 10% of the asset's basis each year.

Real estate has to be depreciated using the straight-line method. There isn't any choice. The Tax Reform Act of 1986 changed depreciation dramatically. Taking away the accelerated depreciation method for real estate was one of the changes. Since the 1986 Act, all real estate and improvements to real estate are purely straight-line. Older assets can continue being depreciated on their old accelerated method schedules, though.

If an item isn't real estate, it is called *personal property*. This shouldn't be confused with *personally used property*. They are two completely different things. Personal property is anything that is not real estate. It isn't attached to land or a building in a way that would cause damage if removed. Personally used property, on the other hand, is property you don't use in a trade or business.

Manufactured cabinets, for example, are personal property. Even though they are attached to your walls, they can be easily removed without damage to the building. Built-in cabinets, on the other hand, might be an integral part of the building structure. If so, they are real property rather than personal property.

In business, personal property will include your:

➤ Manufacturing equipment
➤ Office equipment
➤ Furniture
➤ Telephones
➤ Computers
➤ Cars and trucks
➤ Forklifts

For your personal property, you can use a depreciation method that is faster than straight-line. The depreciation deductions are front-end loaded. In the early years of depreciation, the deductions are more than straight-line depreciation would be. In the later years, the depreciation deductions are less than straight-line depreciation would be.

An accelerated depreciation method recognizes that the value of your equipment falls quickly in the first few years of its life. The depreciation deduction more closely mirrors the trend line of the asset's value.

For personal property, you will take a half-year of depreciation in the first year of an asset's life. This is called the *half-year convention*. Even if you owned the property less than six months, you will get one half of a year's depreciation. The same half-year assumption is used in the last year you own an asset.

The IRS has made the depreciation system easy by giving us tables to use. The tables have percentages that you use each year to figure your depreciation. For example, a three-year asset is depreciated as shown in Table 14.1.

Table 14.1   Three–Year Depreciation Table

Year	Accelerated Depreciation	Straight Line Depreciation
1	33.33%	16.67%
2	44.45%	33.33%
3	14.81%	33.33%
4	7.41%	16.67%

You might ask why there are four years on a three-year table. The reason is the half-year convention. If you only take one-half year in the first year, your depreciation will span four different tax years.

You can slow down your depreciation method if you like. The IRS prints depreciation tables for nearly every option you can consider. To make things even easier, you might try using a software package that will calculate the depreciation for you. Your trusty tax return preparer can also handle this task.

Red Flag

If you load up on your equipment purchases in the last quarter of the year, you can't take a half-year of depreciation. If more than 40% of your new assets were placed in service during the last three months of the year, you have to use a mid-quarter convention rather than a half-year convention.

Real Estate

The depreciation of real estate has taken many dips and twists over the last couple of decades. We have seen real estate depreciation lives go from 15 years in 1983 to either $27^1/_2$ years or 39 years today.

If you have real estate that is being depreciated on an old depreciation life or method, you just keep the old method rolling. If you buy or improve real estate, though, the newer rules apply to you.

You will take $^1/_2$ of a month's depreciation in the month that you place real property in service. For example, if you place a building in service in April of 1998, you will take $8^1/_2$ months of depreciation in 1998.

When you sell real property, you take $^1/_2$ month of depreciation in its final month. If you sell a building in November of 1998, for example, you will claim $10^1/_2$ months of depreciation for 1998.

Residential rental real estate is depreciated over 27.5 years using the straight-line method. Residential real estate includes a rental house, a condominium, or an apartment building. A hotel or motel is not residential real estate.

Nonresidential real estate is depreciated straight-line over 39 years. It doesn't matter if the building that you bought is in shambles or if it is 80 years old. The life is still 39 years and the method is still straight-line.

The 27¹/₂- and 39-year lives apply to a building that you buy or build. These lives also apply to improvements made to a building.

For example, if Nina decides to add a new entrance to her building, this is a building improvement. She has to depreciate the improvement over 39 years. Even though she knows that the entrance will need major work again in the next 39 years, she is stuck with a 39-year life.

Where do you draw the line between a building improvement and a repair? It can mean a huge tax difference since repairs are 100% deductible in the year of the repair.

Paper Trail

If Nina's improvements to her facility make it handicap accessible, she might qualify for the Disabled Access Credit explained in Chapter 4, "Even Better Than Deductions—Tax Credits." As an alternative, she might be able to deduct (up to $15,000) the cost of removing barriers for handicapped or elderly persons. She can't take both the deduction and the credit, though.

Ask this question: "Will the expenditure extend the useful life of your building or add to its value?" If the answer is no, you have made a repair. If the answer is yes, you have made an improvement. In Nina's case, the new entrance won't extend the useful life of the building, but it will increase its value.

Expenses that are for regular maintenance to keep the property in efficient operating condition don't have to be depreciated. They can be deducted as repairs. The following expenses are examples of items that you could deduct as repairs:

➤ Repainting
➤ Mending leaks
➤ Plastering
➤ Repairing a roof

If you replace a roof, that is a capital expenditure that has to be depreciated. If you repair a roof, that is a deductible repair. Most roofs won't last 39 years, so the chances of replacing a roof before the old one is depreciated is pretty good. If you have to depreciate a new roof and replace it within 39 years, you can write off the undepreciated basis of the old roof in the year that the new roof goes on.

Use your judgement on repair items. If challenged, the IRS agent will have to use his or her judgement, too. If you have damage that has to be repaired, keep a copy of your contractor's estimate that gives information about the damage. Taking pictures can sometimes be a good idea, too. If the IRS can see that a window was damaged and that you repaired it, you might have more luck supporting your repair cost.

If you are doing a general upgrade of your property, even the little repair items will have to be capitalized and depreciated. Painting by itself would be deductible, but it is capitalized if part of a general remodeling job. For example, if Nina remodels the office in her shop, she will be painting, repairing damaged spots in the floors and walls, replacing fixtures, etc. Any part of her remodeling that is not personal property (furniture, fixtures, etc.) will have to be depreciated over 39 years.

Turbo Charge Your Depreciation

If you choose, you can take a big chunk of depreciation expense in the year that you place business property in service. This extra depreciation is called Section 179 expense or *additional first year depreciation*. It's called Section 179 expense because the deduction is allowed by Section 179 of the Internal Revenue Code (the tax law).

In 1998, you can claim up to $18,500 of Section 179 expense. The election is only available to personal property (furniture, equipment, etc.) and cannot be taken on real estate. You could have Section 179 expenses coming from different sources such as partnerships, S corporations, and your sole proprietorship. The total amount you can claim on your 1998 tax return for all of the Section 179 expenses combined is $18,500.

There are limits to Section 179 expense other than the annual $18,500 limit:

➤ If you add more than $200,000 of property in one year (other than real estate), your Section 179 expense is reduced. If your additions are more than $218,500 in one year, you get no Section 179 expense that year.

➤ Your Section 179 expense is limited to the net income from your trade or business. In other words, your Section 179 expense can't throw you into a loss.

➤ You can't use Section 179 expense on property that you use 50% or more personally.

The Section 179 expense is a real help for small businesses. A consultant, for example, might have to buy a new computer each year. By using the Section 179 expense, his tax deductions will be right in line with his computer purchase needs.

A Bit Business, a Bit Personal

Some business assets can be used partly for personal reasons. The IRS calls these items *listed property*.

Listed property includes these assets:

➤ Any passenger automobile

➤ Any other transportation vehicle

➤ Property generally used for entertainment, recreation, or amusement (boats, for example)

➤ Some computers and computer equipment

➤ Cell phones or other telecommunications equipment

193

You have to calculate the personal use portion and business use portion of the listed property. You can only take depreciation on the business use portion.

If you use listed property 50% or more for personal reasons, there are two depreciation consequences:

➤ You have to use the straight-line method of depreciation.

➤ You can't take Section 179 expense.

If you start out with an asset being predominantly personal in use and you exceed 50% business use in later years, you are stuck with the straight-line method of depreciation. You won't get an upgrade. If you start with accelerated depreciation and drop to less than 50% business, you have to switch to straight-line depreciation. You are then stuck with straight-line for the rest of the asset's life.

To support your depreciation expense, you'll have to keep records. Keeping a log of your car's use is a challenge. Keep a good appointment book or calendar. It can help. Keeping a log of cell phone use is even a greater challenge. You can get detailed records from your cell phone service provider, but it might cost an extra monthly fee. The extra monthly fee will, of course, boost your deduction for your cell phone. It's a never-ending circle of expenses and deductions!

Red Flag

Keeping a log of business and personal use items for a sample period of time might help you in an IRS audit. The agent doesn't have to accept your sample log as a representation of the whole year's use, though. If your records are well kept, your case for taking the deduction is credible, and you cooperate with the IRS agent, you are more likely to be successful in your audit.

Intangibles

Intangible assets that you acquire in your business can't be deducted or depreciated. Instead, you amortize them. Amortization is like depreciation, except that it is only taken straight-line. If you amortize over 15 years, your tax deduction is $1/15$th each year.

Intangible assets are things that you can't touch and feel. Intangible assets include:

➤ Trademarks

➤ Trade names

➤ Goodwill

➤ Franchises (other than sports franchises)

➤ Copyrights

➤ Patents

➤ Covenants not to compete

Prior to August 10, 1993, you could not amortize most intangible assets. You could only write off the cost of the intangible asset when you got rid of it. This was a terrible result for taxpayers. For intangibles that could be amortized, there were frequent battles over what life to use.

In 1993, the battle lines were cleared out. Intangibles can be amortized over 15 years.

You can't amortize self-created intangibles. For example, you can't amortize the cost of a trademark that you developed. You can, however, amortize the cost of a trademark that you buy.

Depletion

If you are involved in mining or drilling for natural resources, you might be able to take a depletion deduction.

Natural resources include:

➤ Oil

➤ Gas

➤ Coal

➤ Minerals

➤ Gravel

➤ Timber

For example, if you are drilling for oil, you will pay for your interest in the drilling operation. You can't write off your investment in the oil reserves. You can't even take depreciation on your oil reserve investment. Instead, you will take a depletion deduction.

Paper Trail

If you are buying or selling a business, the allocation of the purchase price is important. For the buyer, it could make the difference between five-year depreciation, 15-year amortization, or 39-year depreciation. For the seller, it could make the difference between ordinary income or capital gain. You have to be consistent. The seller and the buyer have to report their purchase price allocation to the IRS. Negotiate wisely and document the allocation.

You will deduct your investment in the natural resources by taking either cost depletion or percentage depletion.

Cost depletion is a method by which you estimate how much of the natural resource you recovered during the year. You allocate your investment in the total reserves to the portion that you recovered and claim a cost depletion deduction.

Percentage depletion is a bit easier than cost depletion. Percentage depletion is a fixed percentage of the royalties that you receive. There are limits, of course. You might need an accountant to calculate depletion, unless you're a hardy self-preparer.

Need Help with Depreciation?

These IRS publications might help you:

➤ Publication 946, How To Depreciate Property

➤ Publication 534, Depreciating Property Placed in Service Before 1987

➤ Publication 535, Business Expenses

You can get IRS publications from the IRS web site www.irs.ustreas.gov. From The Digital Daily page, click on Forms & Pubs.

People Working for You

Anyone who works for you will either be your employee or an independent contractor. We talked about independent contractors in Chapter 13, "Deductions If You Are an Employee." If you pay an independent contractor $600 or more in 1998, you will have to file a Form 1099-Misc.

If you have employees that work for you, a new world of paperwork and tax returns has just been opened for you.

Paper Trail

To file Form 1099 or to file payroll tax returns, you will need a tax-payer ID number for your business. To get an ID number, complete a Form SS-4. You can either call the IRS to get your ID number (see the instructions on the form) or mail in Form SS-4.

The Employer Routine

When you are an employer, there is a series of steps that you will go through like clockwork. Pay attention to your payroll system. Take it seriously. The penalties for not paying payroll taxes can boggle your mind.

When you have employees, you will follow these steps:

➤ When you calculate your employees' paychecks, hold out federal income tax, FICA tax, Medicare tax, and any state and local taxes that apply. You will use each employee's Form W-4 to calculate federal tax withholding. On the W-4, the employee will tell you how many exemptions are being claimed and whether to use married or single tax rates.

➤ Calculate the amount you owe to the IRS for withheld taxes. Add up the federal taxes, FICA taxes, Medicare taxes, and your FICA and Medicare match.

➤ Pay your federal payroll taxes. This is done electronically or by deposit through your local bank. The IRS will determine how frequently you have to pay the taxes that you have withheld.

➤ Calculate the taxes you owe to your state or local government.

➤ Pay your state and local withholdings under your state's rules.

➤ Quarterly, file a Form 941 to report your wages and withholding to the IRS.

➤ Quarterly, take care of your federal and state unemployment tax payments and file the appropriate forms.

➤ Annually, file a Form 940 to report your unemployment tax liability.

➤ Annually, file Forms W-2 with the IRS and the Social Security Administration.

As an employer, you can deduct the gross wages that you pay. You can also deduct the FICA match, Medicare match, and unemployment taxes that you pay on your employees' wages.

Believe it or not, this is a simplified list of your payroll tax filing responsibilities. We haven't covered all of the possible steps. The filing responsibilities are not much simpler for someone with two employees than they are for someone with 200 employees. How do you manage this?

Your Decoder Ring

FICA and **Medicare** taxes together make up your Social Security Taxes. You will pay the 6.2% FICA tax on the first $68,400 of earnings in 1998. You pay the 1.45% Medicare taxes on every dollar of earnings.

Your accounting software may have a payroll module that can help you through the payroll process. A good payroll package will calculate your employees' withholding. The software should produce reports to help you pay the correct amount of taxes and produce some of the payroll tax forms that you will need to file.

Using a payroll service is another option. For a fee, the service will write your payroll checks, pay your taxes, and fill out your payroll tax returns. You submit time records to the payroll service. The service tells you what the total damages are. Funds are transferred to cover the payroll and your taxes. Payroll services can pay for themselves if you have trouble getting your tax payments in on time.

The penalties for not paying withheld taxes can be overwhelming. The IRS is not very sympathetic with employers who hold taxes out of employees' pay and don't hand the tax money over to the IRS.

Pay close attention to your payroll taxes. Make sure the taxes are all paid on time. Make sure your forms are all completed and filed when they are due. If you are the employer, it is your responsibility. If you're the bookkeeper, you can be held responsible, too. This means that the IRS can come after you personally. You don't want to be in this position. The IRS is a very bad place to borrow money for your business.

Red Flag

If you're paying penalties now for late payroll taxes, it's time to make a change. Hire a bookkeeper or switch to a payroll service. Your bookkeeper's salary and the payroll service's fee are deductible business expenses. IRS penalties are not deductible.

Extra Goodies: Fringe Benefits

When you provide things for your employees beyond their paycheck, you've entered the fringe benefit arena. Fringe benefits will give you a tax deduction. Some benefits are taxable to your employees as additional compensation. Other benefits are protected by the tax law and are tax-free to your employees.

Taxable fringe benefits include the following:

➤ Personal use of a car

➤ Membership to an athletic club

➤ Membership to a country club or other social club

➤ Theater tickets

➤ Sporting tickets

➤ Vacation

Tax-free fringe benefits include the following:

➤ Group health insurance coverage

➤ Medical savings accounts

➤ Disability insurance

➤ Group-term life insurance up to $50,000

➤ Cafeteria plan

➤ Adoption assistance

➤ Dependent care plan

➤ Free parking

These fringe benefits each have rules that must be followed. For example, adoption assistance plans are limited to $5,000 ($6,000 for a special needs child). Employee parking is tax-free only up to $175 a month in 1998. For more information about employee benefit programs, read chapter 5 in IRS Publication 535.

Put the Kids to Work

Hiring your children in your business can save taxes in many ways. If you are self-employed and file a Schedule C to report your business income, your kids' wages are deducted with your other employees' wages on your Schedule C.

If your kids are less than 18 years old, you don't have to withhold FICA tax or Medicare tax from their wages. This also means that you don't have to pay the employer's match for FICA and Medicare tax. This payroll tax break can't be used if your business is in a corporation.

The other tax savings from hiring your kids can be substantial:

➤ You save income taxes because of deducting the children's wages.

➤ You save self-employment taxes because the wage deduction reduces your self-employment income.

➤ Your child doesn't pay income tax on the first $4,250 of wages (earned income) in 1998.

➤ Your child can contribute up to $2,000 a year from his or her wages to a Roth IRA.

Contributions to Roth IRAs aren't deductible, but the earnings in the account can be tax-free. In Chapter 23, "IRAs: Saving for Your Own Retirement," we'll discuss Roth IRAs in more detail.

Don't think that hiring your kids is an open checkbook. There are practical limits to hiring your children. You must pay your kids a fair wage for the work that your kids perform. Clearly establish your children's job responsibilities. Set the pay rate at market rate. Pay them what you would pay other unrelated workers. By doing this, you will be prepared if the IRS challenges the deduction for wages paid to your children.

Red Flag

If you are self-employed, you can't pay yourself as an employee from your business. You might want to handle your taxes by withholding like your employees, but you can't do it. You can hire your spouse or your parents, but not yourself.

Forms, Forms, Forms

These are the forms that you will need each employee to complete:

➤ Form I-9, Employment Eligibility Verification. This is a form from the Immigration and Naturalization Service. Every employee must complete a Form I-9. Keep the Form I-9 in the employee's personnel file.

➤ Form W-4, Withholding Allowance Certificate. You will use the filing status and withholding allowances reported on this form to calculate the federal income taxes to withhold from your employee's pay.

➤ Form W-5, Earned Income Credit Advance Payment Certificate. This form can be completed by an employee to get advance EIC payments.

You will have to file the following forms as an employer:

➤ Form SS-4 to get your employer ID number

➤ Form 941 to quarterly report your wages and payroll tax withholdings to the IRS

➤ Form 8109 to make deposits of payroll taxes (unless you pay electronically)

➤ Form W-2 to report wages to your employee, the IRS, and the Social Security Administration

➤ Form W-3 to transmit your Forms W-2 to the Social Security Administration

➤ Form 940 or 940-EZ to report your unemployment taxes to the IRS

➤ Any state forms that might be needed

What Else?

There are a lot of other business expenses that you can claim if you are self-employed. Your deductions will depend on your business, of course.

To claim a deduction, it must be ordinary (typical for your business) and necessary (helpful in your business). There is no complete list of expenses that you can or can't deduct. Each situation can be different. Use your judgement.

Since Nina is in the medical field, buying resource materials that relate to medical matters would be both ordinary and necessary. If Nina wants to expand her business into the construction site safety market, she might have to buy materials about the construction process. At first glance, these materials might not appear to be ordinary for her business, but she is in the business of selling products. These publications will pass the ordinary and necessary test because they help her promote sales.

Insurance

There are many different kinds of insurance that you could be paying for. You can deduct these insurance premiums if they relate to your business:

➤ Fire, theft, or flood coverage of your business property

➤ Insurance to protect your inventory

➤ Insurance on your cars or other vehicles (you can't deduct insurance if you use standard mileage rate to calculate your deduction, though)

➤ Business liability insurance

➤ Business interruption insurance

➤ Overhead insurance

➤ Workers compensation insurance

➤ Federal and state unemployment insurance

You can't deduct these insurance payments:

➤ Life insurance premiums on your own life

➤ Disability insurance to protect against your sickness or disability

➤ Funds that you set aside to protect against a business casualty (self-insurance reserve fund)

You can deduct health insurance premiums that you pay for your employees. If you are self-employed, a portion of your own health insurance premiums is also deductible (see Chapter 19, "Health Plans: Self-Employed Health Insurance and Medical Savings Accounts").

Interest

You can deduct interest that you pay on business loans. To qualify for the deduction, the proceeds of the loan have to be used in your business.

For example, if Nina borrows money from the bank to increase her inventory, she will be able to deduct the interest. If she uses the proceeds from the loan to send her son to college, the interest won't be deductible. Even if her inventory is the collateral for the loan, she can't deduct the interest if the loan proceeds aren't used in her business.

You can also have deductible interest expense if you borrow money to invest in your business partnership. The interest should be claimed on your Schedule E, Supplemental Gains and Losses, in the same section that you report your partnership income.

If you borrow money so that you can make a loan to your partnership, your interest is not a business expense. Instead, you have investment interest expense that is deductible as an itemized deduction. Investment interest expense is only deductible to the extent of investment income. If you can't take all of your investment interest expense in one year, you can carry over the excess amount to future years.

Bad Debts

In your business, you might have to extend credit to your customers. In other words, you have accounts receivable. The receivables can't always be collected. You might be able to take a tax deduction for these accounts receivable gone bad. Your deduction depends on your method of accounting.

If you report your income as you collect payments from your customers, you use the *cash basis* of accounting. If an account receivable goes bad, you can't take a bad debt deduction. You have not reported the income from the sale yet, so you get no write off for the account that turned south.

If, on the other hand, you report income as your sales are booked, you are on the *accrual basis* of accounting. Bad accounts receivable can be deducted when they go bad. The sale has already been included in your income. You will take a bad debt deduction to remove the income that you will never collect.

You can also have a bad debt deduction if you make a business-related loan that becomes uncollectible. A business bad debt is an ordinary loss. Personal bad debts are short-term capital losses.

Nina, for example, might be able to get an important supply from just one source. Her supplier is in financial difficulty. Nina loans money to the supplier in an effort to protect her source for the products. If the loan becomes uncollectible, Nina will be able to claim a *business bad debt*.

Your Decoder Ring

You can't use the **cash method** of accounting if inventories are an important part of your business. Retailers, wholesalers, and manufacturers, for example, can't use the cash basis of accounting. Service businesses that don't have inventories, like carpenters, doctors, and lawyers, can use the cash method.

Business bad debts can be deducted when they become either partially or wholly worthless. Nonbusiness bad debts, on the other hand, are only deductible when they are wholly worthless.

Checking out a New Business

If you spend money to investigate a new business, there are three possible ways that it could be treated on your tax return:

➤ If you are checking out a new business (not similar to your current business) and you do not buy or start the new business, your expenses are not deductible at all.

➤ If you are checking out a business that isn't similar to your current business and you acquire or start the new business, you can elect to amortize your expenses over 60 months.

➤ If you are investigating an opportunity to expand your existing business by purchasing or opening a similar business, the expenses are now deductible. You can deduct the expenses whether you actually go into the new business or not.

No-Nos

You can't take a business expense deduction for the following items:

➤ Political contributions

➤ Lobbying expenses (even if it relates to your business)

➤ Bribes or kickbacks

➤ Charitable contributions (they are itemized deductions instead)

➤ Dues to social clubs

➤ Penalties and fines you pay because you broke the law

You can't deduct payments that are the consequence of actions that are contrary to public policy. The tax code will not give tax benefits to people who break the law. A speeding ticket is never deductible, even if it was incurred when you were driving your car or truck for business.

In spite of the public policy principle, deductions for illegal business activities are allowed. If you run an illegal gaming operation, for example, all of your income is taxable. Your business expenses are also deductible. This might seem to be against public policy, but many criminals are actually prosecuted on tax charges.

A penalty or fine that you pay for late performance on a contract is a deductible business expense. It is viewed differently than a fine for breaking the law.

Partnership Expenses

If your business is a partnership, you might have expenses that you pay out of your own pocket. These expenses are deductible. If you were an employee, the expenses would be miscellaneous itemized deductions. For a partner, the result is different.

A partner can deduct his or her business expenses on Schedule E, Supplemental Income and Loss. The expenses are claimed on the same section of the return that the partnership income is reported.

The best example of these expenses can be found in the legal profession. A lot of law firms are partnerships. The law practice can have partners that are quite diverse in spending habits. Some partners entertain potential clients while other partners will do very little entertaining. Some partners travel for continuing education, while others seek seminars in their hometown.

If the law partnership has a policy requiring each partner to pay for his or her own business meals, entertainment, and transportation expenses, the partner will deduct those expenses on his or her Schedule E. The business expenses reduce the partner's taxable income and his or her self-employment income.

Red Flag

If you have expenses related to your partnership and you are covered by a retirement plan, your retirement plan contribution is impacted. Since the expenses reduce your business income, the **compensation** amount used to calculate your retirement plan contribution is also reduced. If you ignore these expenses, your plan might be considered disqualified for violating discrimination rules.

The Least You Need to Know

➤ A self-employed person can deduct business expenses. When self-employment tax is factored in, the tax savings from business expenses can be significant.

➤ If you sell products in your business, you will have to keep inventories. You will deduct the cost of your products as they move off your shelves.

➤ Depreciation is the way that you claim a tax deduction for business assets such as buildings and equipment. You might be able to take a quick write-off for some of your equipment or furniture, though.

➤ If you hire employees in your business, you will have to comply with the payroll tax withholding and filing rules.

➤ Hiring your children in your business can save taxes.

Chapter 15

Using Your Car for Business

In This Chapter

➤ Calculating the deduction for using your car for business

➤ Handling a car allowance on your tax return

➤ Leasing your business car

➤ Keeping records to support your car expense deduction

If you use your car on the job, you can take a tax deduction for your car expenses. Most people use their cars only partly for business since they also drive their cars for personal reasons. You can only deduct the part of your car expenses that relate to your business use.

If you are an employee, your car expenses are one part of your employee business expense deduction. You might remember from Chapter 13, "Deductions If You Are an Employee," that your business expenses are part of your miscellaneous itemized deductions. Use Form 2106 to report your car expenses.

If you are self-employed and report your business income on a Schedule C, Net Profit From Business, your car expenses are deducted on your Schedule C. If you are a farmer, your car expenses will be reported on your Schedule F, Profit or Loss From Farming. If you are a partner in a partnership, your car expenses will be deducted on Schedule E, Supplemental Income and Loss.

There are two tax goodies that might save you taxes even if you don't use your car in your business. There is a deduction for clean-fuel vehicles and a credit for electric vehicles.

The clean-fuel vehicle deduction can be taken for a car that uses natural gas and hydrogen and fuels that are at least 85% methanol, ethanol, alcohol, or ether. The amount of your deduction depends on the vehicle:

➤ For a car or light truck, the deduction is up to $2,000.

➤ For some trucks and vans with gross weight of more than 10,000 pounds, but not more than 26,000 pounds, the deduction is up to $5,000.

➤ For a truck or van with gross weight of more than 26,000 pounds, the deduction is $50,000.

➤ A bus that can seat 20 adult passengers will get a $50,000 deduction.

The credit for electric vehicles is 10% of the cost of the car. The credit can't be more than $4,000. The credit is claimed on Form 8834, Qualified Electric Vehicle Credit.

In this chapter, we will explore the deductions that you can take for your car that you use in your business. These rules also apply to light trucks and minivans. Heavy trucks, buses, and construction equipment are treated as business property that you will take depreciation deductions for. We discussed depreciation in Chapter 14, "Deductions If You Are Self-Employed."

How Much Can You Deduct?

You can deduct car expenses for traveling away from home for business. You can also deduct car expenses for certain in-town travel. For example, you can deduct the cost of driving from your office to visit a customer. You can't deduct the cost of commuting from your home to work. Check out Chapter 17, "Travel, Meals, and Entertainment," to see which trips in your car you can deduct.

Once you have identified the car trips that you can deduct, how much do you claim? You have to come up with a dollar amount. There are two different ways that you can measure your car expenses to deduct:

➤ By using the standard mileage rate

➤ By calculating your actual car expenses

Standard Mileage Rate

In 1998, the standard mileage rate for using your car for business is 32.5 cents per mile. In 1997, the rate was 31.5 cents per mile. Each year, the IRS adjusts the mileage rate for a cost-of-living increase.

If you use the standard mileage rate, calculating your car expense deduction is easy. Simply multiply the number of business miles you drove during the year by the standard mileage rate. The result is your deduction.

Let's say that Michael drove his car 100,000 miles for business in 1998. His car expense deduction is $32,500.

By opting for the standard mileage rate, you give up the right to deduct your actual car expenses. You can't take both mileage and actual expenses or use partly one method and partly another. You have to make a choice. The choice has to be made the first year you use your car in your business.

If you don't use the standard mileage rate for the first year, you can't use it in later years. In other words, if you use actual expenses for the first year you take a deduction for your car, you have to use actual expenses for every year you use that car. When you get a different car, you can choose again whether you want to use the standard mileage rate or actual expenses.

Some people can't use the standard mileage rate. You can't use mileage if:

➤ You operate more than one car at the same time for business

➤ You use your car for hire (a taxi, for example)

➤ You claimed a deduction for the car in an earlier year using an accelerated depreciation method (ACRS or MACRS)

Don't be confused by the using more than one car at a time rule. You aren't using more than one car at a time if you alternate using different cars.

For example, Melanie has two cars, a sedan and a minivan. Melanie works in a print shop. When she calls on a potential customer, she drives her sedan. When she makes deliveries, she drives the minivan. Melanie can still use standard mileage for her cars because she is never using both cars for business at the same time.

John, on the other hand, has a different situation. John owns a social service agency that makes frequent visits to clients' homes. John has three employees who make the client visits. John owns two cars. They are both available to employees to drive to clients' homes. There are times that both cars are being used by John or his employees to call on clients. John is using more than one car at a time. He can't use the standard mileage rate to claim deductions on either car.

Paper Trail

Before 1998, Postal Service employees with rural routes used a higher mileage rate (47.25 cents in 1997). Rural mail carriers are paid a mileage rate set by collective bargaining. Starting in 1998, this rate becomes the standard mileage rate for tax purposes. Rural mail carriers won't have taxable income or loss for their mileage.

Paper Trail

Even if you claim standard mileage, you can deduct business-related parking fees and tolls. Parking at your place of work is not deductible. Parking at your work is considered part of your nondeductible commute. Parking at customer's businesses is deductible.

Before 1998, you couldn't use mileage for cars that you leased. Starting in 1998, leased cars qualify for the standard mileage rate.

Actual Car Expenses

If you don't (or can't) use the standard mileage rate, you will deduct your actual car expenses instead. To claim the actual expense, you will:

➤ Figure out what percentage of your car use is business-related

➤ Add up all of your car expenses

➤ Apply your business use percentage to your car expenses to get your deduction

There are two important parts to this calculation:

➤ The business use percent

➤ The actual expenses

To get the business use percent, you have to tally miles. Your business use percent is the portion of your total miles that are driven for business.

For example, if you put 10,000 business miles and 40,000 total miles on your car, you used your car 25% for business. Don't count commuting miles as business. Check out Chapter 17 to see which in-town trips you can count as business miles.

Red Flag

The IRS is leery of cars reported as 100% for business. Unless your business is in your home and you use another car for all personal trips, it's not possible to have 100% business use. On your tax return, you have to disclose business miles, personal miles, and business use percent.

Miles is the only measure of business and personal use that the IRS will recognize. Conceivably, you could argue that time spent in the car is more important. It won't matter. Miles is the measure.

Your car expenses include:

➤ Gasoline and oil

➤ Insurance

➤ Repairs and servicing

➤ License

➤ Tires

➤ Depreciation

➤ Lease fees

If you are an employee, interest paid on your car loan is not deductible. Even to the extent your car is used in your business, the interest can't be claimed. If you are self-employed, on the other hand, the business part of your car loan interest can be deducted.

Taxes that you pay on your car are deducted with your other taxes as an itemized deduction. To deduct car taxes, the taxes have to be based on the value of your car (rather than being based on the model year, for example). Sales taxes on your car are never deductible.

Fines and penalties are never deductible. Even if you are on a business call, parking fines and traffic tickets are not deductible.

Choices, Choices: Which Method to Use?

Is standard mileage better? Is the actual expense method the smart way to go? How do you know which way to go? Consider the following:

➤ Which method gives you a higher deduction?

➤ How good are your records? Could you support your actual expenses in an audit?

➤ Are you eligible to use the standard mileage rate?

➤ How much time are you willing to spend keeping records and calculating your deduction?

If you're having a hard time deciding which method to use, test it out. See how much each deduction would be. That might help you make up your mind.

Consider the record keeping you'll have to maintain if you use actual expenses. Remember that if you start off using actual expenses, you can't switch back to the mileage method.

If record keeping is a problem for you, standard mileage might be an attractive option. You'll still have to know your miles, though. If your records put most accountants to shame, let the larger deduction win.

On-the-Job Cars: When Your Employer Shares Your Cost

If your car is one of your business tools, your employer might pay for part of the cost of operating your car. There are three different ways that employers usually help pay for car expenses:

1. By paying a mileage reimbursement for business miles

2. By paying an automobile allowance

3. By providing a company-owned car

Each of these methods effectively shifts some of the financial responsibility for the business car

Paper Trail

What's the best way to keep track of mileage? Whatever method that works for you! If you don't keep detailed records, find short cuts. Map out the miles on your standard routes. Keep your appointment calendar. Mark the miles on the calendar using the mileage that you measured before. Whatever your method is, stick with it. Make it work for you.

to your employer. The income tax impact to you, as the employee, is quite different under these plans.

Sub-Standard Rate Mileage

Some employers set their mileage rates back in the '70s and haven't changed them since. It's become a corporate tradition. Twenty cents a mile was good enough 10 years ago, so it's good enough now, right?

If your employer pays less than 32.5 cents a mile in 1998, you can take an extra deduction for your car.

Your mileage reimbursement shouldn't be included in your W-2 as taxable wages because it's not more than the standard mileage rate. You need to know how much your reimbursement was, though. Keep a copy of your expense reports or ask your employer for a report showing your reimbursement for the year.

Enter your car expenses on Form 2106. You can use either the standard mileage rate of 32.5 cents a mile or your actual expenses. On the Form 2106, there is a line on which you enter the reimbursement that you got from your employer. By using this line, you reduce your car expenses by the reimbursement you got.

Red Flag

Do you ever check your Form W-2? You should. It's easy to make a mistake on a W-2. It is a surprisingly complicated form. Check your W-2. Check it as soon as you get it. Corrections can be made. If you catch it early enough, the form might not have been sent to the IRS yet.

Julie's employer, for example, pays 28 cents for each business mile. In 1998, Julie was paid $2,240 for 8,000 miles. On Julie's business expense Form 2106, she can claim car expenses of $2,600 (8,000 miles at 32.5 cents per mile). The car expenses are reduced by her $2,240 reimbursement. Julie's deduction in 1998 for using her car is $360. This deduction is carried to Schedule A. It will be combined with Julie's other miscellaneous itemized deductions, which are reduced by 2% of her adjusted gross income.

It is that easy. Don't miss out on this deduction thinking you are just stuck with a low mileage rate. Claim the deduction. You are entitled to it.

Super-Mileage Reimbursements

You might be fortunate enough to get mileage reimbursed at more than the standard rate of 32.5 cents per mile. If so, your employer will have to report part of your reimbursement as taxable wages (unless you are a Postal Service employee with a rural route).

The employer should include in your W-2 the reimbursement that is more than 32.5 cents per mile. For example, if you were reimbursed 35 cents a mile in 1998 for 10,000 miles, your total reimbursement was $3,500. If your reimbursement had been at the standard mileage rate, it would have been $3,250. Your W-2 should include $250 as taxable wages because of the *excess* mileage reimbursement.

Figure out exactly what your employer has reported in your W-2. Do your wages include your entire mileage reimbursement, none of your reimbursement, or just the reimbursement over 32.5 cents per mile? In spite of the IRS reporting requirements, employers do report these items in different ways.

If your entire reimbursement was included on your W-2, you should have your employer file a corrected W-2 to include only the excess (over 32.5 cents). Make the request as soon as you notice the error. It might take time to get the corrected form prepared.

If your W-2 includes none of your mileage reimbursement, you have two options:

➤ Ask your employer to file a corrected W-2 so that the excess is reported on your W-2.

➤ Include the excess reimbursement on your tax return as income even though it wasn't included in your W-2.

At this point, you have included the excess reimbursement (above the standard mileage rate) in your income. You can stop here and pay income tax on your excess reimbursement. If your actual car expenses are more than your reimbursement, though, you can claim a deduction for your actual expenses that exceed your reimbursement.

Car Allowances

If you get a car allowance from your employer, the allowance should be included in your Form W-2 as taxable wages. You will then claim a deduction for the business use of your car. You can either use the standard mileage rate or your actual expenses to claim your car expenses.

A car allowance is taxable because it doesn't satisfy the *accountable plan* rules. Under an accountable plan, you have to report all of your expenses to your employer. If you don't spend all of the employer's money on business expenses, you have to return the money to your employer. In other words, you have to account for your expenses to your employer.

When you get an allowance, it's a one-way street. The employer pays you money. That's it. You don't have to justify or account for how you use the money. There is, of course, the expectation that you will use a car allowance to pay for an automobile that you'll use on the job.

Since you don't have to report back to your employer how you spent the money or how you used your car, your car allowance is taxable to you. You can then claim a deduction for your car expenses. Your deduction is a miscellaneous itemized deduction. You can either use the standard mileage rate to calculate your deduction or you can use your actual expenses.

211

Your employer might qualify to use a special non-taxable allowance method to reimburse you for the business use of your car. The alternative method is called FAVR. This acronym stands for *fixed and variable*. As the name suggests, the allowance has two parts:

➤ A fixed payment for the cost of the car
➤ A variable payment for the miles you drive

This method can only be used if there are 10 or more employees using their own cars for company business. This is an allowable reimbursement method only. You can't claim your own automobile expenses using FAVR if you are an employee or if you are self-employed.

Company-Owned Cars

If your employer provides you with a car, you might have a taxable fringe benefit. Unless you pay for your personal use of the car, you will have taxable income.

You might ask how the IRS would know if you use the car for business miles or personal miles. It's pretty easy. You have to account to your employer how you use the car. If you don't account for your business use, your employer has to assume that you used the car 100% for personal driving and all of the car use is taxed to you. Needless to say, it's worthwhile to respond to your employer's request for mileage records to support your business use.

Personal use of your company car includes your commute and any personal or family driving. Business use includes driving to temporary job sites, driving from your office to clients' or customers' locations, and driving between job sites. Business use also includes business trips away from home.

There are three different ways that your employer can value the personal use of a company car:

➤ The annual lease value method
➤ The cents-per-mile method
➤ A fixed value per commute

Under the annual lease value method, an IRS table is used to find the *annual lease value*. This dollar figure is prorated to the portion of the year that the car was provided to you. The personal use percentage is then applied. The result is taxable to you. If you had use of a company car for half of the year and used it 80% for business, your personal use would be 40% of the annual lease value.

If your employer also pays for your gasoline for your personal driving, you have to pay tax on the value of the gasoline too. Five and a half cents per mile is added to the annual lease value. The total taxable fringe benefit is included in your Form W-2.

Under the cents-per-mile method, your employer can value your personal use using the standard mileage rate (32.5 cents for 1998). You can only use the cents-per-mile method if you meet all of these requirements:

➤ You use the car at least 10,000 miles for the year.

➤ You use the car at least 50% for business or you use the car every day in an employer-sponsored car pool to take at least three employees to and from work.

➤ The value of the car is not more than $15,800 for a car first placed in service in 1998.

Under the commuting method, your employer can include $1.50 in your W-2 as taxable wages for each one-way commute in the company-owned vehicle. You can only use the commuting method if all of these requirements are met:

➤ The vehicle is owned or leased by the employer.

➤ The vehicle is used by an employee in the employer's business.

➤ For business reasons, your employer requires you to drive to work in the company-owned vehicle.

➤ Your employer prohibits employees from using the vehicle for personal reasons other than commuting and minimal personal use (like picking up groceries on your way home). There has to be a written policy prohibiting the personal use.

➤ You don't use the vehicle for personal reasons other than commuting and minimal personal trips.

➤ You are not a control employee.

A *control employee* is someone who is either a 1% or more owner of the employer, a director of the employer, an officer whose compensation is $50,000 or more, or an employee whose compensation is $100,000 or more.

If you are a car salesperson, you might be able to use a demonstrator car tax-free. You have to be a full-time salesperson for this tax benefit, among other requirements.

Depreciating Your Car

When you use actual expenses to claim automobile expenses, part of your deduction will be for depreciation. Through depreciation, you write off the cost of your car over several years. Car

Paper Trail

If you provide company cars to your employees, it might be time for professional help. W-2s aren't easy anymore. Company-owned cars can turn up the heat.

depreciation expenses are limited. The IRS tells us what life to use, what method to use, and what dollar limits we must live within.

The depreciation limitations apply to all passenger automobiles. It might seem strange to have to define a passenger automobile, but there is a definition. It's important to have a definition. If a vehicle is not a passenger automobile, it will not be subject to the limits placed on depreciating automobiles.

A passenger automobile is a vehicle that:

➤ Is a four-wheeled vehicle

➤ Was manufactured for use on public streets, roads, and highways

➤ Has an unloaded gross vehicle weight rating of 6,000 pounds or less

➤ Is not used in the business of transporting people or property for compensation

Your Decoder Ring

Motorcycles aren't covered by the passenger auto rules. The four-wheel requirement keeps you out.

The following vehicles don't meet the definition of a passenger automobile. Depreciation can be taken using regular depreciation rules without applying the automobile dollar limits:

➤ Taxicabs

➤ Ambulances

➤ Hearses

➤ Semi-tractors and trailers

➤ Delivery vans

➤ Sport utility vehicles with gross vehicle weight over 6,000 pounds

A passenger automobile is depreciated using a five-year life. On the five-year schedule, your depreciation expense each year is a fixed percent of the basis in your car. Before you use the percentages, you have to apply your business use percent to your car:

Vehicle Depreciation Schedule	
Year 1	20%
Year 2	32%
Year 3	19.2%
Year 4	11.52%
Year 5	11.52%
Year 6	5.76%

For example, Jerry purchases a business automobile for $10,000. He uses the car 80% in his business. The basis to use for depreciation is $8,000. The first year depreciation is $1,600 (20% of $8,000).

It's not quite that easy. You can't use the full depreciation percentages unless your car is used more than 50% in your business. If it is used 50% or less for business, your depreciation will be slower. Use these percentages to calculate your depreciation:

Vehicle Depreciation if 50% or More Personal Use	
Year 1	10%
Year 2	20%
Year 3	20%
Year 4	20%
Year 5	20%
Year 6	10%

By using this table, you have converted from an accelerated depreciation method to a straight-line method. Once the car's business use drops to 50% or less in any year, your depreciation method drops to straight line for the rest of the car's life.

If you use a five-year life, you might ask why the schedule covers six years. Only one-half year of depreciation is taken in the first year the car is placed in service. This is known as the half-year convention. If more than 40% of your assets were placed in service in the last three months of the year, you have to use a mid-quarter convention instead of a half-year convention. The IRS prints tables you can use for the mid-quarter convention.

You can use Section 179 expense on automobiles. Through Section 179 expense, you can claim a larger depreciation deduction in the first year you place an asset in service. For assets other than cars, Section 179 expense limitation is $18,500 in 1998. For an automobile, you won't be able to claim that much.

The depreciation expense (including Section 179 expense) is limited to a fixed-dollar amount each year. Every year, the IRS sets new dollar limits.

The annual dollar limits for passenger automobile depreciation (including Section 179 expense) are determined by when your car was placed in service:

Paper Trail

Depreciation for your vehicle can be calculated on the second page of Form 2106, Employee Business Expenses. The instructions to Form 2106 will help you make the calculations.

Placed in Service	1998	1997	1996 or 1995
Year 1	$3,160	$3,160	$3,060
Year 2	$5,000	$5,000	$4,900
Year 3	$2,950	$3,050	$2,950
Years 4 and later	$1,775	$1,775	$1,775

215

You're not done yet. The dollar limits have to be reduced to your business use percentage. So, if you are in the second year of using a 1997 car, the dollar limit is $5,000. If the car is used 80% in your business, the dollar limit you can use is $4,000 (80% of $5,000).

Let's do an example. Dina bought a new car in 1998 to use in her business. She spent $21,000 for her car. She uses the car 80% in her business. Her first year depreciation could be $21,000 times 80% (business use) times 20% (depreciation rate), or $3,360. The limit for first year depreciation for a car placed in service in 1998 is $3,160. Dina's limit is $3,160 times 80%, or $2,528. It will take Dina almost nine years to depreciate her car because of the dollar limits.

The fun doesn't stop yet. If your business use drops to 50% or less after you have started depreciating your car, you have to *recapture* some of the earlier years' depreciation. This means that if you had been depreciating 80% of your car and your business use drops to 50%, you have to refigure your old year's depreciation at 50% using straight-line depreciation and include the difference between the recalculated amount and the depreciation you actually took in your income. It boggles the mind, doesn't it?

All things considered, the automobile depreciation rules make a pretty good case for using the standard mileage deduction method for your automobile. Don't be hasty in making your decision, though. There are software programs to help you with these calculations. When all else fails, let your accountant worry about it!

Leasing Your Car

If you lease your car, you have a new option in 1998. You can either use standard mileage or your actual expenses. You can't deduct both mileage and your lease payments. The actual expenses include your lease payments.

You will calculate your actual car expenses just like you would for a car you own, but you will use your lease payments instead of depreciation. At first glance, this might seem to avoid the depreciation limits, but leases have their own tax limits.

When Congress cut back the depreciation deductions for cars, they anticipated that leasing could be a way around the depreciation limits. Congress headed this loophole off at the pass. They created a *lease inclusion* amount. By using an IRS chart, you have to include in income a certain dollar amount. This system effectively cuts back your deductions for a leased car.

The lease inclusion amount is determined by the value of your car. If the value is less than $15,800 for a car placed in service in 1998, you don't have to worry about the lease inclusion amount.

To calculate the lease inclusion amount:

➤ Determine the fair market value of your car on the first day of your lease term.

➤ Find the appropriate IRS table for your car.

➤ Find the line on the table that includes the value of your car.

➤ Prorate the table amount by the number of days in the year you leased the car.

➤ Multiply the result by the business use of your leased car.

A car with a value of $30,000 that was first leased in 1997 has a lease inclusion amount for 1998 of $265. If the car is used 80% for business, the lease inclusion amount is $212 (80% of $265). Your 1998 car expense deduction might look like this:

Lease payments	$3,600
Gasoline	$1,100
Repairs	$300
Insurance	$800
Other expenses	$200
Total expenses	$6,000
80% of total expenses	$4,800
Less lease inclusion amount	$212
Net car expense deduction	$4,588

If you make advance payments on your lease, you can't deduct the whole payment. You have to spread the deduction for the advance payments over the lease period. For example, if you make a $5,000 advance payment on a five-year lease, you can include $1,000 each year in your car expenses for the advance payment.

Time for a New Car?

When it's time to get a new car, you can either trade in your old car or sell it. There can be a big tax difference.

As you use a car in business, your basis in the car is reduced by your depreciation. Even if you have used standard mileage, your basis is cut back some every year. When you subtract your depreciation from your car's cost, you get the adjusted basis in your car.

Paper Trail

To read more about leasing a car, read chapter 4 of IRS Publication 463, Travel, Entertainment, Gift and Car Expenses.

When you sell your car, you might have a gain or a loss on the sale. If the selling price of your car is more than your adjusted basis, you will have a taxable gain. For example, if a car with an adjusted basis of $18,000 is sold for $20,000, you have a $2,000 gain.

If your selling price is less than the adjusted basis of your car, you have a loss. To the extent the car is personally used, your loss is not deductible. To the extent that the car is used for business, you will have a tax loss.

If you trade in your car, a very different tax result is achieved. You don't recognize a taxable gain when you trade in your car. Even if your trade-in allowance is more than

Red Flag

A gain on the sale of a car is taxable whether your car was used in business or not. Personal gains are always taxable. Personal losses are not deductible, though. It might not seem fair, but it's the way the tax system works.

the adjusted basis in the old car, no taxable gain is reported. Your basis in the new car is adjusted by the gain you didn't report.

For example, Tony's old car has an adjusted basis of $3,000. Tony trades in his old car on a new car. The new car cost $30,000, but Tony got a $5,000 trade-in allowance, so he paid $25,000 for his new car. Tony won't have a taxable gain on trading his old car. His new car will have a basis of:

Net purchase price	$25,000
Basis of old car	3,000
Basis of new car	$28,000

With car depreciation being so slow, the adjusted basis in your car drops pretty slowly. Your car's value will drop faster than your depreciation. As a result, there are a lot of business car owners whose adjusted basis in their car is much more than the value of their car.

If you are one of these people, you can save taxes by selling your car instead of trading it. If you sell your car, you will have a loss. To the extent your car was used for business, you have a deductible tax loss.

Shannon, for example, has a car that she uses 75% for business. The car has an adjusted basis of $25,000, but a value of $15,000. Shannon is planning to trade in her car on a new $35,000 car. After the trade-in allowance, Shannon will pay $20,000 for her new car.

If Shannon trades in her old car, she will have no loss on the trade. The basis in her new car will be $45,000 ($20,000 paid plus $25,000 basis of old car).

If Shannon sells her old car instead of trading it, she will have a $10,000 loss ($15,000 selling price minus $25,000 basis). Seventy-five percent of the loss, or $7,500, will be allowed on her tax return as a loss on the sale of her car.

You could be in a situation like Shannon. Car depreciation is so slow that depreciation just doesn't keep up with the decline in a car's value. Consider selling your business car rather than trading it. Big tax savings can result from this simple change in plans.

Records, Records, Records

Keeping records on business car use is vital to defending your deduction. The tax law requires you to keep records. You must be able to support the business use of the car. This means supporting the business miles that you drove. You will need these records if you use either the standard mileage method or the actual expense method of claiming your deduction.

If you use the actual expense method of deducting your car expenses, you have to be able to support your actual expenses. Gasoline records, insurance bills, etc., have to be maintained.

The IRS doesn't require that your records be in writing. Having said this, it's hard to have credible records that aren't in writing. I wouldn't want to try to prove business car use without written records. If you're audited, be prepared to produce written records.

To support your business miles, you need to document:

➤ The date you used the car

➤ The place to which you drove

➤ The number of miles that you drove

➤ The business purpose of your trip

Your Decoder Ring

A gain or loss from the sale of business property might be **capital** or **ordinary**. The instructions to Form 4797 can help you through the maze of rules. The difference is important. Net capital losses are limited to $3,000 a year. Ordinary losses aren't subject to the $3,000 per year limit.

One of the best records you can have is a well-kept appointment book or calendar. Your calendar will hold most of the documentation that you need. By adding miles and filling in missing information, you can probably increase your car expense deductions and satisfy the documentation requirement.

If you are audited, the IRS is likely to check your automobile records if you claim mileage on your tax return. Without good records, your deduction will be lost. Agents are usually pretty strict when it comes to automobile deductions.

It's a shame when people lose legitimate car expense deductions because of poor record keeping. It happens all the time, though. Keep the records that you need to support the deduction to which you are entitled.

The Least You Need to Know

➤ You can deduct the business use of your car using either a standard mileage rate or actual expenses.

➤ Some employer automobile reimbursements are tax-free. Car allowances are taxable.

➤ If you use a company-owned car for personal driving, you will have to pay tax on your personal use.

➤ If you own your car, you can deduct depreciation as part of your actual automobile expenses. Depreciation deductions are very limited.

➤ Record keeping is essential to support your deduction for the business use of your car.

Chapter 16

Using Your Home for Business

In This Chapter

➤ Claiming a deduction for using your home in your business

➤ Calculating the deduction for your home office or business

➤ The special rules for in-home daycare

➤ Selling your home after claiming home office deductions

➤ Deducting the things that you use in your business at home

The home office has taken on new life in these days of telecommuting. People who used to work in an office now work at home. By using computers, fax machines, and telephones, many employees have found that most of their work can be done without being in the office.

Some employers are embracing the concept of employees working at home because of the cost savings. In some cities, it is cheaper to outfit a home office than it is to provide a space at the employer's office.

Competition for a trained work force is also fueling the work-at-home trend. Being flexible about work hours and work spaces can give an employer an edge when recruiting or trying to retain an employee. Some employees like to work at home, so the home office is an attractive option. The at-home worker can avoid lengthy commutes and is home when the children are done with the school day. The dress code is pretty easy to live with, too.

Not just employees work at home, though. Self-employed people often work out of their home. Sometimes, the home office is a place where phone calls are made, letters are written, and customers are billed. Other businesses are based in locations in or near the owner's home.

The home-based business seems to be a very modern trend. In fact, it's an old concept revisited. Before there were automobiles, people couldn't work very far from home. In fact, many people lived in the same structure that they worked (restaurants, doctors' offices, law offices, etc.). They did it all without fax machines or Internet connections.

Our tax code was crafted during a time that most people didn't work in their homes, though. Deducting a home office was considered a loophole that the IRS was determined to close. The tax code is finally adjusting to people who work at home. The transition is very slow, though.

In this chapter, we'll talk about home office expenses primarily. If you use the space in your home for business activities other than an office, the tax rules are the same. If you are assembling products, for example, in your home, your deduction for the use of your home is covered by the same rules that cover a home office.

Can You Claim a Home Office?

The home office deduction is available whether you own your home or you rent. You might also be able to claim a deduction for other buildings that are on your property. If you use an unattached garage, a barn, or a greenhouse in your business, it might qualify for a deduction.

You can claim a home office deduction if you are an employee or if you are self-employed. To claim the home office expense, you have to use a portion of your home exclusively and on a regular basis as either:

➤ The principal place of your business

➤ A place of business that is used by your clients, patients, or your customers

If you are an employee, there is another requirement. You must have to use your home office for the *convenience of your employer*. It isn't enough that the use of your home office is helpful.

We'll discuss each of these requirements separately. As you can probably tell by the language, though, there are some pretty stiff requirements. The government doesn't let just anybody claim home office expenses.

Exclusive Use

To claim a deduction for using your home, the space has to be exclusively used on a regular basis for your business. Exclusive use means that you use the space in your home for nothing but business.

222

Some people get a break. You don't have to pass the exclusive use test if:

➤ You use part of your home for storing inventory or product samples.

➤ You use part of your home as a daycare facility.

If you are using your home to store inventory or samples, there are five tests that you have to pass:

1. You keep the inventory or product samples for use in your business.

2. You are in the business of selling products at wholesale or retail.

3. Your home is the only fixed location for your business.

4. The storage space in your home is used on a regular basis.

5. The storage space is a separate, identifiable, space suitable for storage.

Red Flag

Some people are so afraid of IRS audits that they don't claim a legitimate home office deduction. You might increase your odds of audit with a home office, but it's not an automatic sentence. Don't give up deductions out of fear, though. Measure what the deduction will save you before making your decision. Only claim the deduction if it is legitimate. Keep good records.

Examples might be the easiest way to illustrate these rules.

Jim sells musical instruments. His primary customers are schools. Jim doesn't have a store space or a regular office for his business. He makes phone calls and keeps records at his home. His desk is in a corner of his guest bedroom. He uses his desk only for business. Does he have a home office? Yes, but it's not much. The guest bedroom itself is not a home office. Most of the room is used for things other than his business. Only the space where his desk sits is his home office. He has less than 40 square feet of his home exclusively dedicated to his home office.

If, on the other hand, Jim used the closet and some shelving in the guest bedroom to store sample products and the limited amount of inventory he carries, Jim will have a different result. The space that is used to store his products doesn't have to be used exclusively for his business. The fact that guests will stay in this room a couple of times a year doesn't foul up Jim's deduction for using the guest bedroom in his business.

Catherine is a homemaker. She decided to make some extra money selling baskets. Catherine has sales parties in her home and has decorated using the baskets that she sells. The parties are held in her family room. She considers the entire home to be a showcase for her products. Since Catherine's family also uses the family room, there is no deduction for using this room in her business. The concept of using her home as a showcase doesn't work because the *exclusive* use test is not met.

Melinna is a self-employed architect. She works in an office that is behind her home. The building was formerly a potting shed that Melinna has remodeled as her office. Since this space is used only for Melinna's office, she can deduct home office expenses.

Principal Place of Business

If you don't see clients, patients, or customers in your home office, your home office has to be your principal place of business to get a home office deduction. What is meant by *principal place of business*?

Your Decoder Ring

Investment activities don't constitute a trade or business unless you are an investment broker or dealer. Even if your sole source of income is from investments, your home office is not deductible.

Taxpayers and the IRS fought over this definition for years. The battle was so intense that the U.S. Supreme court finally got involved. The Supreme Court set a very high standard in the case of *Commissioner v. Soliman*. They decided that you had to compare your business activities you performed inside your home to those you performed outside your home. If the most important activities were performed inside your home, you would get the home office deduction.

An anesthesiologist is the example to use here. If the anesthesiologist is not provided an office at the hospital, he will have to use an office in his home. He has to do billings, consult with other doctors, do medical research and reading, etc. Under the Supreme Court's standards, the doctor's home office is not deductible. His most important work is done at the hospital, not in his home office.

Congress understood how unfair this strict interpretation was, so they loosened up the rules in 1997. The new rules don't take effect until 1999, but they are a welcome change.

Under the new rules, a home office will be your principal place of business if both of the following statements are true:

➤ Your home office is used to perform management or administrative functions in your trade or business.

➤ You have no other fixed location where you can perform these business tasks.

In the case of our anesthesiologist, he would meet the new standards for home office deductions in 1999 only if he didn't have another office (at the hospital, for example) that he could use. Since he uses his home office for administrative and management functions (billing, phone calls, etc.), and he has no other place to perform these tasks, his home office will be deductible.

This change is a long time overdue, but it's not in force yet. For 1998, our anesthesiologist friend is still stuck with no home office deduction.

If your home business is in a separate structure, it doesn't have to be your principal place of business or a place that you meet customers. You can still claim a deduction for using the structure.

For example, if a mechanic has a separate garage behind his home that he uses only for his business to repair small motors, he will be able to claim a deduction for his garage. He has another place of business (the shop that he works for) and he doesn't meet customers in his garage at home. He uses the home garage for his employer's convenience. His employer is able to save a lot of money by not devoting space in its garage to the repair activity. Since the mechanic's garage is a separate structure, he can take a deduction for the garage even though he doesn't see customers there.

The Meeting Place: Your Home

If you meet with patients, clients, or customers at your home, you can deduct your home office expenses. Since you meet your customers in your home, it doesn't have to be your principal place of business. Even if you have another business location, you can claim your home office deduction.

In order to claim your home expenses, though, the meetings with your customers or clients have to be an integral part of your business. The contact at your home can't be occasional or an unimportant part of your business.

Heather, for example, is a wardrobe consultant. Heather has an office in a department store that she uses in her consulting business. Heather also has a studio in her home that she uses only for her consulting work. Heather meets with a significant number of her clients in her home studio instead of meeting with them in the department store office. While the arrangement with the department store is important to Heather, it is also important for her to meet with customers in her own space to retain her objectivity. Although Heather has another space available, she can deduct her home studio space since she meets there with clients to a significant degree.

Convenience of Employer

If you are an employee, your work in your home has to be for the convenience of your employer for your home office space to be deductible. Unfortunately, there is not a good definition of *convenience of employer*.

Clearly, if the home office is a condition of your employment, the convenience of your employer standard is satisfied. In other words, if you either do the work at home or lose your job, your home office is for the convenience of your employer.

Paper Trail

One of the most confusing things about tax law changes is that Congress sets different effective dates for different changes. This is confusing, but there is a method to the madness. Tax bills have to be **revenue neutral**, meaning that there has to be a tax increase for each tax decrease. By delaying the effective date of tax breaks, Congress can balance the books on tax laws.

One court allowed a deduction for home use that was not a condition of employment, but was necessary for the employee to perform his duties properly. The case (*Drucker v. Comr.*) involved a musician who practiced at least 30 hours a week at home because his employer provided no practice space. The court decided that using the home was a business necessity. Practicing at home was not for the employee's personal convenience, so it was for the employer's convenience.

It helps to support your case if your employer requires you to keep the home office. If there is no explicit requirement to keep a home office, it helps your case if you don't have suitable space provided by your employer to complete your job requirements. The logic is that the use of your home saves the employer the cost of providing suitable space. The use of your home for the job duties is, then, for your employer's convenience.

Paper Trail

Get it in writing. If you must work in your home, get your employer to put it in writing that you have to work at home. The best documentation would be a letter or a memo from your employer. Personnel manuals can be a source of written documentation, also.

How the Math Is Done

There are three parts to calculating the deduction for using your home:

➤ Calculating the business use percentage
➤ Adding up your expenses
➤ Limiting your deduction

We'll cover each of these three steps in the following sections.

The Business Use Percentage

You can only deduct your home office expenses that are allocated to the part of your home you use for business. What does this mean?

This means that you have to determine what portion of your home is used in your business. There are two different ways that you can do this.

➤ By area (square footage)
➤ By the number of rooms

If you use the area method, you simply calculate the square footage of the space you use for business as a percent of your total square footage. For example, if your home office is a 15 foot by 15 foot space, it has 225 square feet. If your home has 2,100 square feet total, your office is 10.71% of the area of your home.

Under the number of rooms method, you calculate the business use percentage by counting rooms. Count up the total rooms in your house and the rooms you use in your business. Draw the business percentage by dividing the number of business rooms by the total number of rooms in your home. If you have a six room home and you use one room for business, 16.67% ($^1/_6$) of your home is used in your business.

Your Decoder Ring

You can only use the number of rooms method to calculate the business use of your home if the rooms in your home are all about the same size. If your rooms are of varying sizes, you have to use square footage to calculate your business use.

There will be expenses for your home office that don't have to be prorated. These are called direct expenses and are fully deductible (subject to an income limit). For example, an electrical outlet in your home office is not working. You have to have it repaired by an electrician. You use the outlet for your computer. The repair expense is fully deductible. You don't have to apply your business use percentage to the repair expense.

On the other hand, you might have to repair your home's heating and air conditioning unit. This repair benefits your entire home, so you can only claim a portion of the repair bill as a home office expense. If your home office uses 10% of your home's square footage, you will claim 10% of the repair bill as part of your home office expense.

Which Expenses to Count

The home business expenses that you can claim include all of the following:

➤ Insurance

➤ Repairs and maintenance

➤ Utilities

➤ Mortgage interest

➤ Real estate taxes

➤ Casualty losses

➤ Depreciation or rent

➤ Security system fees

Each of these expenses are either directly related to your home office or are indirect. For example, you have casualty insurance on your home. This is an indirect expense. If you carry an additional rider on your homeowner's policy to cover your home-based business, the additional premium for this rider is a direct expense.

Direct expenses are fully deducted. Indirect expenses are partially deductible. You will apply your business use percentage to the indirect expenses.

Depreciation expense on your home is calculated using a 39-year life and the straight-line method. Each year, your deduction is $^1/_{39}$th of your home's cost basis.

The Limit

You have to limit your home office expenses to your net business income. In other words, the home office expenses can't create a loss. IRS Form 8829, Expenses for Business Use of Your Home, is used to calculate your deduction limit.

Any expenses in excess of your business income can be carried over to future tax years. You don't lose your deductions; you just have to wait until a future year to use them.

Red Flag

If your home office expenses are limited by your income, you will discover a real *sting*. You have to use mortgage interest and real estate taxes first, leaving your other expenses to be disallowed. Without the deduction for using your home, your mortgage interest and real estate taxes would have been deductible. You might not have saved any taxes at all. Pay attention to the form.

Daycare Facilities

If you run a daycare center in your home, you get special treatment. You can claim a deduction for space in your home that is used partly for your business and partly personally. The *exclusive use* rule doesn't apply to daycare facilities.

This is a real break. It would be very difficult to run an in-home daycare business without having overlapping spaces.

To get the tax break, you must be licensed under your state's daycare licensing requirements. There might also be local daycare licensing requirements that you have to meet. If you are not licensed, you have to follow the regular home business rule that limits your deduction to space that is used exclusively in your business.

What is a daycare facility? A daycare facility is the business of providing daycare for any of the following:

➤ Children

➤ People age 65 or older

➤ Any persons who, due to a mental or physical disability, are not able to care for themselves

Figuring out your business use percentage can be a challenge. If you use the space for business part of the time, how do you do this? You need to consider the number of hours that you use the space in your home for daycare versus personal use.

Let's do an example. Analee has a daycare center in her home for preschool children. Her basement is used for daycare. Her family also uses the basement space. The basement is 1,000 square feet, which is one-third of her home. Analee's daycare center is open 10 hours a day, five days a week, 50 weeks a year. Her daycare is open 2,500 hours a year. Since there are 8,760 hours in a year, the basement is used for business 28.54% of the year.

Any expenses related exclusively to Analee's basement are 28.54% deductible. These are direct expenses. Expenses that relate to Analee's whole house (indirect expenses) are 9.51% deductible ($^1/_3$ of the house times 28.54%). Cleaning expenses in the basement is an example of a direct expense. Utilities and homeowner's insurance are examples of indirect expenses.

Analee will have a lot of other expenses for her daycare center. The cost of food, diapers, toys, and paper supplies will all be deductible, but not as expenses of using her home. These expenses will be claimed directly on Analee's Schedule C, Profit or Loss From Business.

When You Sell Your Home

In 1997, we got a major improvement in the tax law. The tax rules for selling your home were changed significantly.

When you sell your home, you calculate your gain by comparing your selling price to what you have invested in your home (your home's basis). Your basis includes what you paid for your house and any improvements that you have made.

Every two years, you can sell your home and have up to $250,000 of gain ($500,000 if you're married) that you don't have to pay tax on. This break came into being for home sales after May 5, 1997.

If you move because of your job and you've been in your home less than two years, you can use part of the $250,000 exclusion. For example, if you have to move 18 months after you sold your last house, you can exclude up to $187,500 of gain ($^3/_4$ of $250,000) if you are single. If you are married, you could exclude up to $375,000 ($^3/_4$ of $500,000).

When you use your home in your business, you will take depreciation expense for your home. Each dollar of depreciation that you take reduces

Paper Trail

You might take care of children, persons age 65 or older, or a disabled individual. Does this automatically mean you can claim a deduction for the use of your home? No, it doesn't. Using your home is deductible if you are in the business of providing daycare. Taking care of your own kids doesn't count. Taking care of someone else for a fee does count as long as you are properly licensed.

Your Decoder Ring

The **basis** in your home might be less than its purchase price. Under old rules, you avoided tax on a home sale if you reinvested in a new home. The gain from a former home reduced the basis in your home. Find the Form 2119, Sale of Your Home, that you filed when you sold your previous home. The basis in your current home was calculated on that form. Add your home improvements to get the basis in your home.

the adjusted basis in your home. When your adjusted basis goes down by one dollar, your gain goes up by that same dollar.

When you sell your home, you won't be able to use your $250,000 (or $500,000) exclusion to wipe out taxes on the gain that you have because of depreciation that you took after May 6, 1997.

It's example time. Amy uses her home in her business. She sells her house in 1998. Amy has a gain of $24,000 on the sale of her home. Since May 6, 1997, Amy's depreciation expense on her home has been $435. Amy will be able to exclude $23,565 of her gain, but $435 will be taxable.

Forms, Forms, Forms

If you are an employee, your deduction for using your home in business is combined with your other business expenses as miscellaneous itemized deductions on your Schedule A. These deductions are reduced by 2% of your adjusted gross income.

If you are self-employed and report your business income on Schedule C, Profit or Loss From Business, your home office expenses are reported on Form 8829, Expenses for Business Use of Your Home. The allowable deduction is carried forward to your Schedule C. If you are a farmer, your deduction for the use of your home will be taken on Schedule F. If you are a self-employed partner in a partnership, your home office deductions will be taken on Schedule E.

When you sell your home, you will need to file Form 2119, Sale of Your Home.

Paper Trail

The instructions to Form 2119, Sale of Your Home, include a worksheet for adding up your home improvements. These improvements increase the basis in your home, which reduces a taxable gain on the sale of your home. If you're not sure what you can include, remember a simple rule: If you leave it, you can count it.

Other Things in Your Home Business

There are a lot of items you might use in your business at home that aren't covered by the business use of home rules. These expenses are deducted with your other business expenses, not as home office expenses.

For example, our mechanic friend from earlier in the chapter will use tools and supplies to do his work at home. If he has to provide the tools and supplies himself, he can deduct these expenses on his tax return. These expenses are not part of his home office expense; they are regular business expense deductions.

If you are an employee, you will claim these expenses as a miscellaneous itemized deduction. If you are self-employed, the expenses are reported on Schedule C. If you are a farmer, you will report these expenses on Schedule F. If you are a self-employed partner in a partnership, these expenses are deducted on Schedule E.

Keep in mind that you can only deduct these items if they are ordinary and necessary for your business. It's not enough that they are helpful in your business to claim a deduction. For example, if you work at home at night because you don't get your work done during the day, that might not be a compelling enough reason to deduct the items you use at home. If you have to work at home at night to complete the tasks required of you on the job, your expenses will be deductible.

Telephone

There are three parts to your telephone bill. Some parts are deductible if they relate to your business, but some are not.

The first part of your phone bill is the charge for the phone line itself. The cost of the first phone line into your home (including taxes) is never deductible. This is part of the tax law. Even if you only use your home phone for business, the first line into your home is not deductible. You might have to add a separate phone line for fax, computer, or voice purposes. If you need this new phone line for business reasons, it is deductible.

The second part of your phone bill is the monthly charge for extra features. If you purchase features for your home phone for your business (such as call waiting), the cost of the extra features will be deductible.

The third part of your phone bill is the charge for long-distance calls. If the calls are for your business, they are deductible.

You might also pay for advertising in the phone book with your monthly phone bill. If the advertising is for your business, it is a deductible business expense.

Cell Phone

If you use a cell phone in your business, you can deduct the business part of your bill. You might have to do some allocating between personal use and business use.

The cost of the cell phone itself will have to be depreciated. You might be able to write it all off using the Section 179 expense deduction, though. To use Section 179 expense, the phone will have to be more than 50% business use. See Chapter 14, "Deductions If You Are Self-Employed," for depreciation rules.

Computers

Your computer is another asset that might be part business and part personal. If so, you'll have to divide your cost between your business use and your personal use. You

Red Flag

Most cell phones are used partly for personal calls. The IRS knows this. You might have an uphill battle to convince the IRS that your cell phone is 100% business. If your phone is truly 100% business, be prepared to convince an agent if challenged. If you don't have kids at home, your case will be easier to argue. Know your facts and present them honestly. It pays off to be clear and complete in your dealings with the IRS.

Paper Trail

Computer technology makes machinery obsolete before it is fully depreciated. If you depreciate computer equipment and scrap the equipment before it is fully depreciated, you can write off the undepreciated balance of the equipment's basis. If you sell the equipment for less than its remaining adjusted basis, you will have a tax loss that should be reported on Form 4797.

will calculate depreciation on the computer and reduce it to the business use percentage to get your deduction.

Computer supplies that are used just for business are fully deductible. For example, paper, print cartridges, and other consumable supplies that you use for business are deductible.

To measure the business use percentage of a computer, you will need to use a reasonable standard. Time is usually a good measure for computer use. If you use the computer 50% or more for business, you can take depreciation on an accelerated rate and use the Section 179 expense. If the business use is 50% or less, your depreciation can only be taken using the straight-line method and you can't take Section 179 expense.

For doing the 50% use test, you can't count investment use. Your investment use is deductible, though.

For example, your computer use time is:

Business	40%
Investment	20%
Personal	40%

You have not met the 50% threshold, so your depreciation will be calculated using the straight-line method. You can take a deduction for the 40% business use and also the 20% investment use.

If, in another example, your computer use time is:

Business	55%
Investment	20%
Personal	25%

Since your business use is more than 50%, your depreciation is calculated using the accelerated method. You can also use Section 179 expense. You will be able to deduct depreciation for both the business use and the investment use.

Furniture and Equipment

You might use furniture in your business at home. You might use desks, chairs, bookshelves, lamps, and other furniture pieces. Even if you can't claim a deduction for an office in your home, you can claim a depreciation deduction for the furniture that you use in your home office. You might be able to use the Section 179 expense election on your furniture items also.

Equipment items such as machinery and tools can also be depreciated if you use them at home in your business.

The Least You Need to Know

➤ If you use part of your home exclusively for business, you might be able to claim a deduction for the business use of your home. The rules will be relaxing in 1999, making more people eligible for the deduction.

➤ You can't create a business tax loss by deducting expenses for your home. Your home deduction is limited to your net business income.

➤ There are special tax breaks for people who run daycare centers in their homes.

➤ When you sell your home, part of your gain will be taxable if you have claimed a business deduction for your home.

➤ You can claim a deduction for the items you use in your home business (supplies, depreciation, and so on).

Travel, Meals, and Entertainment

If your business activities include meeting the public, you probably have to spend money on travel, meals, or entertainment. Since you are usually a participant in the activity, the IRS is very leery of these expense deductions.

The IRS is afraid that people are trying to deduct personal living expenses as travel, meals, and entertainment. Unfortunately, the IRS has good reason to be skeptical. A lot of people cheat on these items on their tax returns.

To help curb the cheating, there are extensive record keeping requirements. There are also rules that cut back your expense deductions.

To be deductible, these expenses must be *ordinary and necessary*. This means that the expenses have to be common in your trade or business (ordinary). The expenses also have to be helpful or appropriate for your business (necessary).

Eating out on the IRS: Deducting Meals

The tax law allows us to deduct business meals. We can't deduct meals that aren't business-related, though. The distinction between deductible and nondeductible meal expenses is a fuzzy line. The distinction is difficult, in part, because our activities are not always easy to distinguish between business and personal.

The deduction for business meals has been terribly abused by taxpayers. A lot of people have cheated on business meal deductions. Unfortunately, this means that Congress cut back on meal deductions for everyone. Even honest people can't deduct all of their business meal expenses.

The IRS Meets You Half-Way

Although Congress considered cutting out the deduction for meals altogether, they decided to compromise. Only 50% of your meal expenses are deductible.

If your employer reimburses you for business meals, the 50% cutback applies to your employer, not to you.

The 50% limit applies to:

➤ Meals that you buy while traveling away from home, even if you eat alone

➤ Meals that you buy for customers or business associates

➤ Meals associated with business conventions, business meetings, or business luncheons of a business club

➤ The entire cost of the meal including taxes and tip

The cost of travel to and from a business meal is not subject to the 50% limit. This means that the cab fare to get to the restaurant is 100% deductible. The cost of the meal is limited, though, to 50% of the cost of the meal.

There are some meals that don't have to be cut back by 50%. Any of the following meals are fully deductible:

➤ Meals paid by an employer that are included in an employee's compensation

➤ Meals provided in an employer-subsidized eating facility

➤ Meals that qualify as *de minimum* fringe benefits (these are things like occasional food served at work, meals or meal money to enable an employee to work late, and holiday gifts)

➤ Company-paid recreational activities (such as holiday parties or summer picnics)

In 1998, some employees' meals will be cut back 45% instead of 50%. The employees that get higher meal deductions than the rest of us are:

➤ Certain air transportation employees, such as flight crews, dispatchers, mechanics, and control tower operators

The Complete Idiot's Reference Card

1998 Standard Deductions

Filing Status	Deduction
Married, filing joint return	$7,100
Surviving spouse	$7,100
Head of household	$6,250
Single	$4,250
Married, filing separate return	$3,550
Dependent standard deduction minimum	$700
Additional amount for blindness and/or age	$850
Additional blindness/age amount if not married or surviving spouse	$1,050

1998 Mileage Allowances

Mileage Type	Allowance
Business miles	32.5¢ per mile
Charitable miles	14¢ per mile
Moving miles	10¢ per mile
Medical miles	10¢ per mile

1998 Payroll Deduction Limitations

Payroll Deduction	Limitation
Maximum wages subject to FICA tax	$68,400
FICA tax rate	6.2%
Medicare tax rate	1.45%
401(k) maximum salary deferral	$10,000
403(b) annuity maximum deferral	$10,000
Maximum SIMPLE plan salary deferral	$6,000

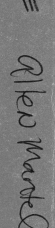

alpha
books

1998 Deduction Floors

Deduction Type	Floor
Medical deductions	7.5% of AGI
Miscellaneous itemized deductions	2% of AGI
Personal casualty losses	10% of AGI

1998 Roth IRA AGI Limitations

Description	Amount
Maximum AGI for Roth conversion (1)	$100,000
Maximum AGI for $2,000 Roth contribution	
If single	$94,999
If married filing jointly	$149,999
If married filing separately	-0-
AGI at which no Roth contribution can be made	
If single	$110,000
If married filing jointly	$160,000
If married filing separately	$10,000

(1) calculated without conversion

1998 Federal Income Tax Brackets and Rates

Taxable Income

Single	Married Filing Jointly/Qualifying Widow(er)	Married Filing Separately	Head of Household	Federal Tax Bracket/ Marginal Rate
$25,350 or less	$42,350 or less	$21,175 or less	$33,950 or less	15%
$25,351–$61,400	$42,351–$102,300	$21,176–$51,150	$33,951–$87,700	28%
$61,401–$128,100	$102,301–$155,950	$51,151–$77,975	$87,701–$142,000	31%
$128,101–$278,450	$155,951–$278,450	$77,976–$139,225	$142,001–$278,450	36%
Over $278,450	Over $278,450	Over $139,225	Over $278,450	39.6%

➤ Interstate truck and bus drivers

➤ Certain railroad employees, such as train crews and dispatchers

➤ Certain merchant mariners

These transportation employees will get higher deductions as time goes on. Their deduction for meals will be as follows:

1998 and 1999	55%
2000 and 2001	60%
2002 and 2003	65%
2004 and 2005	70%
2006 and 2007	75%
2008 and later	80%

What You Can Deduct

Meals that are directly related to your business are deductible (50%, of course). There has to be a business purpose for the gathering. Without a business purpose, the meal is not deductible at all.

Jon, for example, is a banker. He frequently eats lunch with other bankers. If no business is discussed at lunch, the meal is not deductible. If Jon discusses business matters at lunch, his meal is deductible (50%), and he can deduct any meals that he pays for his colleagues.

If you are traveling away from home on business, your meals are deductible (50%). If you pay for other people's meals, though, there has to be a business discussion to deduct their meals.

For example, Christine goes out of town to attend a conference for her job. She meets some of her business friends at the conference and goes out to dinner with them one evening. No business is discussed. Christine picks up the tab for dinner. Christine's meal is deductible since she is out of town on business. The meals she buys for the other people are not deductible since no business was discussed.

Paper Trail

To deduct a business meal, you must discuss business before, during, or after the meal. If you're traveling, this rule doesn't apply. You need to keep a record of the business purpose of the meal. Without this record, the meal is not deductible at all.

The business discussion doesn't have to result in an actual sale to deduct a meal. You could be discussing potential business, actual work in progress, or work that has been completed. Results don't matter for the deduction. It's the activity that counts.

What You Can't Deduct

You, your employee, or your independent contractor has to be present at the meal to take a deduction for the meal. Treating a customer or client to a quiet meal might be a nice gesture, but it won't give you a tax deduction.

Lavish or extravagant meals are not deductible. This is a difficult standard to enforce. Although you can consider the circumstances to determine if the meal is lavish or extravagant, such a subjective rule is difficult to enforce or defend.

Your every-day meals are not deductible. They are considered personal living expenses. If you are away from home on business, though, the meals are deductible. What if you have to go out of town for a day trip? If you do not have to stop for sleep or rest while traveling, your meals are not deductible.

For example, you might have to make a brief visit to a customer in a town that is a two-hour drive away. If you drive to the customer's office, conduct your business, and drive back home, the cost of your lunch along the way will not be deductible.

Let's say, on the other hand, you have to visit that same customer's office to install equipment. The job will take two working days, so you will have to spend the night away from home. Your meals away from home will be deductible.

Entertainment Expenses

Business entertainment is deductible if it is either:

➤ Directly related to your business

➤ Associated with your business

Even after you pass this hurdle, only 50% of your entertainment expenses are deductible.

Entertainment costs that are 50% deductible include:

➤ Entertaining guests at a nightclub, dinner club, or athletic club

➤ Taking guests to the theater

➤ Taking guests to sporting events

➤ Taking guests on hunting or fishing trips

➤ Entertaining guests on a yacht

➤ Hosting a reception or cocktail party for guests (including the cost of renting a room)

Certain club dues and membership fees aren't deductible at all. Even if directly related to your business, membership dues or initiation fees paid can't be deducted if they are paid to a club organized for purposes of:

➤ Business
➤ Pleasure
➤ Recreation
➤ Social

Country clubs, golf clubs, athletic clubs, hotel clubs, airline clubs, and dinner clubs are all organizations whose dues are not deductible. Under no circumstances are these dues deductible.

Trade associations dues are deductible. They are not considered in the same light as social club dues. Other organizations whose dues are deductible if related to your business are:

➤ Business leagues
➤ Chambers of commerce
➤ Real estate boards
➤ Professional associations

Your meals at trade association and business organization meetings qualify as deductible business expenses. The meals are 50% deductible.

Deducting Your Business Travel

If you have to travel for business, you will be able to deduct your travel expenses. Traveling could involve a car trip across town or a flight across the globe.

Red Flag

The deduction for tickets to theater and sporting events is limited to 50% of the face amount of the ticket (including fees and taxes). If you pay a higher rate to a scalper for the tickets, you don't get a higher deduction for the premium that you paid.

Your Decoder Ring

Dues to a chamber of commerce are a deductible business expense. Some taxpayers try to deduct their chamber dues as charitable contributions, but they should be taken as business expenses instead.

If you travel locally, your costs to get there and back are deductible. If you travel out of town, though, you can deduct much more. Your lodging and meals are deductible when traveling away from home.

In-Town Travel

You can deduct the cost of in-town business transportation. This might include using your car, bus fare, taxi fare, or travel by local train.

Deductible in-town trips include:

➤ Going from one in-town workplace to another during your workday

➤ Traveling to visit with clients or customers

➤ Going from your home to a temporary work site (if you have another regular place of work)

You can never deduct the cost of traveling from your home to your regular workplace. This is considered commuting, which is not deductible. Even if you live 60 miles from your job, traveling to your work is a nondeductible commuting expense.

If you have two jobs, the travel from your home to your second job is still commuting and cannot be deducted. If you go from your regular job to your second job, though, that is deductible.

Let's break it down to some simple guidelines (see Table 17.1).

Table 17.1   Local Transportation

Travel	Between	Deduct or Not?
Home	Regular job	No
Home	Second job	No
Home	Temporary job site	Deduct only if have another regular job site
Regular job	Second job	Yes
Regular job	Temporary job site	Yes
Regular job	Customer or client	Yes
Second job	Temporary job site	Yes

If you have to report to a union hall before you go to your regular job site, your trip to the job site is still part of your commute. You can't deduct the travel between the union hall and your regular job site.

If you have to pay to park your car when you are at your regular work site, you can't deduct your parking fees. The parking is considered part of your commute. If you have to pay parking fees to visit a customer, a client, or a temporary job site, your parking is deductible.

If your business is in your home, things change a bit. You don't have a commute. All of your travel expenses to customers, clients, and suppliers are deductible business transportation. You can only use this tax advantage if your home is the principal place of your business.

There are some people who don't have either a regular work place or an office in their home. For these people, travel to their first stop in the morning is considered a nondeductible commute. Travel from their last stop at night to home is the second leg of their commute.

Let's do a few examples.

Sharon works in an office in her hometown. Sharon has to attend a week-long series of meetings for training on new software that is being installed in her office. The cost of traveling between Sharon's home and the meeting site is deductible. The meeting site is a temporary work location.

JoAnn is a physical therapist. She works on patients in three different hospitals, but has a regular office in one of the hospitals. Each of the hospitals is not considered a temporary job site. Instead, they are treated as second job sites. JoAnn can deduct travel between the hospitals. She can't deduct travel between her home and any of the hospitals.

Christopher is an interior designer. He lives above his studio. Christopher has to travel daily to clients' homes and business locations. He also has to visit galleries and suppliers to select materials for his clients. All of Christopher's in-town travel will be deductible.

> **Red Flag**
>
> What if you own your own business and you put an advertising display on your car? Would your car turn into an advertising expense rather than being your personal transportation? What if you have to haul tools in your car? Can you deduct your trips to and from work? Nice tries, but no. Your car is treated no differently, and you still can't deduct your commuting expenses.

Traveling Away from Home

If you are traveling away from home, you can deduct:

➤ Transportation expense, such as airfare, bus ticket, or train ticket

➤ Taxi fare or commuter bus fare for travel between the airport, train station, or bus depot and your hotel

➤ Operating your car to travel away from home

➤ Meals while away from home

➤ Lodging expenses such as hotel or apartment rent

If you aren't traveling away from home, most of these expenses are considered nondeductible living expenses. Traveling away from home is the ticket to your tax deduction. There should be no surprise that there are standards you must meet to be considered away from home on business.

You will be considered as traveling away from home if:

➤ You have to be away from your home for business purposes for substantially longer than an ordinary day's work.

➤ You need to get sleep or rest to meet your job demands while away from home.

For most people, these rules mean that you can deduct your trip if you have to be away from home overnight on business. It could mean more than that to other people, though.

A bus driver, for example, makes a round-trip run between two cities. The entire trip takes 18 hours. When he finishes the first leg of his trip, he has to eat and sleep before his return trip. Even though his sleep time is still in the daytime and the bus driver is gone less than 24 hours, his expenses away from home will be deductible. To do his job, he had to be away for longer than an ordinary day's work and he had to get sleep to complete his task.

If you happen to tire easily, or regularly nap in the afternoon, you won't qualify as traveling away from home. That would be a pretty nice trick, but it doesn't work!

There's No Place Like Home

To get the tax benefits of out-of-town travel, you have to be away from home. To be more precise, you have to be away from your tax home.

Most of us have no problem determining where our tax home is. We usually work in the same general vicinity where we live. That isn't the case for everyone, though. For the people who work in places different than where they live, there is a tax concept known as your *tax home*.

If you are traveling away from your tax home, your travel expenses are deductible. If you are not away from your tax home, your meals and lodging aren't deductible. This distinction can make a huge difference on your tax return. There can be some unexpected results.

Your tax home is not where you live. Your tax home is the place where you regularly work. If you work in more than one place, your tax home is your main place of work.

Some people don't have a tax home at all. These people are considered itinerant for tax purposes and can never deduct business travel expenses. They don't have a tax home, so the IRS considers them to never be away from home.

If you have more than one place where you work, how do you determine your main place of work? You have to look at:

➤ The total time you spend working in each location

➤ The degree of your business activity in each location

➤ The amount of income that you earn from each location

Jan, for example, lives in Tennessee, where she works nine months of the year. Jan makes $22,000 working in Tennessee. During the winter months, Jan works in Colorado. She earns $10,000 for her three months work in Colorado. Tennessee is Jan's tax home. She spends most of her time there and earns most of her money there.

Jan's example was pretty obvious. Let's try some examples that are a bit more challenging.

Pat is a corporate executive. Pat's employer moved its headquarters from Pat's hometown of Boise to Kansas City. Pat's daughter and husband decided to stay in Boise for two years since her daughter is a junior in high school. Pat's tax home is now Kansas City. Pat can't deduct her living expenses in Kansas City. Pat can also not deduct her travel between Kansas City and Boise. This is a classic case of having a tax home different than your main home.

Rob's family lives in St. Louis. Rob is an engineer. He supervises HVAC installations on industrial construction sites. When his work at one job site is completed, Rob moves to the next

Red Flag

If you work in more than one location, you might have to file tax returns in more than one state. Each state has its own filing requirements. There are agreements between states that can help you limit the number of states in which you file. Learn what the rules are in the states that you work.

job site. In 1998, Rob worked on three projects in three different states. The business that Rob works for is located in California. Rob is at home on weekends and holidays. If there are gaps in the time between jobs, Rob does planning and design work from his home. Rob spends his vacation time with his family either at home or traveling. Where is Rob's tax home? There is a solution for Rob.

If you don't have a regular place of work, you might be able to use the place that you live as your tax home. You have to meet all of these three tests:

1. You do some work in the area of your main home and stay in your home when doing business there.

2. When you have to be away from your main home to work, you pay duplicate living expenses.

3. You have not left the area where your main home is located, you have family living in your main home, or you often use your main home for lodging.

In Rob's case, he meets all three of these tests. Rob can treat his home in St. Louis as his tax home. Rob's meals and lodging expenses while he is working out of St. Louis are deductible business expenses. If his employer reimburses him for his expenses while away from home, Rob does not have to pay income taxes on his expense reimbursement.

We've solved Rob's problem, but what about Michelle? She is unmarried and has no children. Michelle is a professional ice skater. She tours 10 months of the year with an ice show. Michelle does not own her own home or rent an apartment. Michelle stays with her parents when she is not working.

Michelle has no tax home. She does not meet test number 2 since she doesn't have duplicate living expenses. This means that Michelle can't deduct her meals and lodging while she is traveling with the ice show. If Michelle would just keep an apartment, the result would be entirely different. She would be able to deduct her traveling expenses while on the road and any employer travel expense reimbursements would be tax-free.

Temporary Jobs—What Are They?

There are two different kinds of job assignments that take you away from your home:

➤ Temporary job assignments
➤ Indefinite job assignments

If a job away from home is temporary, you can deduct your travel expenses, meals, and lodging while away from home. You can also deduct your travel expenses to go back to your home. If your employer pays your travel, meals, and lodging expenses for a temporary assignment away from home, you don't have taxable income as a result of your expenses having been paid.

If the job is indefinite, you can't deduct your travel, meals, and lodging. You can't deduct your travel back home from the job site. If your employer pays your living expenses while away from home, you have taxable income. This can make a huge difference on your tax return.

What is the difference between temporary and indefinite job assignments? A job assignment is temporary if you expect it to last for one year or less and it does last for one year or less.

You have to meet both tests: the expectation of lasting one year or less and the actuality of lasting one year or less. If things turn out so that a nine-month job lasts 13 months, the job is indefinite, not temporary. If you already filed a tax return deducting the expenses for the first nine months, you would have to file an amended return when your actual stay goes beyond a year. At the time, you thought the expenses were deductible. In retrospect, though, they don't qualify.

If a 15-month job ends after 11 months, it is still an indefinite job because it was expected to last more than a year. You can't deduct the expenses for this job since it never qualified as temporary.

It is possible for a temporary assignment to turn into an indefinite assignment because of changed circumstances. When this happens, your tax picture changes. Once the job is indefinite rather than temporary, your expenses are no longer deductible.

If you are away from home for a probationary period of time, this is indefinite. This is not a temporary assignment. You can't deduct your expenses while away from home on this job assignment.

If you are a member of the Armed Forces on permanent duty assignment overseas, you can't deduct expenses for being away from home. Even if you have to maintain your home in the United States because your family can't travel with you, your expenses overseas are not deductible.

There is a special exception for federal employees who are participating in federal crime investigations. If the Attorney General certifies that you are traveling for the federal government in a temporary duty assignment to investigate a federal crime or provide support services for the investigation, your time away from home can exceed a year. Your reimbursed travel expenses will not be taxable to you.

Paper Trail

To support your deduction for a temporary job site, get the terms of the assignment in writing from your employer. You might need to prove that you expected the job to last less than a year.

When You're Not Traveling Solo

If you take a travel companion with you on your business trip, you might be able to deduct the companion's expenses. The person has to be your business companion, though. Personal companions may be helpful, but they won't give you a tax deduction.

You can deduct the travel expenses for someone who meets all of these three requirements:

1. The person is your employee.
2. The person has a bona fide business purpose to accompany you for the travel.
3. The person would otherwise be able to deduct his or her travel expenses.

You might be traveling with a business associate who is not your employee. If he or she meets requirements number 2 and 3 above, you can deduct his or her expenses. A business associate is someone whom you either are doing business with or you expect to do business with. The business associate could be your:

➤ Customer
➤ Client
➤ Partner
➤ Agent
➤ Professional advisor
➤ Supplier

Red Flag

Your employer might insist that your spouse accompany you on a business trip. Even if you have no choice, the travel expenses paid for your spouse will be taxed to you as compensation. The employer's requirement won't overrule the IRS rules.

Business or Pleasure. . . or Both?

It's an American taxpayer's dream. Go out of town to a resort location, do a token amount of work, and write it all off. You're right, it is a dream!

It is possible to mix business travel with pleasure. It's even possible to take travel deductions for mixed-purpose trips. Your deduction depends on the mixing formula.

Mixed-Purpose Travel in the States

If your trip is primarily business, but there is a personal element, you can still deduct your travel. You can't deduct the portion of your trip that is personal. Let's look at an example.

Peggy has to go to a business convention in Sacramento. Her sister happens to live nearby, so Peggy would like to visit with her while there. The convention will last six days. Peggy is planning to stay an extra two days to visit with her sister. Peggy's trip is primarily business. She can deduct her travel to Sacramento. She can deduct her meals and lodging for the days that she attends the convention. Peggy can't deduct expenses for the two extra days that she spends with her sister.

Let's turn the tables a bit. Peggy is going to visit her sister. She will be gone eight days. While she is gone, there is a two-day business meeting in nearby Sacramento that Peggy will attend. Since Peggy's trip is primarily personal, her travel expenses will not be deductible. Peggy's expenses for travel and meals to go to Sacramento for the business meeting from her sister's home are deductible. If Peggy stays overnight in Sacramento for business, her lodging in Sacramento will be deductible.

Travel that is predominantly personal is not deductible. Any expenses that you incur for the business part of your trip can be deducted. You can't turn a vacation into a business trip by scheduling minimal business activity.

Paper Trail

Since the IRS is suspicious of travel to resort locations, keep good records. If you attend a conference or convention, keep the agenda of business meetings and classes. Keep your registration information to prove your participation in the business activities. Your records might come in handy.

Hopping Over the Pond: Travel Outside the United States

If you travel outside the United States, you might be able to deduct your travel costs. There are special rules to follow, though.

Your travel will be considered one of the following:

➤ Travel primarily for vacation

➤ Travel primarily for business

➤ Travel entirely for business

To know the primary purpose for your trip, consider how much time you spend for business and pleasure. If you spend most of your time on business, your trip is primarily business. You might have a more meaningful way to measure the business and personal aspects of your trip. The IRS gives you the flexibility to consider other circumstances, but will rely heavily on how you spend your time.

If you travel outside the United States primarily for vacation, none of your travel expenses are deductible. Even if you conduct some business while gone, none of your travel expenses can be claimed. Your other expenses directly related to the business can be deducted, though. The business expenses might include cab fare, meals, or class registration fees.

If you travel outside the United States primarily for business, but combine personal travel with your business, you can deduct part of your trip. Your expenses related to the business part of your trip (meals, lodging) will be deductible. You will have to allocate your expenses of getting to and from your destination between personal (nondeductible) and business (deductible).

For example, Sam has to visit a business location in Munich to perform on-site inspections and repairs of equipment that his employer manufactures. It will take two weeks for Sam to complete his business in Munich. Sam decides to stay for an extra week to tour southern Germany. Two-thirds of Sam's airfare to Munich and back will be deductible. Sam can deduct his expenses while in Munich working. Sam's expenses for the additional week of personal travel are not deductible.

If the entire trip is business-related, all of your expenses getting to your destination outside the United States and getting back home will be deductible. There are four situations in which you could have a personal element to your travel and still deduct all of your travel expenses to get there and back:

1. You had no substantial control over arranging the trip. You can control the timing of the trip, however. You don't have substantial control if you are an employee whose employer paid for the trip, you are not related to the employer, or you are not a managing executive.
2. You were not outside the United States more than a week.
3. You spent less than 25% of your time on personal activities.
4. You can demonstrate that the vacation was not a major consideration in planning the trip.

Meals and Lodging for Convenience of Employer

There are situations in which an employer might require an employee to live on the employer's property. There are also situations in which an employee is provided meals on the employer's property at the employer's cost.

Ordinarily, lodging and meals are personal expenses. When an employer pays for lodging and meals, the employee has taxable income. There is an important exception, though:

➤ If meals are provided on the employer's premises *for the convenience of the employer*, the meals are not taxable to the employee.

➤ If lodging is provided on the employer's premises *for the convenience of the employer* and it is a condition of employment, it will be tax-free to the employee.

Red Flag

There is a rule change for years that begin after July 22, 1998. If more than half of the meals provided are for the convenience of the employer, all of the meals provided will be tax-free. This is an important easing of the rules.

The exclusion for employer-provided meals and lodging doesn't apply to self-employed people, such as partners in partnerships. They don't have employers, so they can't receive tax-free employee benefits.

To be tax-free, the lodging has to be on the employer's premises. It isn't enough that the employer owns the home that you live in. The living quarters have to be either right on the business premises or very close to it. One court allowed a deduction for a home that was right across the street of a hotel that the employee managed.

What does *convenience of employer* mean? It means that the employer has business motivations to have the employee on the business premises. The IRS gives us some examples in the Regulations that will satisfy the *convenience of employer* test for meals:

➤ A waitress is required to eat her meals at the restaurant during the busy lunch and breakfast hours.

➤ A bank furnishes meals to a teller in the bank building to reduce the time the teller is away from work during busy hours.

➤ A construction site is located in a remote area of Alaska. The employer has to provide meals since there are no other facilities available.

For lodging, the condition of employment requirement is a strict standard. It is not enough that the lodging would be more convenient to the employer, the employer must require it.

Pam, for example, works in a resort area for a real estate management company. Pam's employer requires its managers to live in the buildings that they manage. Pam's lodging will be tax-free to her. If some of the company's managers refuse to live on site and the company tolerates the noncompliance, the test is failed. Pam's lodging would be taxable to her.

If you are an employee of an educational institution, there are special rules. You don't have to recognize taxable income if you pay rent on campus housing if your rent is at least 5% of the value of the property. If the rent payments annually are less than 5% of the property's value, the difference must be included in gross income.

There are special rules for ministers. A minister can receive lodging tax-free. The tax-free benefit could be either of the following:

➤ The rent-free use of a home

➤ A rental allowance paid to the minister (to the extent the allowance is used to pay rent or provide a home)

Military personnel can receive tax-free housing allowances under certain circumstances. The exclusion for military personnel is not governed by the Internal Revenue Code.

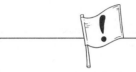

Red Flag

Unless the minister has opted out of the Social Security system, a tax-free housing allowance will be subject to self-employment tax.

Using Per Diems

Instead of deducting your actual expenses while you travel, you can use standard *per diem* amounts. A per diem is a fixed daily amount to cover certain expense. Some employers use per diems to control travel expenses. The employer will pay the employee a set per diem amount. Even if the employee's actual expenses are more than the per diem amount, the employer will only pay up to the per diem rate.

The standard meal allowance can be used if you are self-employed. Some employees can use the standard meal allowance. An employee who is related to his or her employer can't use the standard amount. You are related if your employer is:

➤ Family (brother, sister, half-brother, half-sister, spouse, parent, grandparent, child, or grandchild)

➤ A corporation that you own more than 10% of (either directly or indirectly)

You can also be related to your employer if there are certain fiduciary relationships involving trusts.

The standard meal allowance in 1998 is $32 a day for most locations. There are certain cities that the IRS considers high-cost locations. The standard meal allowance is $40 a day for these cities.

To get more information about per diems, visit these web sites:

➤ For travel in the United States: www.policyworks.gov/perdiem

➤ For foreign travel: www.state.gov/www/perdiems

For the day that you leave on your travels and the day that you return, you can't use a whole day's per diem. You can use a reasonable method to allocate the expenses or you can use $^3/_4$ of the standard amount.

Records, Records, Records

Without the right records, your travel, meals, and entertainment expenses are not worth anything. By law, there are certain records that you must keep. If you don't have the right records, the IRS can deny your deductions. If you are audited, chances are good that you will be asked to produce your documentation. Your deductions can be denied without the necessary records.

The best record keeping system has two parts:

➤ An appointment book
➤ Receipts, canceled checks, etc.

A well-kept appointment book can be invaluable if the IRS challenges your business expenses. Your book will document whom you saw, where you went, and when your activities took place. When you combine this with receipts or canceled checks with dates that match, you have some pretty powerful documentation.

Most of us keep an appointment book of some sort. Unfortunately, many people don't think to keep their appointment book with their tax records. Please keep your book. It might come in handy. If your calendar is kept on a computer system, print it out and keep the hard copy.

The IRS generally requires you to have *documentary* evidence of your expenses. Documentary evidence includes:

➤ Receipts
➤ Canceled checks
➤ Credit card statements
➤ Invoices

The IRS gives you a break in keeping documentary evidence:

➤ If a meal or entertainment expense is less than $75, you don't need a receipt. This break doesn't apply to lodging, so you'll still need a receipt for lodging even if it's under $75.
➤ If you have a transportation expense for which you can't get a receipt, you don't need documentary evidence. For example, if you use a mass transit system that doesn't print receipts for you, a receipt is not needed.

➤ If your employer pays you a per diem rate in an *accountable* plan for your meals or lodging, you won't need receipts. (Accountable plans were explained in Chapter 13, "Deductions If You Are an Employee.")

Your records have to show:

➤ The amount of the expense

➤ The date you had the expense

➤ The place (city and name of restaurant or hotel)

➤ Business purpose of the expense (e.g., entertaining a client or traveling to a convention)

➤ Names of persons (for meals and entertainment)

➤ Business relationship of other persons (for meals and entertainment)

➤ Nature of the business discussion

If you are deducting entertainment expenses, be sure to keep records of the activities. For example, did you have a business meeting before you went to the theater? How long did the business meeting last?

If this seems like a lot of record keeping, it is! Remember that travel, meals, and entertainment deductions have been abused by many taxpayers. Your agent has probably seen more ways to cheat than you can even imagine. The agent will be skeptical, so you need to be prepared.

You will normally need to keep your records for three years after you file your tax return. It's a good idea to keep records up to six years after you file the tax return.

The IRS has three years to audit your return for any reason at all. Your 1996 return was due April 15, 1997, so the IRS has until April 15, 2000, to audit your return. If you filed your return on an extension, the IRS has three years from the date you actually filed your return.

The IRS can go back another three years in limited circumstances. If you have committed tax fraud, the IRS can go back forever.

Your Decoder Ring

The period of time that the IRS has to audit your return is called the **statute of limitations**. If the statute period lapses, the IRS can't audit your tax return unless fraud is alleged. By the same token, you can't file an amended return if the statute has lapsed.

The Least You Need to Know

➤ Fifty percent of your business meals and entertainment expenses are allowed as a tax deduction.

➤ You can deduct business travel expenses, but your cost to commute to your job is not deductible.

➤ If you are away from home on a temporary job (less than one year), your travel, meals, and lodging expenses will be deductible. If you are away from home on an indefinite job (longer than one year), your expenses away from home are not deductible.

➤ If you travel for both business and pleasure, part of the travel expenses are deductible.

➤ Documenting your travel, meals, and entertainment expenses is critical. Without documentation, you can lose your deduction.

Chapter 18

Education Expenses

In This Chapter

➤ Determining when you can take a tax deduction for attending classes or training courses

➤ Using scholarships or employer programs to pay for college

➤ Using education savings bonds or IRAs to pay for a college education

➤ Choosing which tax incentive you will use for your education expenses

---

In today's economy we constantly have to retrain ourselves. Technology changes alone send many of us back to the classroom. It is no longer adequate to train for your life career. We are all expected to stay current in the issues that face our professions.

Some education expenses can be deducted on your tax return. If your education expense would be deductible, your employer can pay the expense for you as a tax-free fringe benefit. Getting reimbursed is even better than getting a deduction because you get 100% of your money back.

There are many different forms that deductible education can take. Education expenses can include traditional classes, training sessions, seminars, or conventions. Self-study and group-study courses can qualify for a deduction.

There are some tax-smart ways to pay for higher education. You can save for college using tax-advantaged savings plans. There are also tax-free ways that you can offset the costs of college.

The ABCs of Education Deductions

To deduct an education expense, you must meet one of these two requirements:

➤ The education must be required (either by your employer or the law) to keep your present job, salary, or status.

➤ The education helps you maintain or improve skills that you need in your present job.

Even if you meet one of these two requirements, you still might not be able to deduct your expenses. You can't claim education expenses if any one of these statements is true:

➤ The education could lead to a degree.

➤ The education is needed for you to meet the minimum education requirements of your present trade or business.

➤ The education is part of a program of study that can qualify you for a new trade or business, even if you don't plan to enter that trade or business.

Mandatory Ed 101

After you have a job, your studying is usually not over. Many jobs require continuing education and training. If that training enables you to keep your present salary, your status, or even your job, the education might be deductible. The training or education must serve a business purpose and it can't qualify you for a new trade or business.

Paper Trail

The requirement to take the additional training or education can be imposed by either your employer or the law. If there is any doubt that your employer required you to take a class, get something in writing. A personnel manual might help. Memos and letters will also help support your tax deduction.

If you work in a personnel department, for example, you might be required by your employer to take at least one continuing education class each year to keep up on employment law matters. If your employer doesn't pay for the course, you can deduct the cost of taking the class. The course is required by your employer, serves a business purpose, and does not qualify you for a new trade or business.

Many professionals have to take continuing education courses to retain their licenses to practice. Since the education is required and it doesn't qualify the professional for a new trade or business, the education is deductible.

A certified public accountant, for example, has to take a minimum number of hours of continuing education to keep his or her license to practice as a CPA. The education that is needed to retain the license is deductible. If education is taken beyond the minimum requirements, the extra education might still be deductible if it helps maintain or improve the CPA's skills.

Teachers will often have special education requirements that might enable them to deduct part of their education. Let's say that your state, for example, requires its teachers to hold a bachelor's degree. The state also requires its teachers to obtain a fifth year of college within 10 years of the date of hire. After a teacher has obtained the bachelor's degree, the minimum job requirements have been met. Unless the fifth year of education will qualify you for a new trade or business, the fifth year of college will be deductible. The fifth year is required for you to retain your job and it is related to your job.

Keeping Your Edge: Education to Hone Skills

Even if education isn't mandated, the knowledge that you gain might be helpful to you on the job. If education helps you maintain your skills or improve your skills, you can claim a deduction for it. As with required education, if the education qualifies you for a new trade or business or will lead to a degree, the education is not deductible.

Classes that might maintain or improve your skills can include:

➤ Refresher courses

➤ Classes on current developments

➤ Classes on new technologies

➤ Classes on new products

➤ Academic courses

➤ Vocational courses

If you are a librarian, for example, you might want to take a class on Internet research techniques. The information from the class will improve your job skills. The training will not qualify you for a new trade or business. The training will be deductible.

To deduct education that maintains or improves your skills, the education has to relate to your present job or your present business. If the course content is unrelated to your business, you can't claim a tax deduction.

Sarah, for example, is a licensed realtor. Sarah is not selling real estate, however. Sarah is public relations director for a not-for-profit organization. If Sarah takes a real estate class to keep up to date on real estate issues, she won't be able to deduct her education expenses. Sarah can only claim education expenses that help her in her current job as a public relations director.

Sarah, on the other hand, might be working temporarily outside her real estate profession because she is between real estate jobs. If her absence from her real estate career is temporary (a year or less), she should be able to deduct her real estate classes, but only if she returns to her real estate career.

Business conventions are deductible as long as there is a sufficient business relationship between your trade or business and the convention. If the topic discussed at the business convention doesn't relate to your business, you can't deduct the convention.

For example, Barbara is a registered nurse. Barbara works in the office of a pediatrician. If Barbara attends a conference on children's health care issues, the cost of the conference will be deductible. If Barbara attends a conference on identifying disease in the geriatric patient, however, the conference will not be deductible since it doesn't relate to Barbara's job.

A convention or seminar held outside North America has a higher standard for taking a deduction. Two tests must be met:

➤ The subject matter discussed at the convention or seminar must be directly related to your business.

➤ It must be as reasonable that the course was held outside North America as it is for it to be held in North America.

Your Decoder Ring

What does it mean for it to be **reasonable** that a course be held outside North America? This is a challenging standard to describe. There is no bright line test. You can consider the course sponsor's location, the residence of most of the attendees, or the location of prior meetings.

The direct relationship test is met if the classes relate to your specific job duties or responsibilities. In Barbara's case, the classes must relate to pediatric nursing issues. General medical conferences would not be sufficiently related to her job to be deductible.

Cruise ship conventions have special rules. You can only deduct up to $2,000 a year for cruise ship expenses. The convention must also meet these tests:

➤ The meeting must be directly related to your business.

➤ The ship must be registered in the United States.

➤ All ports of call must be located in the United States or its possessions.

Classes You Can't Deduct

You can't deduct classes that lead to a college degree. Even if the classes relate to your job or you don't plan to use your new degree to change jobs, the college study is not deductible.

You can't deduct the classes that are needed to meet the minimum education requirements of your present trade or business. For example, you might be working as a teacher's aid in an elementary school. Your school system changes its education requirements for teacher's aids. You now have to obtain a bachelor's degree. Your classes to obtain a bachelor's degree will not be tax-deductible since they are needed for you to meet the minimum education requirements of your job.

Part of a program of study that can qualify you for a new trade or business is not deductible. Even if you don't plan to enter that trade or business, you can't deduct the classes.

Beth, for example, works as a legal paraprofessional. She prepares tax returns as part of her job. Beth decides to enroll in the school of accounting at a local college. She will take enough classes that she will have an accounting degree when she is done with her coursework. Even though Beth doesn't plan to change jobs after she gets her accounting degree, her course work will qualify her for a new profession, so she can't deduct the classes.

Investment seminars are not deductible. There is a specific provision in the tax law that denies a deduction for any expenses related to investment seminars. You can't deduct the registration fees, travel, meals, or lodging.

You can't deduct travel as a form of education. For example, a French teacher might travel to France to experience the culture and practice the language. The teacher's travel is not deductible. If the French teacher was going to France to take a class that is not offered anywhere else, the travel expenses could be deducted. In this case, the travel itself is not the education. The teacher is traveling to take a specific course of study.

Adding Up Your Education Deduction

If a class is deductible, you can claim all of your expenses to take the class. Deductible expenses include:

➤ Tuition

➤ Lab fees

➤ Books

➤ Supplies

➤ Research expenses

➤ Typing or photocopy charges

➤ Transportation (including 32.5 cents per mile to use your car)

➤ Travel

Your Decoder Ring

The IRS broadly defines **trade** or **business** for teachers. Teaching elementary school, teaching high school, serving as a guidance counselor, and becoming a school administrator are all considered part of the education business. Training to enable you to move from one position to another will not qualify you for a new trade or business, so you can deduct your education expenses.

Paper Trail

There is an exception to the prohibition on deductions for investment seminars. If you work as an investment advisor, investment dealer, or investment broker, investment seminars will be deductible. If you are not in the investment business, though, the seminars are not deductible. Even if the sole source of your income is from investments, you can't deduct investment seminars.

➤ Lodging away from home to attend class

➤ Meals wile away from home (subject to the 50% cutback)

These expenses can really add up. If you are taking deductible classes, don't miss out on all of the deductions that you can take. In particular, if you have to be away from home to take a class or attend training sessions, be certain that you don't leave any of your deduction on the table.

How to Claim Education Deductions

Your deduction for education expenses depends on your job. If you are an employee, your education expenses are part of your miscellaneous itemized deductions. Remember that these expenses have to be reduced by 2% of your adjusted gross income.

Your Decoder Ring

Self-employment taxes are your Social Security taxes on self-employment income. Since you have no employer to match your Social Security taxes, you have to pay both parts of the Social Security taxes. Your self-employment taxes are calculated on Schedule SE of Form 1040.

If you are self-employed, your education expenses will give you handsome tax savings. Your income taxes and your self-employment taxes will both be reduced.

If you report your business income on Schedule C (proprietorship), your education expenses are deducted on Schedule C. If you are a farmer, your education expenses are deducted on your Schedule F. If you are a partner in a partnership, your education expenses are deducted on your Schedule E.

Performing artists and handicapped individuals have special provisions for deducting their business expenses. These special rules were explained in Chapter 13, "Deductions If You Are an Employee." Essentially, a qualifying performing artist can claim his or her expenses in arriving at adjusted gross income instead of claiming them as miscellaneous itemized deductions. A handicapped individual's impairment-related expenses to attend deductible classes are not subject to the 2% of AGI floor.

Tax-Smart Ways to Pay for Education

Our tax system holds a variety of opportunities to cut your taxes while you cover the cost of college for you or your children. You can earn tax-free income on your college savings. You can shift some income tax from you to your child. You can get tax credits or use IRA funds penalty-free under the different education tax incentives.

You can only use one tax benefit to pay for a dollar of college expense. If you have more than one possible tax benefit available to you, you will have to make some choices. You can use more than one tax benefit in a year, but not on the same dollar of education expense.

In Chapter 4, "Even Better Than Deductions—Tax Credits," we discussed the new education tax credits: the HOPE Scholarship Credit and the Lifetime Learning Credit. In Chapter 8, "Paying Interest," we discussed the new deduction for interest paid on student loans. You don't want to pass up a tax-saving opportunity, so check out those new tax-saving options.

Scholarships

You don't have to pay income tax on a scholarship that is used to pay tuition, books, supplies, and equipment. The scholarship could be from a variety of sources including your school, a state tuition program, a scholarship fund, or a nonprofit organization.

Scholarships received for room and board are taxable. The scholarship is treated as earned income for purposes of calculating your standard deduction, though. This might make a difference if you can be claimed as someone else's dependent. See Chapter 3, "Your Tax Freebee—The Standard Deduction," for a discussion of calculating your standard deduction.

If you work for a school, you might be eligible for undergraduate tuition waivers. This would allow you or your family to attend school at a reduced rate. This benefit won't be taxable to you as long as the program doesn't give preferential treatment to the school's highly compensated employees. If you qualify for a reciprocal tuition waiver program, you might get reduced tuition at another school. These programs are also tax-free as long as they don't discriminate in favor of highly compensated employees of the school.

Tuition waivers for graduate students might be taxable. If you are a teaching or research assistant, you may be able to get tuition waivers for graduate courses tax-free, though. If the tuition waiver is a substitute for cash wages, you will have to pay tax on the tuition waiver. If you are paid a fair wage for your work, the tuition waiver will be tax-free.

Let Your Boss Pay

Some businesses pay for their employees to attend school. This is known in tax lingo as *employer-provided education assistance*. Your employer can pay for your tuition, fees, books, and supplies for undergraduate courses. Payments up to $5,250 a year will be tax-free to you. The classes don't even have to be job-related.

If your employer pays for graduate courses, you will have to pay income tax on the payments. This taxable employee benefit is treated as additional wages paid to you.

Your employer gets a tax deduction for the educational assistance that you are paid. If it's tax-free educational assistance, your employer will take a regular business expense deduction for the expenses that are paid. If it's a taxable payment (such as graduate courses), it will be included on your Form W-2 and will be deducted by your employer as wages paid to employee.

Education Savings Bonds

One way that you can finance higher education expenses in a tax-smart way is to use savings bonds. If you own savings bonds, you don't have to report the interest income until you cash in your bonds. You can choose to report the interest income each year if you wish. Most people prefer to wait until the bonds are cashed, though, to report their interest income.

Some people can get an extra tax advantage from savings bonds. You can cash EE bonds and not pay tax on the interest if you meet the following tests:

➤ The savings bonds were issued after December 31, 1989.

➤ The savings bonds were issued to a person who was at least 24 years old when the bonds were issued. This means that the bonds need to be in the parent's name rather than the child's name.

➤ The redemption proceeds (both principal and interest) are used to pay for qualified higher education expenses.

➤ Your modified adjusted gross income (AGI) is less than $108,350 on a joint return or $67,250 on a single return.

Red Flag

The exclusion for employer-provided educational assistance expires on June 1, 2000. If a class begins after June 1, 2000, and your employer pays for the class, you will have to pay tax on the amount paid. It's entirely possible that the tax law could change between now and the year 2000. There is no way to predict law changes, though.

Qualified higher education expenses include tuition and fees paid for higher education for you, your spouse, or your dependent. If the redemption proceeds from the savings bonds (interest and principal combined) are more than your education expenses, part of your interest will qualify for the exclusion.

The income threshold for getting the savings bond exclusion keys off of your adjusted gross income, including the savings bond interest but before you subtract foreign earned income, if any. This is your modified AGI.

There is a phase-out range in which you will get part of your savings bond interest tax-free. For married couples filing jointly, the phase-out range is modified AGI of $52,250 to $108,350 in 1998. For single taxpayers the phase-out range is $52,250 to $67,250. Within the phase-out range, a portion of your interest is tax-free.

Paper Trail

If you've thought about going back to college at some future date, you might be interested in using savings bonds for yourself. Proceeds used for your education or your spouse's education will qualify.

260

Using an IRA for College

You can use IRA funds for higher education and save tax dollars. There are two education-related IRA opportunities:

➤ Education IRAs

➤ Penalty-free IRA distributions

You can put up to $500 a year into an education IRA for a child under age 18. As the account grows, you don't have to pay income tax on the earnings. When the IRA funds are distributed to pay for higher education expenses, the distribution can be tax-free.

There is an income limit for making contributions. You can make the full $500 contribution if your adjusted gross income (AGI) is not more than $95,000 if you are single and $150,000 if you are married and file jointly. Between $95,000 and $110,000 of AGI on a single return, a partial contribution is allowed. On a joint return, the partial contribution is available if your AGI is between $150,000 and $160,000. Above $110,000 (single) or $160,000 (joint), you can't make any education IRA contributions.

If you set up an education IRA for your child, and the child doesn't use the funds for college, you have two choices:

➤ You can change the account over to benefit another family member (who is under age 30).

➤ You can distribute the education IRA funds to your child.

The education IRA will have to be rolled over to another child's account or paid out within 30 days of the child's 30th birthday. If your child takes money out of the education IRA and doesn't use it for education, the earnings are taxed, and there is a 10% penalty.

There is a new opportunity in 1998 to use IRA funds to pay for education expenses. IRA distributions to pay for higher education for you, your spouse, your children, or your grandchildren will be exempt from the 10% premature distribution penalty. You still have to pay income taxes on the distribution, though.

Paper Trail

If your income is too high to fund an education IRA for your child, but you really like the idea, see if Grandma and Grandpa are willing to help. Your parents might be under the AGI limits. If so, they can fund your child's education IRA. The contribution limit is still $500 per year per child (even if more than one person contributes for the child).

State Tuition Programs

Some states have programs that allow parents to save money for their child's college education. The parents put money into the state program. When the child goes to college, the money is used to pay for the education expenses.

Red Flag

You have to pay a 10% penalty on IRA distributions if you take money out of your IRA before age 59¹/₂. You can avoid the penalty on distributions after death, after disability, or as part of a series of payments to pay down your IRA. The new education tax break adds another exception to the list. You only pay the 10% penalty on the taxable part of an IRA distribution. As you withdraw nondeductible contributions, the penalty doesn't apply.

Red Flag

Many parents who save for their children's education want to avoid paying income taxes at the parent's tax rate on the college fund's earnings. They put the funds in the child's name. An often unanticipated result is that the fund is controlled by your child when he or she is no longer a minor. Using a state tuition program avoids this consequence.

The state program funds can be used for tuition, fees, books, supplies, or room and board. If the fund isn't used by your child for college, you can get your money back with interest. At that time, you'll have to pay income tax on the earnings. Some states offer different investment options for your funds.

As the money grows, you don't pay income tax on the earnings. When the money is used for your child's college expenses, the child pays tax on the fund's earnings that are paid out. Even though you own the fund, your child will pay the income taxes (at your child's tax rate).

These state programs are becoming very popular. Each state has its own eligibility rules. The programs are worth checking out.

Choices, Choices: Which Tax Goodie to Choose?

There are so many different education tax incentives that you can easily be confused. Don't get tangled up in the different rules, though. You have to coordinate your options. You can only use one tax benefit for one dollar of education expense. You can use more than one tax benefit in a year, though.

How do you sort it out? Following these steps might help:

1. Determine which tax benefits you might qualify for.
2. Identify the overlapping benefits. These will be the areas in which you will have to make choices.
3. Calculate the tax savings you get from each benefit.

As a general rule, your first choice should be an option that will shift the cost of the education to someone else. For example, a scholarship is better than a tax credit.

Your second choice might be tax-free earnings. These options include education IRAs, education savings bonds, and state tuition programs. If you have these types of savings plans in place, you can use them for your education tax-free. You will have to compare these options to tax credits though. Some careful timing might help.

Let's say that Bill is a sophomore in college. He can either pay for his college by withdrawing funds from his education IRA or by taking out a student loan. If Bill uses his education IRA, he will not be able to claim his HOPE Scholarship Credit. A good plan for Bill would be to borrow the money for his sophomore year so that he can claim the HOPE credit. For his junior year, Bill can use his education IRA funds. His junior year tuition won't qualify for the HOPE credit since this credit is only for the first two years of college.

Red Flag

When comparing deductions to credits, don't forget about the 2% of AGI floor. If your education expenses are part of your miscellaneous itemized deductions, they have to be reduced by 2% of your adjusted gross income. Even if you are in a high tax bracket, this floor could take away your tax deduction, making the tax credit more valuable than the tax deduction.

If you have to choose between a deduction and a credit, look at your tax rate. For example, if you qualify for the Lifetime Learning Credit (see Chapter 4), you can claim a 20% credit. If you take the credit, you can't claim a deduction for the education expense. You have to make a choice. If you are in the 15% tax bracket, the credit will be better than a tax deduction. If you are in the 28% tax bracket or higher, the deduction will save you more money than the credit.

Remember that the tax credits (HOPE and Lifetime Learning) can't be taken on books and transportation expenses. You can use the credit on your tuition and claim a deduction on your books and transportation expenses. By coordinating these programs, you could use two tax advantages at the same time.

The Least You Need to Know

➤ You can deduct education expenses that help improve your job skills.

➤ You can't deduct classes that earn you a degree or will qualify you for a new trade or business.

➤ There are many tax-smart ways to pay for education, including scholarships, tax credits, state scholarship funds, savings bonds, and IRAs.

➤ You will have to choose which tax benefit to use for an education expense. With planning, you can coordinate your tax benefits.

Part 4
Deductions Even If You Don't Itemize

We saved the best for last with the deductions explained in this part of the book. If you can take the deductions explained in these final chapters, you will reduce your adjusted gross income. All kinds of good things happen on your tax return when you reduce your adjusted gross income.

Since so many of our tax goodies evaporate as AGI increases, finding a way to reduce AGI can have a big impact. As AGI drops, medical expense deductions increase. Miscellaneous deductions increase. Personal exemptions can increase. The list can go on and on.

IRAs and retirement plans provide a way to save for your own retirement. You simply can't count on Social Security to take care of you in your old age. We each have to save and plan for our own retirement. With an IRA or a retirement plan, Uncle Sam helps us save with some great tax advantages.

There are a lot of new options in IRAs. The new Roth IRA is a fabulous program. Ironically, the Roth IRA doesn't even give you a tax deduction. We'll still talk about Roth IRAs, though. They're just that good!

Chapter 19

Health Plans: Self-Employed Health Insurance and Medical Savings Accounts

---

In This Chapter

➤ Deducting health insurance premiums if you are self-employed

➤ Understanding health insurance premium deductions for shareholders in S corporations

➤ Using a medical savings account (MSA) to pay your medical expenses in a tax-advantaged manner

➤ Determining if you qualify to use an MSA

Medical insurance coverage is a real financial concern for our country. There are a lot of uninsured and underinsured people. Our government is struggling to deal with problems associated with health insurance coverage.

Even though health insurance coverage issues are difficult to resolve, Congress is able to impact health issues through the tax code. In the last few years, there have been some pretty dramatic changes in tax deductions for health insurance.

If you work for a large company, you can be fairly assured of being able to plug into your company's health insurance plan. You can also be assured of having access to tax-advantaged means to pay for your coverage.

Cafeteria plans are very popular in larger companies. A cafeteria plan enables an employee to pay for health insurance with pre-tax dollars. Funds can also be set aside to pay for uninsured medical expenses. We talked about cafeteria plans in Chapter 5, "Pay Yourself First and Lower Your Taxes."

Small businesses and self-employed people have fewer options. It can be very difficult to find health insurance at decent rates for small employee groups. Self-employed people can't participate in cafeteria plans, and small businesses often can't afford the costs of operating these plans.

Fortunately, there are a couple of tax advantages that can help soften the health insurance woes of the small business owner. There is a special deduction available for health insurance premiums paid by self-employed individuals. In 1997, we also saw the introduction of medical savings accounts, known as MSAs.

Self-Employed Health Insurance

Your health insurance premiums are ordinarily deducted as part of your itemized deduction for medical expenses. You will remember that medical expenses are only deductible to the extent that they are more than 7.5% of your adjusted gross income. If you don't itemize, you don't get a tax benefit from your medical expenses.

If you are an employee, rather than being self-employed, you can take advantage of attractive tax breaks for health insurance plans. Your employer can take a full deduction for your medical insurance premiums, and you get this benefit tax-free. You might be able to take advantage of a company-sponsored medical reimbursement plan or your company's cafeteria plan. Self-employed individuals can't take advantage of any of these tax benefits.

To help correct this inequity, self-employed people can deduct a portion of their health insurance premiums. The deduction is taken in arriving at adjusted gross income. In other words, the deduction is above-the-line. You can take the deduction whether you itemize or not, and the deduction is not subject to the 7.5% of AGI floor.

How to Claim Your Deduction

The deduction for self-employed health insurance premiums is taken on page one of your Form 1040 in the "adjusted gross income" section of the form.

Each year a portion of your self-employed health insurance premiums is deductible. In 1998, 45% of your premiums can be deducted. The deduction will increase over time. Eventually, 100% of the premiums will be deductible. The following schedule illustrates the percentage of health insurance premiums that can be deducted by a self-employed person:

1997	40%
1998 and 1999	45%
2000 and 2001	50%
2002	60%
2003 to 2005	80%

2006	90%
2007 and after	100%

Congress might increase the deduction to 100% sooner than the year 2007. Serious discussion is afoot in Washington to allow self-employed people to deduct more of their health insurance premiums sooner than the law now allows. Until a change is actually enacted, though, the schedule above will stand.

The portion of your insurance premium that you don't claim on page one of your Form 1040 can be taken as an itemized deduction with your other medical expenses.

For example, if your premiums are $300 a month, you will pay $3,600 a year for your coverage. $1,620 (45% of $3,600) will be deducted as your self-employed health insurance premiums. The remaining $1,980 of your premiums can be added to your other medical expenses for calculating your itemized deductions.

Who Is Self-Employed?

The self-employed health insurance deduction is available to these people:

➤ Sole owners of unincorporated businesses (proprietorships)

➤ Partners in partnerships

➤ LLC members who actively participate in the LLC business and are treated for tax purposes like partners

➤ Farmers who file on Schedule F

➤ Employee-shareholders of S corporations who own more than 2% of the S corporation stock

Red Flag

There is an income requirement for claiming the self-employed health insurance deduction. Unlike other income limitations, you can lose the deduction if you have too little income. You have to have enough taxable income from the business to cover your self-employed health insurance deduction.

If you are a more-than-2% shareholder of an S corporation, you are caught in a tax pickle. For all fringe benefits purposes, you are treated as a self-employed person. This means that the S corporation can't deduct your health insurance premiums, and you can't participate in a medical reimbursement plan or a cafeteria plan.

If an S corporation shareholder does receive health insurance benefits, the IRS has set these procedures in place to follow:

➤ The health insurance premiums paid by the corporation are included in the employee-shareholder's Form W-2 as taxable wages.

➤ The corporation takes a tax deduction for the insurance premium payments as wages (not as an employee benefit program).

➤ The employee-shareholder claims the self-employed health insurance deduction for a portion of the premiums (45% in 1998).

➤ The remaining premiums (55% in 1998) are claimed as a medical deduction on the Schedule A, Itemized Deductions.

Which Medical Premiums Qualify

To claim the self-employed health insurance premium deduction, you can't be eligible to participate in a subsidized health plan sponsored by your employer or your spouse's employer. In other words, you or your spouse can't be eligible to have any of your health insurance premiums paid by an employer.

For any month that you or your spouse could be covered by an employer-subsidized plan, you can't claim a deduction for your self-employed health insurance premiums. Even if you could be covered, but choose to opt out, you lose your self-employed health insurance premium deduction.

Phil, for example, is self-employed. For the first three months of 1998, his wife, Christy, was covered by her employer's health insurance plan. Christy's employer paid part of her health insurance premiums. Starting in April of 1998, Christy left her job and was no longer eligible for the subsidized health insurance coverage. Phil paid his own health insurance premiums through all of 1998. He can only claim the self-employed health insurance premiums for his coverage from April through December. Any premiums he can't deduct as self-employed health insurance premiums can be claimed with Phil and Christy's medical expenses if they itemize.

Medical Savings Accounts

The medical savings account is a new option for some self-employed people and employees of small businesses. An MSA is like an IRA, but is used to pay medical expenses.

You contribute money to your MSA fund. The earnings (interest, dividends, capital gains) of the fund are not taxed as long as the money stays in the MSA. When you need the funds to pay medical bills, you can withdraw money from your MSA tax-free.

The contributions you make to an MSA are deducted as an adjustment in arriving at adjusted gross income. It is an above-the-line deduction. You don't have to reduce your deduction by the 7.5% of AGI floor that applies to other medical expenses. To claim a deduction for your MSA contribution, you must complete Form 8853 and attach it to your tax return.

Medical savings accounts are available under a pilot program. The program is running from 1997 through the end of the year 2000. The number of people who can benefit from an MSA is limited to 750,000 during the test period. It is possible that the test period could be extended, but is currently scheduled to expire December 31, 2000.

Starting in 1999, another four-year pilot program will begin. It is for eligible seniors and is called MedicarePlus Choice MSAs. This program will run through the year 2002.

Who Can Use an MSA?

Self-employed people and employees of small businesses (fewer than 50 employees) can establish medical savings accounts.

Employers that are growing get a break. If your number of employees passes the 50-employee limit, you can continue to contribute to your MSA program. Once your work force reaches 200 people, you can finish out that year using MSAs. You will not be eligible to sponsor an MSA program the year after you have 200 employees.

Paper Trail

For more information about MSAs, read IRS Publication 969, Medical Savings Accounts.

To establish an MSA, you must be covered only by a high-deductible health plan. If you are an employee (rather than a self-employed person), your health insurance must be provided through an employer-sponsored policy.

A high deductible policy is one with an annual deductible between $1,500 and $2,250 for an individual policy and between $3,000 and $4,500 for a family policy. The annual out-of-pocket expenses under your health insurance plan cannot exceed $3,000 for single coverage and $5,500 for family coverage.

If you are eligible to get your health insurance through an employer-sponsored cafeteria plan, you can't have an MSA.

Contributions to Your MSA

Either you or your employer can make contributions to your MSA. If your employer makes the contribution, it is a tax-free benefit. You won't claim the deduction on your tax return. The payment won't be included on your W-2 as taxable wages.

If you make the contribution to your MSA, you can claim a deduction for the contribution. The deduction is claimed on page one of your tax return.

Your annual contributions to an MSA cannot be more than:

➤ 65% of your deductible under a single health insurance policy

➤ 75% of your deductible under a family health insurance policy

Red Flag

In any one year, you can only have MSA contributions from you or your employer. You can't both make contributions to your MSA in one calendar year.

If you contribute too much to your MSA for a year, you are subject to a 6% excise tax on the excess contributions. There is a remedy, though. You can avoid the excise tax if you withdraw the excess contribution (including investment income it has earned) by the filing date, including extensions, for your tax return.

For example, Lucinda contributed too much to her MSA in 1998. She only went over her allowed contribution by $50. Lucinda will be filing her 1998 tax return by April 15, 1999. Lucinda can avoid the 6% excise tax if she takes all of the following steps:

➤ Withdraws $50 from the MSA by April 15, 1999.

➤ Withdraws the interest earned on the $50. The earnings will probably be less than $2 on the excess contribution.

➤ Includes the interest income that is withdrawn from the MSA on her 1999 tax return.

➤ Lucinda will not claim a 1998 tax deduction for the $50 excess contribution and she will not report the withdrawal in 1999 as taxable income.

How to Use Your MSA Funds

Distributions from your MSA that are used to pay qualified medical expenses are tax-free. MSA sponsors provide different methods by which you can reach your MSA funds. You might be able to write checks off of your MSA so that payments can be made directly from the MSA for your medical bills. Some plans even use MSA debit cards that you can use to pay your doctor, hospital, or pharmacist.

Qualified medical expenses include any medical bills for which you could claim an itemized deduction. The medical expense cannot be reimbursed by any other health insurance or medical reimbursement plan.

Doctor and dentist visits, for example, are deductible medical expenses. These bills can be paid from an MSA. Cosmetic surgery, on the other hand, is not deductible, so it can't be paid from an MSA. Chapter 6, "When You Need More Than an Apple a Day," has a complete discussion of deductible medical expenses.

In general, qualified medical expenses for MSA withdrawals don't include your health insurance premiums. The following premiums do, however, qualify for payment out of your MSA:

➤ Long-term care insurance

➤ COBRA continuation coverage

➤ Health insurance coverage while you are receiving unemployment compensation

If you pay a medical bill out of your MSA, you won't be able to claim a deduction for that same medical expense. The itemized deduction for medical expenses can only be taken for medical bills that are not reimbursed by any medical plan. Your MSA reimbursement will knock out the deduction. This isn't a bad result, though, because your MSA contribution was deducted already and the earnings have grown tax-free.

If you make a distribution from your MSA that is not for the payment of qualified medical expenses, you will have to pay income tax on the distribution. You will also pay a 15% penalty in addition to your income tax. The penalty is 15% of the amount that you withdrew from the MSA but did not spend on qualified medical expenses.

You can avoid the 15% penalty tax on distributions if you meet one of these three tests:

➤ You are age 65 or older when the distribution is made from your MSA.

➤ The MSA distribution is made after your death.

➤ The MSA distribution is made after you become disabled.

Investing Your MSA Funds

You can set up your MSA at a bank, insurance company, or other financial institution. The financial institution will be the trustee or the custodian of your account.

You won't have many choices for investing your MSA funds when you start your account. Your account's trustee or custodian will tell you how the funds will be invested. Most likely, your funds will earn interest like a savings account would.

There is a new opportunity in 1998, though. Once your account reaches $3,500, you can transfer your MSA to a self-directed investment sub-account.

Your Decoder Ring

If you leave your job, you might be able to continue your health insurance coverage (at your expense) for an interim period of time. This is known as **COBRA** coverage. If you are eligible for COBRA coverage, your employer has to give you notice of your COBRA rights. The term COBRA comes from the tax bill that established COBRA rights. The tax bill was the Consolidated Omnibus Budget Reconciliation Act.

Paper Trail

If you want to move money from one MSA to another, you have 60 days to make the move. You can withdraw the money from one MSA, and as long as you put the money into your new MSA within 60 days, you will avoid income tax on the rollover. You can only conduct one rollover per year.

Special MSA Advantages

If you can't take advantage of employer-sponsored medical plans, it is worth checking out an MSA. Medical savings accounts have some benefits that other medical plans don't offer. The advantages of the MSA include:

➤ The MSA is your account. The account is in your name and is owned by you. Unlike cafeteria plans, you will never risk forfeiting the funds in your account.

➤ When you die, your fund will be paid out to your beneficiary.

➤ If you change jobs, you take your MSA with you.

➤ The earnings of your MSA will not be taxed as your fund accumulates. If the fund is used to pay for qualifying medical expenses, you never pay income taxes on your MSA earning.

➤ Your MSA funds are available to you at any time.

➤ Your funds can be distributed penalty-free after age 65 or after you are disabled.

➤ You can save money on your health insurance premiums by buying a high-deductible medical insurance policy.

➤ An MSA can be transferred tax-free to your former spouse under a divorce decree or legal separation agreement.

Your Decoder Ring

It is desirable to have **portable benefits**. A portable benefit is one that you can take with you when you leave your job. An MSA is a portable benefit because the account is in your own name.

The Least You Need to Know

➤ A self-employed person can deduct 45% of health insurance premiums even if he or she doesn't claim itemized deductions.

➤ If you own more than 2% of an S corporation for which you work, you can take the self-employed health insurance premium deduction.

➤ Medical savings accounts can be used by self-employed individuals and employees of small businesses.

➤ To use a medical savings account, you must be covered by a high-deductible health insurance policy.

➤ Your medical savings account belongs to you, so you can take it with you if you change jobs.

Chapter 20

Workers on the Go: Deducting Your Moving Expenses

In This Chapter

➤ Deducting the cost of moving to a new home

➤ Sorting out which expenses qualify for the moving expense deduction

➤ Dealing with state taxes in the year that you move

➤ Reporting the sale of your house on your tax return

If you move, you might be able to claim a tax deduction for your moving expenses.

This deduction has been moved around itself over the last few years. Moving expenses used to be an adjustment in calculating adjusted gross income (above-the-line). They were then moved to the itemized deduction schedule (below-the-line). Now moving expenses are once again an above-the-line deduction.

If you remember claiming moving deductions the last time that you moved, things might have changed a bit since then. You used to be able to deduct temporary living expenses and the cost of selling your old home or buying your new home. These expenses are no longer deductible.

There used to be dollar limitations for certain types of moving expenses. We no longer have the dollar limitations either.

The moving expense deduction today is fairly streamlined. The most critical facet of the deduction is figuring out if you qualify for the deduction at all.

Paper Trail

Be sure to report your change of address to the IRS. File Form 8822, Change of Address, with the IRS Service Center for your old address. The addresses for the IRS Service Centers are on the back of Form 8822.

Qualifying for the Moving Expense Deduction

Your moving expenses are only deductible if you work at your new location. Both employees and self-employed people can take the moving expense deduction. If you move after retirement and don't take work at your new location, you can't deduct your moving expenses.

It just wouldn't be a proper tax rule if there weren't exceptions to the rule. It should then come as no surprise that some retirees can claim moving expenses after retirement:

➤ If you are a member of the Armed Forces moving from your last post of duty to your home in the United States, your moving expenses can be deducted.

➤ If you are a retiree who lived and worked outside the United States, you can deduct your move back into the States after permanent retirement.

➤ You can deduct moving expenses if you are the surviving spouse or dependent of a person whose main job location was outside the United States at the time of his or her death. You must begin your move within six months after the death.

You don't need to have a new job lined up before your move to deduct your moving expenses. You can deduct your move if you find work after you have moved to your new location. You don't need to have a new employer to deduct your move, either. If you are transferred to a new location and still work for the same company, you can qualify to deduct your move.

You can deduct moving expenses if you were unemployed before your move. You do need to start working at a new job in enough time to meet the time test explained later in this chapter.

There are two tests that you must meet to deduct your moving expenses. You must meet both a distance test and a time test. The distance test is a measure of how far away you moved. The time test is a measure of how long you worked in your new location after the move.

The Distance Test: Little Moves Don't Count

The moving expense deduction is supposed to be used by people who move because they change jobs. To prevent people from deducting moving expenses when they just change homes (not jobs) the distance test was put in place.

To meet the distance test, your new job location must be at least 50 miles farther from your old home than your old job location was from your old home. Let's do an example.

Gracie takes a new job. She is planning to move to a new home because of the job change. Gracie's old home was 10 miles from her old job location. Her new job is 65 miles from her old home. Gracie's new job is 55 miles farther away from her old home than her old job was (65 miles minus 10 miles). Gracie has met the distance requirement for claiming her moving expenses.

Resto, on the other hand, is also planning a move. Resto's old house was 55 miles from his old job. When he changes jobs, he will be working in a town that is 100 miles away from his old job. His new job location is 75 miles from his old house. Since the distance between Resto's old house and his new job (75 miles) is not more than 50 miles greater than the distance from his old job to his old house (55 miles), Resto can't deduct his moving expenses.

Paper Trail

Members of the Armed Forces get a break. If they move because of a permanent change of station, they do not have to meet either the distance test or the time test.

The Time Test: You Have to Stick to Your Job

To deduct your moving expenses, you have to work full-time at your new job location for 39 weeks of the 12 months after your move.

If you are self-employed, you have to meet two time tests:

Paper Trail

If you don't have a job before you move, how do you do the distance test? You can measure the distance from your old home to your new job. If the distance is at least 50 miles, you have met the distance test.

➤ You must work full-time 39 weeks during the first 12 months after your move.
➤ You must also work full-time in your new location 78 weeks during the first 24 months after your move.

There are legitimate excuses for not meeting the time test. If you don't pass the time test for any of the following reasons, you can still meet your time test:

➤ Your death
➤ Disability
➤ Termination from your job for a reason other than willful misconduct
➤ Transfer to another job location for your employer's benefit

When you file your tax return for 1998, you might not have yet met your time test. What should you do? You have three choices:

➤ You can claim the moving expense deduction on your 1998 tax return. If you end up not meeting the time test, you will have to file an amended return to remove the moving expenses.

➤ You can file your 1998 tax return without the moving expense deduction. Once you have met the time test, you can file an amended return to claim your moving expenses.

➤ You could obtain an extension of time to file your 1998 tax return. This will give you additional time to determine if you meet the time test.

Your Decoder Ring

What is an **amended return**? You have up to three years from the filing date of your tax return to make a change to the return. You make the change by filing an amended tax return. For individuals, an amended tax return is filed using Form 1040X. There is a space on the return to explain why you are amending the return. It is helpful to be specific and thorough in your explanation. Don't forget to amend your state return, too.

Which Moving Expenses Are Deductible

There are a lot of expenses involved in moving from one place to another. You won't be able to deduct all of your expenses, but here are the ones you can:

➤ The cost of moving your possessions to your new home

➤ The cost of traveling from your old house to the new house

The cost of moving your possessions can include:

➤ Payments to a moving company to pack and move the things in your house

➤ Renting a moving truck or van

➤ Shipping your possessions to your new home

➤ Shipping your pets to your new home

➤ Storing and insuring your possessions (only for 30 days after they are removed from your old home)

The cost of traveling to your new house includes:

➤ Ten cents per mile for each car that you drive from the old house to the new house

➤ Instead of mileage, actual expenses of transporting your car to the new house

➤ Lodging for you and your family if you have to spend the night along the way to your new home (meals aren't deductible, though)

➤ Lodging on the day of the move because your furniture isn't in your new house yet

You can't claim a deduction for:

➤ House hunting trips

➤ Temporary living expenses

➤ Meals

➤ Utility deposits

➤ Security deposits

➤ Lease expenses

➤ Expenses to clean or repair your old home or your new home

➤ Costs of selling your old home (commissions, fees, etc.)

➤ Costs of buying your new home

If Your Employer Pays

Some employers will pay your moving expenses as an enticement. They want you to accept the job offer or accept the transfer to a new location. Your employer might pay your expenses directly or might reimburse you for the moving expenses that you had to pay.

If your employer pays for a moving expense that you could claim as a tax deduction, you have received a tax-free benefit. Laura's employer, for example, pays the cost of her moving van when she is relocated to another state. Since Laura could have deducted the cost of the moving van, she has received a tax-free benefit. Laura won't be able to get a double benefit, though. She can't claim a deduction for the moving expenses that her employer paid.

Paper Trail

Moving expenses are claimed on Form 3903. Use Form 3903 to calculate your deduction and enter the moving expense deduction on page one of your tax return.

If your employer pays for an expense that you can't deduct, you have received a taxable fringe benefit. The payment for your expenses will show up on your W-2 in your taxable wages. In Laura's example, her employer also paid her realtor's commission when she sold her old home. Expenses of selling your home are not deductible as moving expenses. Laura will have to pay income tax on the amount of commissions paid by her employer.

State Taxes on the Move

For most people, calculating the federal tax deduction for moving expenses isn't too difficult. Once you know that you meet the time and distance tests, you have to add up your moving expenses. You fill out the Form 3903 and you have your moving expense deduction. Keeping papers organized after a move so you know where to find the moving bills can be the greatest challenge of the process.

If you moved across state lines, the real fun begins when you prepare your state tax return. Unless you are lucky enough to be moving between two states that have no state income taxes, you have some work ahead of you. You will quickly learn that you can't file the same state tax forms that you filed in the past. Most states require a part-year tax return be filed in the year that you move out of the state. Your new state might also require a part-year tax return for the year that you move into your new state.

Red Flag

If you own rental property in your old state, your state filing responsibilities are not over. You will still have to report the rent income to your old state. A nonresident tax return will be used to report the rent income. There are agreements between states that help avoid double-taxation by giving credit for taxes paid to the other state.

Knowing how to approach this task might help. Here are a few pointers:

➤ Start early. You will need forms and instructions. They might take time to get.

➤ Call both states' revenue departments and request their part-year resident state tax forms and instruction booklets.

➤ Read each state's instruction booklet to know how you should complete your tax return.

➤ Remember that the two state returns might not add up to your federal tax return. The states' rules might be different enough that the two halves won't equal the whole.

➤ If this isn't your cup of tea, have someone prepare your tax returns for you. It costs more to do part-year returns, but it can be well worth the fee.

Selling Your House

If you have moved, you have probably sold your home. The tax rules for home sales are now very easy. Under old rules (before May 7, 1997), you could avoid paying tax on the gain from selling your home if you bought a more expensive home than the one you sold. This tax rule encouraged people to trade up to a more expensive home with each move.

For homes sold after May 6, 1997, we have new tax rules. If you owned and lived in your home two of the last five years, you can exclude $250,000 of gain. If you are married, you can exclude up to $500,000 of gain. This gain exclusion can be used once every two years.

You can exclude your gain on the sale of your home even if you don't buy a new house. You don't have to buy up to a more expensive home like the old tax rules required. These new rules truly simplified the taxes when you sell your home.

If you were in your old home for less than two years because of a job-related move, your health, or other unforeseen circumstances, you can exclude a portion of your gain.

Michele, for example, was transferred to a new job location. She bought her house only six months ago. When she sells her home, she won't meet the two-year ownership and occupancy test. She was only in her home $1/4$ of the two-year required time period. Since Michele's move was job-related, she can use $1/4$ of her $250,000 gain exclusion amount. If her gain is less than $62,500 ($1/4$ of $250,000), Michele will pay no income tax on her home sale gain.

When you calculate the gain on the sale of your house, count up all of your expenses and home improvements. Realtor's commissions when you bought your house are part of the cost of your old home. Improvements that you made to your home are part of the home's cost. These expenses and improvements will reduce your gain.

Red Flag

If you are lucky enough to have a gain over $250,000 ($500,000 if you're married), there are no tax relief provisions for you. You'll have to pay tax on the gain over $250,000 (or $500,000). The good news is that the highest capital gains tax rate is 20%. Double-check your home improvements if you have a big gain. Improvements can slice your taxable gain.

Even if your home sale gain is tax-free, you still have to report the sale to the IRS. Use Form 2119 to calculate and report your gain. The Form 2119 needs to be attached to your tax return in the year that you sell your home.

The Least You Need to Know

➤ If you meet a distance test and a time test, you can deduct the cost of moving your household goods and personal effects.

➤ You can deduct moving expenses if you are self-employed or if you are an employee.

➤ If you move to another state, you might have to file a part-year state tax return in both your old state and your new state.

➤ When you sell your home, $250,000 of gain from selling your house can be tax-free. If you are married, you can exclude up to $500,000 of gain.

➤ You have to own and live in your house for two of the last five years to exclude the gain on the sale of your home.

Chapter 21

Alimony

In This Chapter

➤ Identifying payments that qualify as alimony

➤ Deducting alimony that you have paid

➤ Reporting alimony that you have received

➤ Paying back the tax benefits of alimony

Divorce brings a host of issues that must be dealt with. Income taxes are just one of those issues. Income taxes, though, do have the power to motivate people to take actions they might not otherwise take. In divorce proceedings, income taxes often play a significant role.

In the best of circumstances, the couple would negotiate a property settlement and determine their continuing financial obligations to each other in a mutually beneficial manner. Divorces are seldom negotiated under the best of circumstances, however. Unfortunately, what is helpful to one person may be detrimental to the other. A payment structure that will save one spouse taxes will often cost the other spouse taxes.

1984 was a pivotal year for divorce tax rules. The playing field was completely changed. After 1984, property settlements in divorce or legal separation became tax-free. Neither the husband nor the wife will recognize taxable income or loss because of a property settlement. This greatly simplifies the negotiation process.

Child support payments are also tax-free. The person receiving child support doesn't pay income tax on the payments. The person making the payments isn't able to take a tax deduction for the child support.

Alimony is another story. The person who pays alimony can take a tax deduction for his or her alimony payments. The person who receives alimony has to pay income tax on the alimony payments. This clearly creates potential for adversarial negotiations.

Paper Trail

To read about alimony for pre-1985 divorces, see IRS Publication 504, Divorced or Separated Individuals.

In this chapter, we're going to talk about the alimony rules for divorces or legal separations after 1984.

Before we begin our discussion of what qualifies as alimony, it's important to mention that we're talking in this book about the tax rules only. Some states' laws do not provide for alimony payments. It is still possible for divorcees in those states to negotiate payments that qualify as alimony under the income tax laws. Your state might call your payments property settlement, but if they meet the tax definition of alimony, you will be able to take the alimony deduction.

Alimony: Which Payments Can Be Deducted

To be considered alimony, a payment must be made under a divorce or separation instrument. The following are examples of instruments that qualify:

➤ A divorce decree

➤ A decree of separate maintenance

➤ A written instrument incident to a decree of divorce or separate maintenance

➤ A written separation agreement

➤ A court order or decree that requires you to make payments for the support or maintenance of the other spouse (including temporary decrees, interlocutory decrees, and temporary alimony decrees, called decrees of alimony *pendente lite*)

Payments made under a divorce or separation instrument will be treated as alimony for tax purposes if they meet all of the following requirements. These requirements apply to divorce or separation instruments executed after 1984:

➤ The payments are in cash.

➤ Your divorce decree or separation agreement doesn't say that the payments are not alimony.

➤ You aren't living in the same household as your former spouse.

➤ Your payments (of cash or property) stop when your former spouse dies.

➤ The payments are not treated as child support.

Alimony doesn't have to be paid directly to your former spouse. Cash payments to other people for your former spouse's benefit can qualify as alimony. The payments are treated as if you paid the cash to your former spouse, and then your former spouse paid the other person. Payments that might be made to third parties include the following:

Red Flag

You might have to make alimony payments before you are divorced. If you want to deduct your alimony, you can't file a joint income tax return with your spouse. You must file separately.

➤ Medical bills paid directly to the doctor, hospital, or pharmacy for your former spouse

➤ Housing costs that you pay for your former spouse (rent, utilities)

➤ Taxes that you pay for your former spouse

➤ Tuition that you pay for your former spouse

➤ Payment of life insurance premiums for policies that are owned by your former spouse

If you don't want payments to be treated as alimony, you and your former spouse can agree to this in your divorce or separation agreement. If you agree to treat the payments as not being alimony, you can't deduct the payments you make to your former spouse. Your former spouse won't include the payments as income on his or her tax return.

The alimony rules will prevent you from living with your former spouse and treating your payments as alimony. Even if you live in a separate part of the home, if you are in the same household, your alimony payments won't be deductible. This rule prevents people from taking advantage of the alimony deduction rules for tax gain while still living together.

If you have to continue making payments after your former spouse dies, none of your payments are alimony. Even the payments before death are not alimony.

Let's say, for example, that Richard has to pay his ex-wife $10,000 a year for 15 years after their divorce. If his ex-wife dies, the remaining payments have to be made to their children. Since the payments can continue after his ex-wife's death, Richard's payments are not alimony. None of Richard's payments (even the ones before death) are deductible as alimony because the payment structure fails the alimony test.

Richard can't deduct any of the payments even if his wife lives more than 15 years. Even though his wife lived long enough that the payments didn't stop, it won't change the fact that the structure of his payments failed the "stop at death" test.

Some divorce agreements can get complicated. There might be payments that stop at death and other payments that continue after death. If you have this type of an arrangement, part of your payments might not be treated as alimony.

Paper Trail

Believe it or not, people do crazy things to save taxes. They divorce just before year-end to file as single tax-payers only to remarry the next year. They divorce to claim alimony deductions but still live together as husband and wife. As the IRS identifies these abuses, Congress plugs up the holes in the Tax Code. That's partly why taxes are so complicated. We all have to live with the consequences.

Pat, for example, is paying $30,000 a year to his ex-wife. The divorce decree provides that the payments will stop after 15 years. If Pat's ex-wife dies within that 15-year period, Pat has to continue making payments of $20,000 a year to a trust set up for his children. Pat's payments are treated as two separate payment streams.

$20,000 per year will be paid for the entire 15-year period. Even if Pat's ex-wife dies, the $20,000 payments continue. None of the $20,000 payments will be deductible alimony.

$10,000 per year will only be paid as long as Pat's ex-wife is alive. This portion of his payments satisfies the "stop at death" requirement to be deductible alimony. Pat can deduct $10,000 a year as alimony.

Any payment that is called child support in your agreement or decree is not deductible. There are also payments that might be treated as child support. If your payments are reduced because of events that relate to your child, they will be treated as child support.

Barb, for example, has to make payments to her ex-husband of $500 a month for the next eight years, and $250 a month for years nine and 10. Barb has two sons who live with her ex-husband. The sons are ages 10 and eight. Since half of Barb's payments are eliminated when the older son turns 18 and the remaining payments end when the younger son turns 18, the payments will be treated as nondeductible child support.

To figure out if your payments are really child support rather than alimony, the IRS will look for changes in your payments that relate to events in your child's life. Payments that change when the following events occur in your child's life are likely to be treated as child support:

➤ Reaching a certain age

➤ Dying

➤ Marrying

➤ Leaving school or graduating from school

➤ Leaving the household

➤ Becoming employed

These can be very difficult standards to measure. How can you prove that a change in your payments is not a result of an event in your child's life? The payment change could be a coincidence of timing. If the payments could appear to be child support, but they really aren't, you need to be prepared. You need to be able to show that there was another reason for the payments changing at the time that they changed. You need to demonstrate that a change in your child's life has nothing to do with the change in your payments.

You won't be able to explain away a reduction in payments that is within six months of your child's reaching age 18, age 21, or the local age of majority. You also can't explain away reductions that happen in stair steps when your children reach ages between 18 and 24 (like in the example of Barb above).

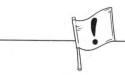

Red Flag

Negotiating alimony is a tricky business. A good divorce attorney who specializes in family law matters will know if your payments will be alimony or not.

House Expenses: How to Treat Them

You might still own a home jointly with your spouse after you are legally separated or after your divorce is final. If you still own the home jointly, you might have to pay the costs of maintaining the home. Some of your payments to maintain the house might qualify as deductible alimony.

You might have to make all of the mortgage payments on a home that is owned jointly with your former spouse. If so, you have two tax deductions:

➤ You can deduct half of the mortgage interest as an itemized deduction on Schedule A.

➤ You can deduct half of the payments (principal and interest) as alimony.

Your former spouse must report the alimony income (half of the mortgage payments) on his or her tax return. Your spouse can also deduct half of the mortgage interest as an itemized deduction on Schedule A.

Real estate taxes and insurance on your home are handled a bit differently. The income tax treatment depends on the type of joint ownership that you have.

Joint ownership can take different forms. You can own property as tenants in common. This means that each of you can sell your half interest to someone else. On death, your half of the property goes to whomever you name in your will. If your home is owned jointly as tenants in common and you have to pay all of the real estate taxes and insurance, you can deduct half of the taxes and insurance as alimony. The other half of the real estate taxes will be deducted as an itemized deduction. The other half of the insurance isn't deductible at all.

You might own the home as tenants by the entirety or as joint tenants. In these cases, your former spouse would receive the house automatically on your death and vice

Your Decoder Ring

The different types of **joint owner-ship** (tenants in common, tenants by the entirety) are legal terms rather than tax terms. Your attorney can tell you the type of ownership you have by knowing your state law and examining your deed. Don't make assumptions about ownership. Check it out with your attorney.

versa. This is called having *rights of survivorship*. If this is how you own your home, you will deduct all of your real estate taxes as an itemized deduction. You won't be able to take a deduction at all for the insurance that you pay on the house. You won't claim any of your payment of real estate taxes or insurance as alimony.

Payments You Can't Deduct

Certain payments that you make to your former spouse are never considered alimony. Alimony does not include any of the following payments:

➤ Child support

➤ Noncash property settlements

➤ Payments that are for your former spouse's part of community income

➤ The use of property (the right to live in your home, for example)

➤ Payments to maintain property that belongs to you

None of the payments listed above can be deducted on your tax return. You might get the short end of the stick on the property settlement. It doesn't matter for your income taxes. You can't claim a loss for an unequal property settlement.

If you receive property in your divorce, you will pick up the old cost basis in the assets. Be sure that you get the records that you need to support your basis.

Evangeline, for example, will receive a portfolio of stocks as a property settlement in her divorce. When Evangeline sells one of these investments, she will calculate her capital gain or loss using the original purchase price for the investment. The value placed on the investments for the property settlement won't have any bearing on Evangeline's taxable gain or loss. She will want to be sure to secure the records that support her basis in the investments. Obtaining the records at a later date could be difficult.

Deducting Alimony You Paid

You don't have to itemize your deductions to claim alimony. The deduction for alimony is taken in arriving at your adjusted gross income (above-the-line).

On page one of the Form 1040, there is a line for your alimony deduction in the adjusted gross income section of the tax return. You can't file a Form 1040A or a Form 1040EZ if you deduct alimony.

When you deduct alimony, you have to enter your former spouse's Social Security number on the tax return. If you are paying alimony to more than one person, you will need to attach a separate schedule showing the name, Social Security number, and alimony paid to each of your former spouses.

Reporting Alimony You Received

If you receive taxable alimony, you must include the alimony on your tax return. There is a line on page one of the Form 1040 to report your alimony income.

You need to attach a statement to your tax return that includes the Social Security number of the person who paid the alimony to you. If you don't disclose the Social Security number, you could be fined $50.

Red Flag

If you don't report your former spouse's Social Security number to the IRS on your tax return, you may have to pay a $50 penalty, and your alimony deduction can be disallowed.

Guess what the IRS does with all of these Social Security numbers? It tries to match up the information. The IRS compares the alimony deductions to the reported alimony income. If your former spouse deducts alimony paid to you, the IRS will make sure that you reported the alimony income. If you and your former spouse disagree as to how the payments should be treated for tax purposes, you could end up with the IRS involved.

You should resolve the tax treatment of alimony payments as part of your divorce proceedings. Don't leave this issue for later.

Paying Back Your Tax Benefits

Property settlements in divorces are ripe for tax abuse. Alimony is deductible, but property settlements are not. Why not rearrange the payments for your property settlement so that the payments look like alimony? Sounds like a good plan, right?

Congress was afraid that the temptation to restructure property settlements to look like alimony would be pretty strong. Because of this fear, an anti-abuse provision was added to the Tax Code.

Paper Trail

Dependency exemptions should also be resolved during your divorce proceedings. If the custodial parent is going to release the exemption to the other parent, get this resolved and get the proper forms signed. We discussed dependency exemptions in Chapter 2, "Personal Exemptions."

The anti-abuse provision requires you to recapture alimony payments that don't pass muster. If your alimony decreases during the first three years, you might trigger the recapture rules.

You will have to recapture alimony in the third year if the alimony you paid in either the second year or the third year decreases by more than $15,000 from the prior year. There is probably no simple way to explain the recapture rules, but an illustration might help.

The alimony paid during the first three years of divorce is as follows:

Year 1	$60,000
Year 2	$40,000
Year 3	$20,000

Alimony Recapture Calculation

1. Alimony paid in 2nd year		$40,000	
2. Alimony paid in 3rd year	$20,000		
3. Floor	$15,000		
4. Add lines 2 and 3		$35,000	
5. Subtract line 4 from line 1			$5,000
6. Alimony paid in 1st year		$60,000	
7. Adjusted alimony paid in 2nd year (line 1 less line 5)	$35,000		
8. Alimony paid in 3rd year	$20,000		
9. Add lines 7 and 8	$55,000		
10. Divide line 9 by 2	$27,500		
11. Floor	$15,000		
12. Add lines 10 and 11		$42,500	
13. Subtract line 12 from line 6			$17,500
14. Recaptured alimony (add lines 5 and 13)			**$22,500**

You might have to recapture alimony if your payments are reduced or terminated for any of the following reasons:

➤ A failure to make the payments

➤ A change in your divorce decree or separation agreement

➤ Your spouse has less need for support

➤ You are not able to provide the support

The alimony recapture is calculated in the third calendar year that you make payments. When you do the calculation, you don't have to include the following payments:

➤ Payments made under a temporary support order

➤ Payments that are a fixed part of your income

➤ Payments that are reduced or stopped because of your former spouse's death or remarriage

Let's say, for example, that you have to pay your ex-spouse $24,000 a year until he remarries or dies. He remarries two years after you were divorced, so you don't have to make any alimony payments in year three. Clearly, your payments have reduced by more than $15,000. Since the reduction in payments is a result of his remarriage, though, you don't have to recapture your alimony deductions.

Your Decoder Ring

Recapture is a tax term. To take away the tax benefit you got from a tax deduction in a prior year, you may have to recapture the deduction by including it as income on a later return. For alimony, you might have deducted alimony on your previous tax return. To recapture the alimony, you would include it as taxable income on your current year's tax return.

If you have to recapture alimony that you paid, you will include it on the alimony income line on page one of your tax return. Include your former spouse's name and Social Security number and write in the word *recapture* on the line of the tax return.

If you are receiving alimony that has to be recaptured, you have a deduction coming. You will claim the deduction on the Alimony Paid line of the Form 1040. Write *recapture* on the line and enter your former spouse's Social Security number.

The Least You Need to Know

➤ Alimony payments are deductible. Property settlements and child support payments can't be deducted.

➤ If you receive alimony, you have to include the alimony in your taxable income. Property settlements and child support payments will be tax-free to you.

➤ Deductible alimony payments have to be made in cash.

➤ Deductible alimony payments have to stop when your former spouse dies.

➤ If your alimony payments drop in amount during the second and third years by more than $15,000, you might have to recapture some of your alimony payments.

Self-Employment Tax

In This Chapter

➤ Determining if you have to pay self-employment tax

➤ Calculating your self-employment tax

➤ Reporting your self-employment tax on your tax return

➤ Deducting part of your self-employment tax

All workers in the United States have to pay into the Social Security system. If you are an employee, your Social Security taxes are withheld from your pay. Your employer matches your Social Security taxes dollar for dollar.

Your Social Security taxes pay for a host of benefits. Since you have to pay into the system, you will be able to enjoy the benefits if and when you need them. The benefits provided by your Social Security taxes include the following:

➤ Old age and retirement benefits

➤ Disability benefits

➤ Survivor benefits

➤ Medicare benefits

If you are self-employed, you don't have a paycheck from which Social Security taxes can be withheld. You also don't have an employer to pay your Social Security match. It is your responsibility to pay all of your own Social Security taxes. The tax that you will pay is called the *self-employment tax*.

Your Decoder Ring

Your Social Security taxes actually have two parts. Your **FICA** taxes pay old age, disability, and survivor benefits. Your **Medicare** taxes pay for hospitalization insurance under the Medicare system.

If you have to pay self-employment tax, you will be able to claim a deduction for half of your self-employment tax. Your deduction is not an itemized deduction. Your deduction is an adjustment in arriving at your adjusted gross income.

Do You Have to Pay Self-Employment Tax?

There are two parts to determining if you have to pay self-employment tax:

> ➤ First, you have to earn the type of income that is taxable for self-employment tax.

> ➤ Second, you have to be in the type of business structure that will cause you to be considered self-employed for tax purposes.

We'll cover each of these requirements separately. Remember that you must have both the type of income and the type of business structure that will cause you to be subject to self-employment tax.

Defining Self-Employment Income

Self-employment income, in general, is the fruit of your own labor. Since there are many different ways that you can earn income, there are many different types of self-employment income.

You will pay self-employment tax on the following types of income:

> ➤ Net income from your sole proprietorship

> ➤ Fees received by you for services that you performed

> ➤ Fees for serving on a corporation's board of directors

> ➤ Your share of partnership trade or business income

> ➤ Guaranteed payments received from your partnership that are for services that you performed

> ➤ Commissions paid to insurance agents

> ➤ Commissions paid to retired insurance agents that are based on a percentage of commissions earned before retirement

> ➤ Payments to retired insurance agents that are based on renewal or deferred commissions

> ➤ Wages received by a church employee who earns $108.28 or more in a year and does not have Social Security taxes withheld from his or her pay

You will not pay self-employment tax on the following types of

➤ Investment income (interest and dividends)

➤ Rent income from real estate

➤ Capital gains

➤ Pension or profit sharing plan distributions

➤ IRA distributions

➤ Social Security benefits

➤ Renewal commissions paid to the survivor of an insurance agent

➤ Retirement benefits earned by clergy (including rental value of parsonage allowance)

These lists don't cover all of the types of income that you might earn. In general, though, if you are not an employee and you receive income in exchange for services, the earnings will probably be subject to self-employment tax. There are special exemptions and exclusions, so it is worth checking out your own special circumstance. Check with a tax professional if you have an unusual or difficult situation. Self-employment taxes are expensive. You want to be sure that you have reached the appropriate conclusion.

Red Flag

If you receive a 1099–Misc for fees that you receive, the IRS will look for self-employment tax (Schedule SE). If you don't calculate the self-employment tax, the IRS will send you a notice requiring either payment or an explanation.

People Who Have to Pay Self-Employment Tax

If you have business income that is not earned as an employee, you might be subject to self-employment tax. You don't have to work full-time to be subject to self-employment tax. Part-time work is subject to self-employment tax just like full-time work.

Retirees who have self-employment income also have to pay self-employment tax. Even if you are drawing Social Security benefits, you still have to pay into the system if you have self-employment income.

The following types of business owners have to pay self-employment tax on their business income:

➤ Sole proprietors

➤ Partners in partnerships that engage in trade or business

➤ Farmers

Limited partners don't pay self-employment tax on their share of the partnership's income. A limited partner, by definition, is not engaged in the trade or business of the partnership.

S corporation shareholder doesn't pay self-employment tax on his or her share of the trade or business income of the corporation. If the shareholder receives fees for rendering services to the corporation, though, the fees are subject to self-employment tax.

For example, Jenna owns a 20% interest in an S corporation. In 1998, Jenna's share of the S corporation earnings is $25,000. Jenna also received a $3,000 fee for serving on the S corporation's board of directors. Both the $25,000 share of the S corporation earnings and the $3,000 director's fee are taxable income to Jenna and will be reported on her Form 1040. The $25,000 S corporation income is not subject to self-employment tax, but Jenna will pay self-employment tax on the $3,000 director's fee.

A *limited liability company* (LLC) member might have to pay self-employment tax on his or her share of the LLC earnings. It will depend on the involvement of the LLC member. The IRS and Congress are having a hard time dealing with LLC members and their self-employment tax responsibilities. We should see some clarification in the next couple of years. If you have questions about your particular position in an LLC and whether self-employment tax applies, you should seek professional tax advice.

Your Decoder Ring

A **limited liability company** (LLC) is a type of business entity. The LLC owners, called members, have liability protection like corporate shareholders have. The LLC is treated for tax purposes like a partnership. Each member will pay tax on his or her share of the LLC's income. An LLC member will receive a Schedule K-1 informing the LLC member what to report on his or her personal tax return.

Need a Break? Who Won't Have to Pay SE Tax

There are some self-employed people who don't have to pay self-employment taxes. There are special provisions in the tax laws that give them a break. We all need a break every now and then.

People who don't have to pay self-employment tax include:

➤ A self-employed person with self-employment income of $400 or less

➤ A newspaper carrier or vendor who is under age 18

➤ A notary public

➤ Certain clergy and certain church employees

➤ An owner of farm ground who uses sharecroppers or rents the ground to farmers

➤ Certain executors or personal representatives of estates

➤ A former insurance salesperson who meets certain requirements

➤ Certain public officials

Fitting into one of these categories doesn't blanket all of your income in self-employment tax immunity. You can't avoid self-employment tax on income from director's fees by becoming a notary public, for example. Only the notary public fee income is covered by the self-employment tax exemption.

A member of a religious order who has taken a vow of poverty is automatically exempt from self-employment tax. Other clergy can be exempt from self-employment tax if they file Form 4361, Application From Self-Employment Tax for Use by Ministers, Members of Religious Orders, and Christian Science Practitioners. Unless these exemptions are met, a clergy member will have to pay self-employment tax on his or her earnings.

Paper Trail

If you are an employee, you don't pay self-employment tax on your wages. Instead, you have Social Security taxes withheld from your pay. Even if you are an employee, though, you can still have to pay self-employment taxes from other sources.

You might be a church employee, but not a member of clergy. If your church has elected to be exempt from Social Security and Medicare taxes, you do not have to pay self-employment tax if your annual earnings are less than $108.28 for the year. If you earn $108.28 or more for the year, you will have to pay self-employment tax on your wages.

If you own farm ground but you don't farm it yourself, you might not have to pay self-employment tax on the farm income. Some farming arrangements are treated like rental agreements instead of active businesses.

Jackie, for example, owns farm ground. Jackie doesn't do any work on the farm herself. Instead, she has engaged a farmer to work the fields. Jackie pays the farmer a fixed percentage of the crops that are sold. Jackie will not pay self-employment income on her farm profits.

You might receive a fee for serving as executor or personal representative of a deceased person's estate. Ordinarily, executors or personal representatives don't have to pay self-employment tax on their fees. You will have to pay self-employment tax on your fees, though, if you are in any of these situations:

➤ You are a professional fiduciary.

➤ The estate includes an active business that you are actively participating in and your fees are related to operating the business.

➤ The estate requires extensive managerial activity by you for a long period of time.

Your sister, for example, named you as her personal representative. You will receive a fee from the estate for your services. Your sister's estate doesn't involve a business that you have to manage. You are not in the business of serving as a trustee or a personal representative. You don't have to pay self-employment tax on the fee you will receive from your sister's estate.

Paper Trail

If you own farm ground but are not actively involved in the farming activity, you should not use Schedule F to report your farm income. Use Form 4835 instead of Schedule F if your income from the farm is based on the farm's income. If you rent your farm ground for a flat charge, report your ground rent directly on Schedule E.

Former insurance salespersons might not have to pay self-employment tax on payments they receive after retirement. New rules went into effect in 1998. If you are a retired insurance salesperson, you won't have to pay self-employment tax if you meet all of these requirements:

➤ Your payments were received after your agreement to perform services for the insurance company has ended.

➤ You performed no services for the insurance company this year after the contract ended.

➤ You signed a noncompete agreement that covers at least one year after your contract ended.

➤ Your payments depend primarily on insurance policies that you sold or were credited for the year before your retirement.

➤ The amount of your payment does not depend on how long you worked for the insurance company or how much you made with the company.

Public officials generally do not pay self-employment tax on the income that they earn in their official positions. Public officials of a state or local government, though, must pay self-employment tax on their fees if both of the following statements are true:

➤ The public official is paid solely on a fee basis.

➤ The person is eligible for (but not covered by) Social Security under an agreement between the federal government and his or her state.

Doing the Math

To calculate your self-employment tax, you have to add up your income from self-employment activities. Losses can offset profits.

For example, Bud has two sources of self-employment income. He receives $8,000 in fees for being a corporate director and he has a $2,000 loss from his sole proprietorship. Bud's net self-employment income is $6,000.

There are three ways to calculate your net earnings from self-employment:

1. The regular method
2. The farm optional method
3. The nonfarm optional method

Under the regular method, you will multiply your net self-employment income by 92.35%. This will give you the net earnings subject to self-employment tax.

There are two parts to calculating your self-employment tax:

➤ Net earnings up to $68,400 in 1998 are taxed at 12.4%

➤ All earnings are taxed at 2.9%

Red Flag

If you have a loss from a business activity, be sure to check the passive activity loss rules. You must materially participate in the business activity to claim your losses on your tax return.

The 12.4% tax on the first $68,400 pays for your old age, survivors, and disability insurance benefits. This is the Social Security, or FICA, portion of your self-employment tax. The 2.9% tax on all of your self-employment income pays for your Medicare (hospitalization) insurance.

For example, Josie has self-employment income of $84,000 in 1998. Under the regular method, her self-employment tax is calculated as follows:

Net self-employment income	$84,000
Times 92.35%	77,574
$68,400 times 12.4%	8,481.60
$77,574 times 2.9%	2,249.65
Total self-employment tax	$10,731.25

You might have self-employment income and also have wages. You will have paid FICA tax on your wages. When you calculate your self-employment tax, you will get credit for the FICA tax that you paid on your wages. You won't have to pay the 12.4% part of the self-employment tax on the entire $68,400. You only have to pay the Social Security tax once on $68,400.

In Josie's case, let's say that she had wages of $50,000 in 1998 in addition to her self-employment income. Her self-employment income was $84,000, which is reduced to 92.35%, or $77,574. Josie's self-employment tax would be calculated as follows:

Earnings limit for FICA tax	$68,400
Wages subject to FICA tax	50,000
Remaining FICA tax limit	$18,400
$18,400 times 12.4%	$2,281.60
$77,574 times 2.9%	2,249.65
Total self-employment tax	$4,531.25

Tax planning for most people involves paying the least amount of self-employment tax as possible. Most people try to control their self-employment tax because it is so expensive. Other people, however, want the coverage that the Social Security system provides. The optional methods of calculating self-employment tax allow these people to increase their self-employment tax.

Your Decoder Ring

Not everyone can earn Social Security benefits. You must pay into the Social Security system to earn your benefits. You can pay in by having FICA taxes withheld from your wages or by paying self-employment tax. If you have questions about your Social Security benefits, contact the Social Security Administration (SSA). Even though the IRS helps collect the taxes, SSA handles keeping the records and paying the benefits.

You will use the optional methods if:

➤ You want to get credit for Social Security benefit coverage and would not otherwise get credit.

➤ You want to claim a child or dependent care credit (using the optional method will increase your earned income used for this credit).

➤ You can claim the earned income credit (using the optional method could increase your credit).

You qualify to use the nonfarm optional method if you meet all of these tests:

1. Your net nonfarm profits are less than $1,733.

2. Your net nonfarm profits are less than 72.189% of your gross nonfarm income.

3. You have had self-employment income of $400 or more in two of the last three years.

4. You have not used the optional method more than four previous times. There is a five-year lifetime limit.

The farm optional method doesn't have the same qualification tests. There isn't a lifetime limit, and you don't need self-employment income in prior years. You only need to have gross farm income of less than $2,400 and net farm profits under $1,733.

When you use an optional method, you pay more self-employment tax than you would under the regular method. For examples of how to calculate the optional methods, see IRS Publication 533, Self-Employment Tax.

Paying Your Self-Employment Tax

Your self-employment tax is paid with your federal income taxes. The tax is reported on your individual income tax return. You don't write a separate check. Both taxes are paid at the same time.

The IRS doesn't want to wait until April 15th to get your self-employment taxes. They want the taxes to be paid throughout the year. You make your payment using an estimated tax voucher Form 1040-ES. If you don't pay enough each quarter, you could be subject to a penalty for underpayment of your estimated taxes.

The Self–Employment Tax Deduction

If you pay self-employment tax, you can take a deduction for half of your self-employment tax. You will claim the deduction in the adjusted gross income section of page one of your tax return. You don't have to itemize your deductions to claim the self-employment tax deduction.

Paper Trail

There are exceptions to the penalty for underpayment of estimated taxes. To learn more about underpayment penalties and their exceptions, check out the instructions to Form 2210 and IRS Publication 505, Tax Withholding and Estimated Tax.

The deduction for half of your self-employment taxes is Congress's way of helping close the tax gap between employees and self-employed individuals. If you are employed, your employer can deduct the half of your Social Security taxes that it pays (its match). The deduction for half of your self-employment taxes helps level the playing field to give the self-employed individual a tax deduction that an employer can take.

If your unincorporated business (sole proprietorship or partnership) has employees, it will pay the Social Security match on their wages. A business deduction is taken for the Social Security match. If you are a sole proprietorship, the wages and payroll taxes are deducted on your Schedule C. A partnership will deduct its wages and payroll taxes on its tax return, Form 1065.

Forms, Forms, Forms

If you are subject to self-employment taxes, you might need these forms:

➤ Schedule SE, Self-Employment Tax

➤ Form 2210, Underpayment of Estimated Tax by Individuals, Estates, and Trusts

➤ Schedule C if you are a proprietor

➤ Schedule E if you are a partner in a partnership

➤ Schedule F if you are a farmer

IRS Publication 533, Self-Employment Tax might come in handy. You can find IRS Publications on the Internet. Access the IRS's Internet web site at http://www.irs.ustreas.gov.

The Least You Need to Know

➤ The self-employment tax is the method by which self-employed persons pay into the Social Security system.

➤ If you have income that you have earned by your own labors that is not a salary or a wage, you might have to pay self-employment tax.

➤ There are some special exemptions from self-employment tax. Some people (clergy, for example) can opt out of the Social Security system altogether.

➤ Self-employment taxes are paid with your personal income taxes. You might need to make estimated tax payments to avoid underpayment penalties.

➤ You can claim a tax deduction for half of your self-employment tax. The deduction can be taken even if you don't itemize your deductions.

Chapter 23

IRAs: Saving for Your Own Retirement

In This Chapter

➤ Sorting out the types of IRAs that you can use

➤ Determining how much you can contribute to your IRA

➤ Calculating how much you can deduct for your IRA contribution

➤ Distributing funds from your IRA

➤ Converting your IRA to a Roth IRA

Each of us must save money for our own retirement. Social Security is not designed to be the sole source of your retirement income. It is up to each of us to provide the funds we will need to live on once we no longer are working.

Company-sponsored retirement plans are a great source of retirement funds. Pension plans, profit sharing plans, and 401(k) plans help fill the gap in your retirement savings needs.

If you are self-employed, you can establish your own retirement program. Your retirement plan will cover you and your employees. The programs available for self-employed people are discussed in Chapter 24, "Retirement Plans If You Are Self-Employed."

You might not have a retirement plan to help with your retirement savings. You also might want to save a bit more than your company plan will allow. An *Individual Retirement Account* (IRA) is one way that you can save retirement funds on your own.

An IRA is a personal retirement savings account with tax advantages. You might be able to deduct the contribution that you make to your IRA. Your earnings in the IRA are tax-deferred. You pay no income tax on your IRA's interest, dividends, or capital gains as your account is growing. Although most IRA distributions are taxable, distributions from certain IRAs are only partially taxable. Some IRA distributions are even tax-free.

Paper Trail

Don't report the interest that your IRA earns as tax-exempt interest. You shouldn't report the interest earned by your IRA at all. You shouldn't get Form 1099 for your IRA's investment earnings. If you get a Form 1099 in error, contact the issuer of the 1099 to get the Form 1099 corrected.

An IRA is the perfect example of a *portable retirement plan*. If you change jobs, your IRA is not impacted. Your account is your own personal retirement program.

IRAs might appear to be a simple retirement savings option. Appearances are often deceiving. The tax rules for IRAs are actually quite complicated. Sorting through the different types of IRAs, figuring out how much you can contribute, and figuring out how much you can (or need to) distribute from your IRA can be difficult.

We will walk through some of the IRA rules. We won't cover all of the IRA requirements, but we'll cover enough to get you thinking about your own IRA program. If you can find the right IRA to suit your savings needs, you can effectively take part of your retirement savings into your own hands.

Obviously, the earlier you start saving for your retirement, the more effective your savings program will be. If you didn't start early, don't despair. Just get started, even if you are starting late.

The Types of IRAs You Can Have

When IRAs were first introduced, there was just one kind of IRA that you could have. All IRA contributions were deductible, and all IRA distributions were taxable. Since then, an entire system of IRAs has developed. There are many different types of IRAs that you can have.

IRAs come in the following varieties:

➤ Traditional deductible IRAs
➤ Traditional nondeductible IRAs
➤ Traditional spousal IRAs (both deductible and nondeductible)
➤ Roth IRAs (regular and spousal)
➤ Education IRAs
➤ Simplified Employee Pensions (SEP IRAs)
➤ Savings Incentive Match Plans for Employees (SIMPLE IRAs)

SEP and SIMPLE IRAs will be discussed in Chapter 24. Education IRAs were discussed in Chapter 18, "Education Expenses." We'll cover the remaining types of IRAs in this chapter.

Although there are many different kinds of IRAs, you might have to make some choices. For example, you can't contribute the full $2,000 to both a traditional IRA and a Roth IRA for one year. Your choice will be directed, in part, by the tax advantages of the different types of accounts.

Having a variety of options gives you the chance to design your IRA funding to meet your personal needs. Sometimes too many choices can be confusing, though. We'll try to help you narrow down your options.

Try these steps to help you make your selection:

Your Decoder Ring

An **IRA** is an account that you open at a bank, insurance company, or other financial institution. Your IRA can be invested in time deposits (certificates of deposits), stocks, bonds, mutual funds, or even annuities. The documents that you sign when you open your IRA will clearly identify the account as an IRA.

1. Figure out to which IRAs you are qualified to make a contribution.
2. Weigh the tax advantages of each IRA to see which account will give you the greatest tax benefit.
3. Do it!

How Much You Can Contribute

To make an IRA contribution, you have to satisfy certain requirements. The different types of IRAs have different rules. In all cases, IRA contributions can only be made in the form of cash, check, or money order. You can't contribute property, such as stock, to an IRA.

For a traditional IRA (deductible or nondeductible), you have to abide by the following rules:

➤ Your IRA contribution can't be more than $2,000 each year.

➤ Your IRA contribution can't be more than your earned income.

➤ You can't contribute to an IRA if you are age $70^1/_2$ or older at the end of the year.

There are exceptions to these rules for other types of IRAs.

➤ You might be able to contribute more than $2,000 to a SEP IRA or a SIMPLE IRA (see Chapter 24).

➤ You can contribute more than your earned income to a spousal IRA.

➤ You can contribute to a Roth IRA past age $70^1/_2$.

You can make your IRA contribution at any time during the year. You also have up through April 15 of the following tax year to make your contribution. Your 1998 IRA contribution, for example, can be made any time in 1998 through April 15, 1999.

Paper Trail

When you make your IRA contribution, you will need to indicate what year your contribution is for. This is particularly important for contributions made between January 1 and April 15. You'll need to let your IRA sponsor know what year the contribution is for so that they can properly report your IRA contribution to the IRS.

Red Flag

There is a 6% penalty for contributing too much to your IRA. Form 5329 is used to calculate the penalty. If the excess contribution is withdrawn by April 15 of the year after the contribution is made you will avoid the penalty. Any earnings that the excess contribution has earned must also be distributed to you.

The IRA Earned Income Limitation

If you make a traditional IRA contribution, you can't contribute more than your earned income for the year. This means that a retiree can't continue to make IRA contributions unless he or she still has some income from working.

Wages, salary, and self-employment income all count as earned income for making an IRA contribution. Retirement benefits, capital gains, rental income, interest income, and dividend income are not earned income for making an IRA contribution.

Bettye Ann, for example, is single and 65 years old. She is collecting her pension, which pays her $10,000 a year. Bettye Ann is also collecting Social Security benefits and works part-time earning $1,800 in 1998. If Bettye Ann wants to make an IRA contribution for 1998, she can only contribute $1,800. Neither her pension nor her Social Security benefits count as earned income for making her IRA contribution.

If you are a member of the clergy and have elected out of the Social Security system, you can still make an IRA contribution. Your earnings count for making your IRA contribution even though you don't have to pay self-employment tax.

If you have a loss from self-employment and you also have wages, you can still make your IRA contribution. The loss from your self-employment won't offset your wages or salary income when testing if you can make an IRA contribution.

Kay, for example, has wages of $18,000 in 1998 that are reported on her Form W-2 from her employer. Kay is also starting up her own small business. Kay's Schedule C for 1998 has a loss of $21,000. Kay can still make a $2,000 IRA contribution in 1998. Her Schedule C loss won't wipe out the earned income that she has from her wages when calculating her earned income for IRA purposes.

Taxable alimony that you receive will count as earned income for making an IRA contribution. See Chapter 21, "Alimony," for our discussion of alimony.

Spousal IRA Contributions

You might have chosen not to work outside the home while your spouse is working. Congress has recognized that you need to save for your retirement, too. The spousal IRA might be an option for you to explore.

You can contribute up to $2,000 to a spousal IRA. There is an earnings requirement similar to the traditional IRAs earnings requirement. Your spousal IRA contribution can't be more than the result of the following formula:

➤ Add together your taxable compensation and your spouse's taxable compensation

➤ Subtract your spouse's IRA contribution

The result is the earned income limit for making a spousal IRA contribution.

Patty and Dennis, for example, each want to make $2,000 IRA contributions. Patty doesn't work outside the home. Dennis is retired, but works part time. Neither Patty nor Dennis has reached age 70$^{1}/_{2}$. If Dennis earns at least $4,000 on his job, both Patty and Dennis can contribute the full $2,000 to their own IRAs. If Dennis earns less than $4,000, their combined IRA contributions can't be more than Dennis's earned income.

Before 1997, the combined contribution for a working and nonworking spouse could not be more than $2,250 per year. Being able to contribute up to $2,000 for each spouse is a distinct enhancement for the spousal IRA.

Paper Trail

IRAs can be held only in your own name. You can have more than one IRA account, but you can't have a joint IRA with your spouse. When you set up your account, you will need to designate a beneficiary. Your IRA is paid to your beneficiary on your death. Be sure to complete the beneficiary designation form.

To make a contribution to your spousal IRA, you have to be less than age 70$^{1}/_{2}$ by the end of the year. After age 70$^{1}/_{2}$, you can't make a spousal IRA contribution.

Let's say, for example, that Bob is age 71 and he is retired. Bob made $1,500 working at a part-time job in 1998. Bob's wife, Mary, is age 69. Mary is also retired and does not work outside the home. Bob can't make a 1998 IRA contribution since he is over age 70$^{1}/_{2}$. Mary can make a $1,500 IRA contribution for 1998, though, since she is not yet age 70$^{1}/_{2}$ and Bob has $1,500 of earned income.

Roth IRA Contributions

Roth IRAs are new for 1998. The Roth IRA is a totally different type of IRA. You can't deduct contributions to your Roth IRA, but there is opportunity to receive tax-free distribution of your Roth IRA earnings.

Unlike traditional IRAs, you can contribute to a Roth IRA no matter what your age, even beyond age 70$^{1}/_{2}$.

You can make a Roth IRA contribution only if you have earned income. The same earned income rules that apply to traditional IRAs apply to Roth IRAs as well. Roth IRAs, though, have an upper income limit.

If you are single, you can make the full $2,000 Roth IRA contribution if your adjusted gross income is less than $95,000. Between $95,000 and $110,000 of AGI, your Roth contribution is phased-out. At $110,000 of AGI, you can't make any contribution to your Roth IRA.

If you are married, you can make the full $2,000 contribution to a Roth IRA if your adjusted gross income is less than $150,000. Between $150,000 and $160,000 of AGI, your Roth contribution is phased-out. At $160,000 of AGI and above, no Roth IRA contribution can be made.

If you are married filing separately, you can make a partial Roth IRA contribution if your adjusted gross income is less than $10,000. At $10,000 of AGI and above, you can't make a Roth IRA contribution at all.

In the phase-out range, you can make a partial Roth IRA contribution. Let's say, for example, that you file a joint return with your spouse, you have $80,000 of earned income, and your 1998 AGI is $155,000. You are mid-way through the phase-out range of $150,000 to $160,000, so you and your spouse can each make a $1,000 Roth IRA contribution for 1998.

Red Flag

The Roth IRA limit for married taxpayers who file separately is severe. Filing separately prevents you from making a full $2,000 Roth IRA contribution. This is just one factor that will influence your decision whether to file separately or jointly.

You can't contribute more than $2,000 a year to your Roth IRA and your traditional IRA combined. You will have to make a choice. Which is better? How do you decide which IRA to use?

If you are struggling with the decision between funding a Roth IRA or a traditional IRA, these pointers might help:

➤ If your traditional IRA contribution would not be deductible, choose the Roth IRA instead. Your Roth IRA earnings can be tax-free, but the earnings in your traditional nondeductible IRA will be taxable when they are distributed to you.

➤ The Roth IRA will usually save more taxes than a traditional IRA in the long run since the earnings can be tax-free.

Contributions to Education IRAs

You can contribute up to $500 a year to an Education IRA that is established for a child who is under age 18. The contribution is not deductible on your tax return.

You can only make a full $500 Education IRA contribution if your AGI is less than $150,000 on a joint return or less than $95,000 if you are single. If you are married and file a joint tax return, you can make a partial Education IRA contribution if your AGI is between $150,000 and $160,000. The phase-out range for single taxpayers is $95,000 to $110,000. See Chapter 18 for a discussion of the Education IRA and how it works.

Deducting Your IRA Contributions

Your contributions to a Roth IRA and an Education IRA are not deductible under any circumstances. Contributions to a traditional IRA, though, might be deductible.

Each of the following factors has a bearing on your traditional IRA contribution's deductibility:

➤ Participation in a company-sponsored retirement plan
➤ Filing status
➤ Adjusted gross income

If neither you nor your spouse participates in a company-sponsored retirement plan, you can deduct your full $2,000 contribution to your traditional IRA. It doesn't matter how much money you make. Your contribution is fully deductible.

What is meant by participation in a company-sponsored plan? Participation means that a contribution is being made to your account or you are earning additional benefits. Even a small contribution to your company plan can have a bearing on your IRA contribution's deductibility. Your company might only contribute $25 for you to the company retirement plan. For IRA purposes, though, you are a participant in your company plan and your IRA contribution might not be deductible.

If your company has a plan, but you are not earning any benefits from it or your account isn't being credited with a contribution for the year, you are not participating in the plan. Company-sponsored plans include the following:

➤ Qualified pension, profit sharing, stock bonus, or money purchase pension plan
➤ 401(k) plan
➤ Union plan
➤ Qualified annuity plan
➤ Government Section 457(b) plan
➤ Tax-sheltered 403(b) annuity plan
➤ SEP plan
➤ SIMPLE plan

If either you or your spouse is covered by a company-sponsored retirement plan, your filing status and adjusted gross income will work together to determine how much of your IRA contribution is deductible.

We ought to be precise here and clarify that it isn't actually your AGI that will matter; it is your *modified adjusted gross income*. For most of us, our modified AGI will be the same as our AGI, but it will vary for some people. Modified AGI is your adjusted gross income without taking the deductions for the following items:

➤ Your IRA contribution

➤ Foreign earned income exclusion

➤ Foreign housing exclusion or deduction

➤ Exclusion of series EE bond interest from Form 8815 (education savings bonds)

➤ Exclusion of employer-paid adoption expenses

If you are covered by a retirement plan at work, your 1998 IRA contribution deduction might be limited. The following table illustrates how filing status and AGI work together to determine the deductibility of your IRA contribution:

Filing Status	1998 Modified AGI	IRA Deduction Status
Single or Head of Household	Up to $30,000 Over $30,000 to $40,000 Over $40,000	Fully deductible Partially deductible Not deductible
Married Filing Jointly or Qualifying Widow(er)	Up to $50,000 Over $50,000 to $60,000 Over $60,000	Fully deductible Partially deductible Not deductible
Married Filing Separately	Up to $10,000 Over $10,000	Partially deductible Not deductible

If you are not covered by a retirement plan at work, but your spouse is covered by a company plan, your contribution can be limited. This is sometimes called the *spousal taint*. Beginning in 1998, most taxpayers won't have to be concerned about spousal taint. If you are high-income, though, your contribution can be limited. The following table illustrates your 1998 IRA contribution deduction limits if your spouse is covered by a company-sponsored retirement plan:

Filing Status	1998 Modified AGI	IRA Deduction Status
Married Filing Jointly	Up to $150,000 Over $150,000 to $160,000 Over $160,000	Fully deductible Partially deductible Not deductible
Married Filing Separately	At any AGI	Fully deductible

If you use a computer program to prepare your tax return, the program should calculate your IRA contribution deduction. There should be a screen on which you will answer questions about participation in a company-sponsored plan. Be sure to answer all of the questions on this screen or your IRA contribution deduction calculation might not be correct.

Reporting Your IRA Contribution

If you make a deductible IRA contribution, you will claim your deduction on page one of your Form 1040. There is a line on the tax return to enter your contribution deduction.

If you make a nondeductible contribution to a traditional IRA, you must attach Form 8606, Nondeductible IRAs (Contributions, Distributions, and Basis), to your tax return.

You should receive a Form 5498 from your IRA sponsor showing all of the IRA contributions that you made in 1998. You will get the Form 5498 by June 1, 1999, which is after your tax return is due. It will be important for you to keep your own records for preparing your tax return since the Form 5498 may not be sent to you until after April 15.

Paper Trail

The instructions to your Form 1040 contain a worksheet that you can use to calculate your IRA contribution deduction. IRS Publication 590 also contains examples of IRA contribution deduction calculations.

IRA Distributions

The tax rules for IRA distributions differ depending on the type of IRA that you have. As a general rule, if you deducted your contribution to the IRA, you will have to pay tax when you take a distribution. If you didn't deduct your contribution, you can receive your funds back tax-free.

Red Flag

If you fail to attach Form 8606 to your tax return, you may have to pay a $50 penalty.

Earnings in IRA accounts have always been taxed when distributed to the IRA owner. The new Roth IRAs and Education IRAs have changed this general rule. You can have tax-free distribution of earnings from these two IRAs.

Traditional Deductible IRA Distributions

For a traditional deductible IRA, all distributions are taxable. Since you deducted your contributions to the account and your earnings on the account have not yet been taxed, all of the distribution will be taxed.

You can also have to pay a penalty if an IRA distribution is made before you are age 59$^1/_2$. There are exceptions to the penalty in certain circumstances. See Chapter 25, "Penalties on Savings Accounts to Watch for," for a discussion of IRA distribution penalties.

Traditional IRAs have minimum distribution rules. You must start withdrawing your IRA by April 1 the year after you reach age 70$^1/_2$. Your account must be paid out in a manner such that it will be depleted by the end of your normal life expectancy.

There are different distribution options available to you for withdrawing your traditional IRA funds. You should consult a professional tax advisor before April 1 after you reach age 70$^1/_2$ to review your options. The penalty for withdrawing too little from your IRA is 50% (yes, half) of the amount you should have withdrawn, but failed to take out. This penalty should not be taken lightly.

Distributions from Your Traditional Nondeductible IRA

A traditional nondeductible IRA must also begin its distributions by April 1 after the year you reach age 70$^1/_2$. The 50% penalty for distributing too little from your IRA applies to your nondeductible IRA.

Part of your distribution from your nondeductible IRA will come to you tax-free. Since you didn't deduct your contribution when it was made, you don't have to pay tax when your contribution is taken out. All of your earnings are taxable, though.

Unfortunately, you can't choose to call your distribution either a nontaxable distribution of your contribution or a taxable distribution of earnings. There is a formula that you must follow. To apply the formula, all of your traditional IRA funds are added together. As you withdraw funds from your IRA, a prorated portion is not going to be taxed. The untaxed portion is determined by a fraction: your remaining nondeductible contributions divided by your total IRA funds.

Form 8606, Nondeductible IRAs (Contributions, Distributions, and Basis), will walk you through the calculation. Use Form 8606 to determine how much of your distribution from your nondeductible IRA will be taxed to you. Form 8606 has to be attached to your tax return.

Roth IRA Distributions

Distributions from your Roth IRA can be completely tax-free if you satisfy a five-year holding period and meet one of the following four requirements:

➤ The distribution is after you have reached age 59$^1/_2$.

➤ The distribution is after your death.

➤ The distribution is after you have become disabled.

➤ You use the distribution to pay for qualified first-time homebuyer expenses.

If your Roth IRA distribution doesn't satisfy these tests, a part of the distribution might be taxable. Roth IRAs have a most unusual opportunity, though. You can treat the distribution from the Roth IRA as coming from your contributions first. Until you have distributed all of your contributions, your distribution will be tax-free.

David, for example, contributed $2,000 to his Roth IRA in both 1998 and 1999. In the year 2000, David withdraws $1,500 from his Roth IRA. Clearly, David hasn't met the five-year holding period requirement to get tax-free distribution of earnings from his Roth IRA. Since David's distribution is not more than his nondeductible contributions to his Roth IRA, though, his distribution will be completely tax-free.

Your Decoder Ring

The home you buy using the IRA distribution to pay for qualified first-time homebuyer expenses doesn't have to be your first home that you ever owned. A **first-time homebuyer** is a person who has not owned a home in the last two years.

When you take a distribution of your Roth contributions, they are tax-free because you didn't deduct the contributions when they were made. Even if you are under age $59^1/_2$, the distribution of your Roth IRA contributions is penalty-free.

Education IRA Distributions

Distributions from Education IRAs can be tax-free. If the distribution is used to pay the cost of qualifying higher education, the entire distribution (including earnings) is tax-free.

If the Education IRA isn't used for higher education expenses, you can transfer the balance to an Education IRA for another family member.

Check out Chapter 18 for a discussion of Education IRAs.

Converting Your IRA to a Roth IRA

You might have a traditional IRA and wish that it was a Roth IRA instead. Roth IRAs have the advantage of possible tax-free distribution of earnings.

Red Flag

Taking a distribution of Roth IRA contributions before age $59^1/_2$ is penalty-free, but be careful if you have converted a traditional IRA to a Roth IRA. You will pay a 10% penalty if you withdraw converted IRA funds from your Roth IRA within five years of the conversion and you are under age $59^1/_2$. The distribution is income tax–free up to the amount of the conversion, though, because you paid tax on the conversion. This penalty was changed by a 1998 tax law to close an apparent loophole.

You can convert your traditional IRAs to a Roth IRA. There is a tax cost to the conversion, though. You have to pay income tax on the value of your traditional IRA when it is converted.

Your Decoder Ring

The income that you recognize when converting a traditional IRA to a Roth IRA is **ordinary income**. None of the conversion is taxed as capital gain. If your traditional IRA had nondeductible contributions in it, you won't have to pay tax on the conversion up to the amount of those nondeductible contributions.

In 1998, there is a special benefit for people who convert their IRAs to Roth IRAs. If you convert your IRA in 1998, you can spread out the taxable income from the conversion over four years.

Tawnie, for example, has a $30,000 IRA that she converted to a Roth IRA in 1998. Tawnie can include $7,500 of income from the conversion on her tax return in 1998, 1999, 2000, and 2001.

You don't have to use the four-year spread for converting to a Roth IRA. You can choose to report all of the conversion income on your 1998 tax return. You might want to do this if your 1998 tax return will be in a much lower rate than the next three years will be.

You can convert your IRA to a Roth IRA if either of the following statements is true:

➤ Your adjusted gross income for the year of the conversion (without the Roth conversion) is not more than $100,000.

➤ You do not file your tax return as married filing separately.

These rules mean that people with AGI over $100,000 and people who are married but file separate tax returns are not eligible for a Roth conversion. If you want to convert your IRA to a Roth IRA, you will have to be sure that you meet these two tests in the year that you convert.

If you convert your IRA to a Roth and later discover that you didn't qualify, the conversion can be undone.

If you have to pay income tax on the conversion, why would you choose to convert? You convert to have the opportunity to avoid paying income tax on your IRA's future earnings.

The conversion to a Roth IRA is a fairly simple process. Your old IRA will be terminated and the funds will be transferred to a newly opened Roth IRA. Your bank or financial institution can easily guide you through their conversion process.

Now you know that you can convert and you know that it isn't a difficult process. How do you know, though, if you should convert your IRA to a Roth IRA? This is a much harder question to answer.

Roth conversion is not for everyone. Consider the following factors when making your decision:

➤ If you convert, you should have enough cash outside your IRA to pay the income taxes on the conversion.

➤ You should consider how many years you have until retirement. The younger you are, the more favorable a Roth IRA will be.

➤ Consider your tax rate. Will your tax rate in retirement be significantly less than your tax rate is now?

Red Flag

If you convert your IRA to a Roth IRA, check your estimated tax situation. You might need to pay estimated taxes to avoid underpayment penalties. Don't forget about your state estimated taxes also.

The tax rate issue is seldom a deciding factor. Since you can only convert if your AGI is not more than $100,000, you won't be in the higher tax bracket in the year that you convert. Available cash and the number of years until retirement are usually the two determining factors in making a Roth IRA conversion decision.

There are Roth IRA conversion software packages that will analyze the pros and cons of a conversion for you. Your broker or your CPA might be able to run an analysis for you. You can also find a lot of information about Roth IRAs on the Internet.

The Least You Need to Know

➤ You can contribute up to $2,000 a year to an IRA as long as you have at least $2,000 of earned income and you are not yet age $70^1/_2$.

➤ You can contribute up to $2,000 to an IRA even if you don't work but your spouse does work and has made enough money to cover your combined IRA contributions.

➤ Your IRA contribution might not be fully deductible if you or your spouse is covered by a company-sponsored retirement plan.

➤ Roth IRAs are new for 1998. Your contribution is not deductible, but your earnings can be distributed tax–free in the future. You can contribute to a Roth IRA even if you are over age $70^1/_2$.

➤ Your traditional IRAs can be converted to a Roth IRA if your AGI is not over $100,000 and you don't file separately from your spouse. You will pay tax on the conversion, but your future earnings could be distributed tax–free in the future.

Chapter 24

Retirement Plans If You Are Self-Employed

In This Chapter

➤ Using a Simplified Employee Pension (SEP) to fund your retirement savings

➤ Checking out the SIMPLE plan as an easy option

➤ Looking at the Keogh plan requirements

If you are self-employed, you don't have employee benefits available to you like employees have. It's up to you to provide benefits for yourself and for your employees.

There are programs you can implement to provide retirement savings and to provide tax savings at the same time. To take advantage of these retirement savings programs, you will have to meet qualification tests.

Each different type of retirement program has different qualification tests. These tests will primarily require you to provide benefits for your employees that meet eligibility requirements.

As a self-employed person, you can choose from these types of retirement plans:

➤ Simplified Employee Pension (SEP)

➤ Savings Incentive Match Plan for Employees (SIMPLE plan)

➤ Keogh plan (also known as an H.R. 10 plan)

Each of these retirement plans has these tax advantages:

➤ Contributions to the plans are tax-deductible.

➤ Earnings in the retirement plan account grow tax-deferred. You don't have to pay income taxes on the earnings until you take a distribution from your retirement account.

➤ If you are an employee, contributions that are made by your employer to your retirement account aren't taxed to you now. Your taxes are deferred until you begin withdrawing your retirement funds.

If a retirement plan has the characteristics of deductible contributions, tax-deferred earnings, and deferred tax to employees for contributions, it is called a qualified retirement plan. To be qualified, your plan has to comply with rules that prevent it from discriminating in favor of high-income employees and the owners of the business.

SEP and SIMPLE plans have relatively few qualification requirements. These plans are easy to administer and have minimal paperwork. Keogh plans, on the other hand, have a lot of qualification requirements and significant paperwork. Why would you choose a Keogh plan? You can contribute more money to a Keogh plan than to an SEP or a SIMPLE plan. You can also design your Keogh plan in a way that might lower the cost of contributions to your employees' accounts. It's a classic trade-off.

SEP Plans

A Simplified Employee Pension (SEP) plan is a retirement plan that has very little paperwork and is not complicated. An SEP plan is an option to consider if you want a program that is easy to administer.

Under an SEP plan, the self-employed person sets up an IRA. Each of your eligible employees will also open his or her own IRA. You, as the self-employed person, will make a contribution to your own IRA for your SEP contribution. You, as the employer, will also make a contribution directly to your employees' SEP-IRAs.

Paper Trail

In an SEP plan, only the employer can make contributions to the plan. Employees can't make contributions to their own SEP IRAs. If you want employees to participate in the plan contributions, check out SIMPLE plans instead.

You can deduct the contribution that you make to your own SEP-IRA. The deduction is taken on page one of your Form 1040. You can also deduct the contribution that you make for each of your employees under the SEP plan. If you are a sole proprietor, the contribution that you make for your employees is deducted on your Schedule C.

If your business is in a partnership, the SEP contribution is claimed on the partnership tax return, Form 1065. The contributions made for each of the partners are passed through to each partner on the Schedule K-1. Each partner will claim a deduction for his or her own SEP contribution on page one of the Form 1040.

Who Can Use SEPs

You can use an SEP plan whether you have employees or not. SEP plans are available to sole proprietors, partnerships, and corporations.

The simplest form of an SEP plan is set up using a Form 5305-SEP. You cannot use the simplified Form 5305-SEP to set up your SEP plan if any of the following statements applies to you:

➤ You already maintain another qualified retirement plan

➤ You have ever maintained a defined benefit retirement plan, even if it is now terminated

➤ You have any employees who are eligible to participate in your SEP plan but he or she has not established an IRA

➤ You use the services of leased employees

➤ You are a member of an affiliated service group, a controlled group of corporations, or trades or businesses under common control (50% or more), unless all of the eligible employees of all of these groups participate in the SEP plan

➤ You, as the employer, do not pay the cost of the SEP contributions

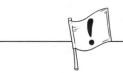

Red Flag

If you have an eligible employee who won't participate in your SEP by setting up an IRA, you simply can't use the SEP plan. If an employee refuses to participate, you don't have any choice but to check out alternative retirement plans.

Before 1997, you could set up an SEP plan that was like a 401(k) plan. These plans were called SARSEPs. Your employees could make contributions to their own SEP-IRAs through a salary reduction. After 1996, you can't set up a new SARSEP. You will instead use the new SIMPLE plan. If you have a pre-1997 SARSEP, you can continue using it.

Employees Eligible for Your SEP

In your SEP plan you have to cover each of your employees who is eligible to participate. You must cover each employee who has met these three eligibility requirements:

➤ The employee has reached age 21.

➤ The employee has worked for you in at least three of the last five years.

➤ You paid the employee at least $400 in compensation for the year.

You can be more liberal in your SEP plan coverage than the law requires. For example, you can cover employees who have worked for you just one year instead of making them wait three years. You can't hold employees out of the plan longer than the eligibility requirements provide, though.

319

You don't have to include employees in your SEP who are covered by a union agreement that has bargained for its retirement benefits.

SEP Plan Contribution

The contribution that you make for your employees to their SEP-IRAs is calculated as a percent of their compensation. Each year, the SEP contribution for each employee can't be more than 15% of the employee's compensation. You can't use more than $160,000 of compensation in 1998 to calculate a contribution, so an SEP contribution can't be more than $24,000 in 1998 (15% of $160,000).

Let's say, for example, that Paul has established an SEP plan for his sole proprietorship. He has one employee who qualifies for the SEP plan. His SEP provides for a contribution equal to 10% of the employee's contribution. If Paul's employee earned $25,000 in 1998, Paul will make a $2,500 SEP contribution to his employee's SEP-IRA.

Paper Trail

In our example, a $2,500 contribution is made, but aren't IRA contributions limited to $2,000 a year? In an SEP plan, the regular IRA contribution rules don't apply, so the SEP contribution can be more than $2,000 a year. The IRA is merely the funding vehicle for the SEP, which is the key to making this plan truly simple.

Your own contribution to your SEP-IRA is calculated using the same percent of compensation that you use for your employees. If you are self-employed, your contribution is not as easy to calculate, though.

Your SEP contribution is a percent of your net earnings from self-employment. To calculate your net earnings, start with your self-employment income. If you file a Schedule C, your net profit on the Schedule C is your starting point. If you are a partner in a partnership, your share of the partnership trade or business income is your starting point. From your income, subtract the following amounts:

➤ One-half of your self-employment tax
➤ Your own contribution to the SEP

We will continue to use Paul as our example. Let's say that Paul's Schedule C for 1998 showed a net income of $60,000. Paul's self-employment tax was $8,478.

Paul's SEP plan provides for a 10% contribution. Paul's 1998 contribution is $5,069. This is how the calculation works.

Paul's self-employment income	$60,000
Less one-half of SE tax	4,239
Less Paul's SEP contribution	5,069
Net self-employment earnings	$50,692

Ten percent of Paul's net self-employment earnings is $5,069.

If you're wondering how this calculation can be made, there are three different ways it can be done:

➤ Remember your high school algebra word problem solving techniques (your teacher always did say those word problems would come in handy).

➤ Better yet, use IRS Publication 560 (it has a chart you can use).

➤ Even better yet, let your tax preparation software or your CPA make the calculation for you.

If you are planning to make the full 15% contribution to your SEP account, the percentage is really about 13.04% of your earnings minus half of your self-employment taxes. Play with the math and you'll find that 13.04% works.

The SEP contribution can be significant if you are a high-earner. Let's say that Don is a computer consultant. He makes $120,000 a year in his self-employed consulting practice. Don's 1998 self-employment tax is $11,962. Don can contribute up to $14,872 for his 1998 SEP contribution. The SEP contribution really adds up for the high-income person. Remember that the highest earnings you can count in 1998 for an SEP, though, are $160,000 a year. Once you hit this earnings level, your benefits max out.

Your contributions to a SEP plan can only be made in cash. This means that you can't use stock or any other property to make your SEP contribution.

You have until April 15 of 1999 to make a 1998 SEP contribution. Even if your tax return is extended, the time to make your SEP contribution is still fixed at April 15.

SIMPLE Plans

SIMPLE plans were new in 1997. Like an SEP plan, each employee sets up his or her own IRA to participate in a SIMPLE plan. The contributions are made directly to the SIMPLE IRA.

A SIMPLE plan can also be used as part of a 401(k) plan. Most SIMPLE plans, though, are funded using SIMPLE IRAs.

When you use a SIMPLE plan, your employees can choose to make a contribution to their own SIMPLE plan accounts. The contribution will reduce taxable wages just like a 401(k) plan salary deferral would.

Who Can Use SIMPLE Plans

SIMPLE plans can be used only by employers who had 100 or fewer employees who received at least $5,000 in compensation in the previous year. Corporations, partnerships, and self-employed individuals can all use SIMPLE plans.

If your business has more than 100 employees with at least $5,000 of compensation and you want to allow salary deferrals, you will have to use a 401(k) feature in a Keogh

Paper Trail

SIMPLE plans replaced the old SARSEPs because they provide for employee deferrals. An old SARSEP plan can continue, but new SARSEPs cannot be established after 1996.

plan instead of using the SIMPLE plan. Not-for-profit organizations can also use tax-sheltered annuities as a retirement plan option.

Who Can Participate in Your SIMPLE Plan

An employee can participate in a SIMPLE plan if he or she meets all of these requirements:

➤ The employee was paid at least $5,000 of salary or wages during any two prior years.

➤ The employee is expected to make at least $5,000 during this year.

➤ The employee elects to have part of his or her compensation contributed to the SIMPLE plan through a salary reduction agreement.

Once an employee is qualified to participate in your SIMPLE plan, the employee can participate for the following two years also.

Karolyn, for example earned more than $5,000 during 1996 and 1997. She can participate in her employer's SIMPLE plan for 1998. If Karolyn's wages drop below $5,000 in 1999, she can continue to participate in the SIMPLE plan in 2000 and 2001.

You can use less restrictive eligibility requirements, but you can't deny participation to any employee who has met the three eligibility tests. You can exclude union employees who are covered by a retirement plan that has been collectively bargained, though.

SIMPLE Plan Contributions

Contributions to SIMPLE plans can only come from two sources:

➤ Employee salary deferrals

➤ Employer matching contributions or nonelective contributions

Each year, the contributions to a SIMPLE IRA are limited to $12,000. Half of the contribution comes from the employee as a salary deferral. The other half of the contribution comes from the employer as a match. Obviously, if you are self-employed, you are responsible for both the employee and the employer contributions to your own SIMPLE account.

A SIMPLE salary deferral is similar to a 401(k) plan deferral. The employee chooses to take a portion of his or her pay and put it into the SIMPLE plan. Salary deferrals to a SIMPLE plan are limited to $6,000 a year. The employee must make his or her salary deferral election 60 days before the beginning of the year.

When an employee defers salary into a SIMPLE plan, there is a tax benefit. The employee doesn't have to pay income taxes on the amount put into the plan or claim a deduction on his or her tax return. The employee's wages reported on Form W-2 will already be reduced by the salary deferral. This makes the process easy for the employee to manage.

Employer contributions to a SIMPLE IRA plan can be calculated under either of these two methods:

Paper Trail

Although salary deferrals under a SIMPLE plan are not taxed for income tax purposes, Social Security taxes still apply. If you haven't yet met the FICA wage limit, FICA taxes will be withheld. You must also pay Medicare taxes on the amount that you put into your SIMPLE plan.

➤ The employer matches the employee's deferral dollar-for-dollar. The match will generally be limited to 3% of the employee's pay. In two years of a five-year period, the match can drop, but can't be less than 1% percent of pay.

➤ Instead of a matching contribution, the employer can contribute 2% of each employee's pay if the employee earned at least $5,000 during the year.

If the SIMPLE plan is part of a 401(k) plan (instead of using IRAs), the employer must make its contribution under one of these two methods:

➤ A matching contribution that can't be more than 3% of the employee's compensation

➤ A contribution equal to 2% of pay for each employee who made at least $5,000

The employer's contribution must be made before the due date (including extensions) for filing the employer's tax return. If the employer is a sole proprietorship, the contribution must be paid by the due date of the owner's Form 1040.

Following the rules is critical in these plans. There are penalties and other nasty consequences that the IRS can invoke if you don't follow the rules. It's important to use competent advisors when you use these plans and make sure that you are complying with your plan's contribution and coverage requirements.

Keogh Plans

Keogh plans can only be used by sole proprietors or partnerships. Corporations can't use them. Keogh plans are very similar to the types of plans that are available to corporations, though.

You would choose to use a Keogh instead of an SEP or a SIMPLE plan if you want more flexibility in designing your retirement plan. There is a trade-off. You will have to comply with more elaborate qualification requirements and reporting requirements.

Paper Trail

The SIMPLE plan's contribution deadline is more flexible than the SEP contribution deadline. Under the SEP, the contribution is due by the filing date of your tax return without extensions. Under a SIMPLE plan you can buy more time by extending your tax return. It isn't advisable to wait to make your retirement plan contributions, though. You are losing out on the opportunity to earn tax-deferred investment earnings.

Red Flag

It's easy to make mistakes in Keogh plans. If you choose to use one, be sure to use a qualified professional to help design and administer your plan. Mistakes can be costly.

Who Can Use Keogh Plans

You can set up a Keogh plan if you are in business, but your business is not in a corporation. You don't need to have employees to use a Keogh plan. If you have employees, though, you have to cover each employee that qualifies to participate.

To use a Keogh plan, you have to comply with all of the following qualification requirements:

➤ The plan must be written.

➤ Minimum participation standards must be met.

➤ Minimum coverage requirements must be met.

➤ Contributions or benefits must be nondiscriminatory.

➤ The plan must comply with contribution and benefits limits.

➤ The plan must meet minimum vesting standards.

➤ Distribution requirements must be complied with.

➤ The plan cannot alienate your participants' benefits.

➤ Top-heavy requirements must be met.

This list of qualifications is quite impressive and should not be taken lightly. If you don't have employees in your business, complying with the qualification standards should not be difficult. If you have employees, though, you must be diligent in your compliance. You don't want to violate any of the qualification requirements.

Employees Eligible for Your Keogh Plan

Your plan document will define which employees are eligible to participate in your Keogh plan. When you set up your plan, you will choose from different design features that enable you to control which employees can participate

In spite of the ability to design your own participation requirements, there are some employees that you have to cover. If an employee meets both of the following two tests, you can't exclude him or her from your Keogh plan:

➤ The employee has reached age 21

➤ The employee has at least one year of service (you can increase the requirement to two years of service if the employee's benefits are *fully vested*)

Keogh Plan Contributions

There are two basic types of Keogh plans:

➤ Defined contribution

➤ Defined benefit

In a defined contribution plan, the employer's contribution to the plan is spelled out as a percent of each participant's compensation. For example, you might contribute 4% of each participant's pay to the retirement plan.

The plan administrator will keep track of the contributions that are made for each employee and will keep track of the investment earnings in each employee's account. When the employee is ready to retire, the account balance is available to pay the employee's benefits.

There are two types of defined contribution plans:

➤ Profit-sharing

➤ Money purchase pension

In a profit-sharing plan, the employer will decide each year how much will be contributed to the plan. The employer can contribute up to 15% of the employees' compensation. If the employer chooses, though, there can be no contribution for any given year.

Paper Trail

IRS Publication 560 explains each of the Keogh plan qualification requirements.

Your Decoder Ring

If your retirement account is **fully vested**, you have the right to take your entire plan balance when you leave your job. If the account isn't fully vested, you have to give up (forfeit) part of your account's balance if you leave your job. SEP and SIMPLE IRAs are always fully vested since the account is actually held in your own name. Keogh plans, though, can use vesting schedules. You earn additional vesting in your account balance for each year of service that you have with your employer.

In a money purchase pension plan, on the other hand, the annual contribution is based on a fixed percentage of employees' pay. Your plan, for example, might provide for a contribution each year equal to 10% of each participating employee's pay.

Contributions to money purchase and profit-sharing plans combined can't be more than 25% of pay or $30,000 for 1998 (whichever is less). You can't count more than $160,000 of compensation in 1998 for making contributions to retirement plans.

You can have both a profit-sharing plan and a money purchase pension plan. The combination is actually quite beneficial. If you pair a profit-sharing plan with a

Red Flag

Flexibility in Keogh plans comes at a price. Your plan has to be properly maintained. Annual reports must be filed each year (Form 5500). Participant account balances have to be tracked. Your plan must be amended when the tax laws change. Maintaining a Keogh plan is more expensive than an SEP or a SIMPLE plan. Some employers, though, think the price is worth paying for the plan flexibility.

10% money purchase plan, your contribution can be as little as 10% or as much as 25% of pay. There is a lot of flexibility.

A 401(k) plan is also a defined contribution plan. The contributions to your 401(k) account can come from both the employees and the employer.

In a defined benefit plan, the structure is a bit different. Instead of spelling out what will be put into the plan, your plan document will spell out what each employee will receive from the plan when he or she retires.

A defined benefit plan, for example, might provide that each employee receive retirement benefits equal to 25% of final pay. To know how much money the employer has to put into the plan to fund these benefits, an actuary is used. The actuary projects what it will cost the plan to provide the benefits that have been promised. The employer will then make a contribution each year to the defined benefit plan to cover the projected benefits.

Some employers choose to use defined benefit plans because they have more liberal (possibly larger) contributions. If you are self-employed and you don't have any employees in your plan, you might consider a defined benefit plan if it will allow you to shelter more money from income taxes.

Some employers also choose to use defined benefit plans because high investment returns will reduce the amount of money that the employer has to put into the plan. If the plan's assets grow faster than the actuary anticipated, the employer will have to put less money into the plan in future years to keep the benefits funded.

Defined benefit plans are not as commonplace as defined contribution plans because they are more expensive and more difficult to administer. In the right scenario, though, a defined benefit plan could be just the right answer to a retirement planning need.

Forms, Forms, Forms

If you sponsor a retirement plan for yourself and your employees, there are some forms that you will need to become familiar with. The trustee of your plan might take care of some of these forms for you. Be sure that the forms are all taken care of, though. It's your responsibility to get all of the proper forms filed on time.

The forms that you might need include the following:

➤ Form 1099-R, Distributions From Pensions, Annuities, Retirement or Profit-Sharing Plans, IRAs, Insurance Contracts, etc. This form is filed if a distribution from your Keogh plan is made to one of your plan participants.

➤ 5304-SIMPLE, Savings Incentive Match Plan for Employees of Small Employers (SIMPLE). This form is not actually filed with the IRS. You will complete this form when you establish your SIMPLE plan.

➤ 5305-SEP, Simplified Employee Pension-Individual Retirement Accounts Contribution Agreement. This form is completed when you set up your SEP plan. You will not file this form with the IRS.

➤ 5305-SIMPLE, Savings Incentive Match Plan for Employees of Small Employers (SIMPLE). This form is not filed with the IRS, but is completed when you establish your SIMPLE plan.

Red Flag

If you have to file a Form 5500, it is due by the end of the seventh month after your plan year ends. For a calendar year plan, the Form 5500 is due by July 31. Don't miss the deadline. There is a penalty for each day that the Form 5500 is late.

➤ Form 5500-C/R, Return/Report of Employee Benefit Plan (with fewer than 100 participants). This form is to be filed annually with the IRS by a Keogh plan that covers you and your employees.

➤ Form 5500-EZ, Annual Return of One-Participant (Owners and Their Spouses) Retirement Plan. This form is to be filed annually with the IRS for your Keogh plan if you and your spouse are the only participants and you meet other requirements.

The Least You Need to Know

➤ You can use an SEP or a SIMPLE plan to provide retirement benefits that are easy to administer.

➤ SEP contributions are made to IRAs set up by each participant. Only the employer can make an SEP contribution, which is limited to 15% of pay or $24,000 in 1998, whichever is less. If you are self-employed, the limit works out to 13.04% of your earnings.

➤ SIMPLE plan contributions come from both the employee and the employer. Each employee can contribute a portion of his or her pay to the plan to be matched by the employer.

➤ Keogh plans are the most flexible retirement plans that self-employed persons can use. Keogh plans are the most complicated and the most expensive to maintain, but provide design features not available in an SEP or a SIMPLE plan.

Chapter 25

Penalties on Savings Accounts to Watch for

In This Chapter

➤ Deducting penalties that you might pay on savings account withdrawals

➤ Recognizing when you might have to pay a penalty on an annuity

➤ Avoiding the penalties on IRAs and retirement plan distributions

---

There are investment and tax incentives if you save money for your retirement. When you invest your money using a long-term horizon, you have more time to let your money grow. By investing your money for the long term, you can get a greater return on your investment. If you choose to save money in a qualified retirement plan product, you will also shelter the investment earnings from income taxes.

The incentives work just fine until you need the money earlier than you planned. You can end up paying penalties if you withdraw your money early. Penalties might be owed to the company that is holding your investment. Penalties might also be owed to the IRS. In the worst case scenario, you might owe penalties to both.

Savings Account Penalties

One of the first investment products that people use is often a certificate of deposit. You can usually get relatively good interest rates on CDs, but the rate is sensitive to the term of the certificate.

You might, for example, get a higher rate of interest if you sign up for a five-year CD than if you sign up for a 12-month CD. All is well with the five-year CD unless you need to cash in the certificate early.

Early withdrawals from CDs often come at a price. You might forfeit part of your interest earnings if you withdraw your funds early.

If you have to pay a penalty for early withdrawal of your savings, you do get a tax break. You can deduct the penalty on your tax return. The deduction is taken on page one of your Form 1040 in the adjusted gross income section of your tax return. You don't have to itemize your deductions to claim a deduction for your penalty on early withdrawal of savings.

Red Flag

The deduction for penalty on early withdrawal of savings is often overlooked. Some people just don't know that they can take the deduction. Others forget that they paid the penalty. Look carefully at each of your Forms 1099–INT. The penalty will be reported on the 1099–INT. Don't lose out on the deduction.

Penalties on Annuities

Annuity products have tax-shelter benefits that other investment products just don't have. An annuity is a promise made to you by the annuity company to make a stream of payments to you at a future date. In exchange for that promise, you make payments into the annuity plan.

The Annuity Tax Shelter

Before the annuity begins making payments to you, the account grows. You don't have to pay income taxes on the annuity account's earnings when they are accumulating inside the annuity. You only have to pay income taxes on the annuity's earnings when the account is paid out to you.

The tax law provides tax shelter inside annuities because these products help people save for their retirement. You can't deduct your investment when you buy the annuity, but you get the tax savings as the account grows, so there is incentive to save for your retirement.

Penalties on Annuities

All is fine with an annuity unless you decide to end the arrangement early. If you take out your annuity funds early, you can face two penalties. First, the company from whom you bought the annuity might charge you a penalty. Unlike the penalty paid on early withdrawal of savings accounts, the penalty on early withdrawal of annuities is not tax deductible.

Second, you owe a penalty to the IRS if you withdraw your annuity before you are age $59^1/_2$. The penalty is 10% of the amount that you have to include in your taxable income because of cashing in the annuity.

330

You calculate the penalty on your annuity on Form 5329, which should be attached to your Form 1040. The penalty is not deductible on your tax return.

Penalties on IRAs and Retirement Plans

IRAs and qualified retirement plans are full of penalty opportunities. Two of the most frequently assessed penalties are the early distribution penalty and the excess accumulation penalty.

We used to have two other penalties on IRAs and retirement plans that were, thankfully, terminated by Congress. There was a penalty if you distributed a large amount from your retirement funds in one year. There was also a penalty if you died with large retirement funds. These penalties are gone. Hopefully, we'll never see them again.

Paper Trail

You can exchange one annuity product for another annuity before you are age 59^1/$_2$ without paying the 10% IRS penalty. You will also not have to pay any income tax when you exchange one annuity product for another.

None of the penalties on IRAs and retirement plans are deductible on your tax return. The penalties are calculated on Form 5329, which is attached to your Form 1040.

Premature Distributions

Congress doesn't want us to take out our IRA funds or our retirement funds too early. They want these funds to be tied up so that they will actually be available for our retirement.

To meet this end, there is a 10% premature distribution penalty. The penalty applies if you withdraw retirement funds before either age 59^1/$_2$, death, or disability. The 10% penalty can be assessed on distributions from IRAs, SEPs, SIMPLE IRAs, Keogh plans, profit-sharing plans, pension plans, 401(k) plans, and so on.

The premature distribution penalty is 10% of the amount that you have to include in your taxable income. Each of the following payments isn't subject to the penalty because they are not subject to income taxes:

➤ The return of your nondeductible contributions to your IRA

➤ An IRA or retirement plan distribution that is rolled over to another IRA or retirement plan account

How to Avoid the Premature Distribution Penalty

You can avoid the penalty on your IRA distribution or your qualified retirement plan distribution if you meet one of the following exceptions:

Red Flag

A 25% penalty (rather than 10%) applies to an early withdrawal from a SIMPLE plan that is made in the first two years of beginning your participation in the plan. If you are making a SIMPLE plan contribution, make sure you are willing to make it stick.

Your Decoder Ring

The **penalty exclusion** for taking a series of equal payments (the annuitization exception) applies to each separate account. You can, for example, divide an IRA into two separate IRAs. Begin taking regular distributions every year from one of the IRAs while leaving the other IRA intact. This will enable you to take some distributions before age $59^1/2$ without penalty while still preserving part of your IRA funds. You have to satisfy the requirements of the annuitization exception to avoid the penalty. Check with your tax professional for those requirements.

➤ Your distribution was received after you reached age $59^1/2$.

➤ You took a distribution after you were totally and permanently disabled.

➤ You took a distribution due to the account owner's death.

➤ You received a distribution from your retirement plan because you separated from service (retired or quit) at age 55 or later. This is known as the early retirement exception, and it doesn't apply to IRA distributions.

➤ You took a distribution as part of a series of substantially equal periodic payments. This is known as the *annuitization exception*.

➤ Your distributions are not more than your medical expense deduction. This is a new exception for 1997 and later.

➤ The distribution is made to your ex-spouse as part of your divorce under a qualified domestic relations order. The QDRO exception doesn't apply to IRAs.

IRAs qualify for the following additional exceptions to the 10% premature distribution penalty:

➤ Distributions made to unemployed individuals for health insurance premiums

➤ Distributions used to pay qualifying higher education expenses

➤ Distributions up to $10,000 for first-time homebuyers

The penalty relief for unemployed individuals applies if:

➤ You lost your job.

➤ You have received unemployment compensation for 12 consecutive weeks.

➤ The IRA withdrawals were made either in the year that you received your unemployment compensation or the year after.

➤ You made your IRA withdrawals no later than 60 days after you were reemployed.

The higher education exception is new for 1998 and is available to you if you withdraw funds from your IRA to pay for higher education expenses (tuition, fees, books, supplies, or equipment) for you, your spouse, your children, or your grandchildren. If the student is in school at least half time, the IRA funds can also be used to pay for room and board.

If you use tax-free funds to pay higher education expenses, you can't also take advantage of the penalty-free IRA distribution for the same expenses. You can often combine scholarships and distributions for maximum effect, though.

Let's say, for example, that you have a scholarship that covers all but $1,000 of your tuition. You withdraw $1,500 from your IRA for your education expenses. You can use $1,000 of the IRA funds to cover the remaining tuition and the other $500 can be used to pay fees, books, and supplies. By combining the two programs, you get nice coverage. You can use two different tax advantaged opportunities in the same year.

The first-time homebuyer exception is also new for 1998. You can withdraw up to $10,000 from your IRA ($10,000 is your lifetime limit) without penalty if you use the funds to buy, build, or rebuild a first home that is the principal residence of:

> ➤ You or your spouse

> ➤ Your child or your spouse's child

> ➤ Your grandchild or your spouse's grandchild

> ➤ Your parent or other ancestor

> ➤ Your spouse's parent or other ancestor

A first-time homebuyer is someone who has not owned a home within the last two years. As with education IRA withdrawals, the distribution from your IRA still might be taxable if you qualify as a first-time homebuyer, but you could avoid the 10% penalty. If more than $10,000 is withdrawn, both income taxes and the 10% penalty would apply if you are not yet age 59$^{1}/_{2}$ or disabled.

Red Flag

Remember that IRA distributions might be penalty-free, but they still might be taxable. Distributions from traditional IRAs to pay education expenses are taxable under the regular IRA rules even though they are penalty-free. Education IRAs and Roth IRAs have tax-free distribution opportunities.

This is a pretty impressive list of exceptions. If you need to reach your retirement funds and you might qualify for one of these penalty exceptions, it is worth checking out. The rules are complicated, though, and they are tricky. IRS Publication 590 might help. A CPA who specializes in retirement plans can be of great help to you also.

Penalty for Failing to Distribute Funds

IRAs and qualified retirement plans are great tax shelters. These plans are so good that some people never want to take their money out. To handle this situation, there is a penalty for failing to withdraw your retirement funds fast enough.

333

You must begin withdrawing your IRA or your qualified retirement plan funds by April 1 of the year after you reach age $70^1/_2$. You don't have to withdraw your entire account by then. You just have to begin making your withdrawals on a schedule.

Your distributions need to be made over a period that is not longer than your *life expectancy* and the life expectancy of your beneficiary. If both you and your beneficiary die according to your life expectancies, your IRA would be fully distributed in the year that the remaining person dies.

Your Decoder Ring

What is your **life expectancy**? The IRS gives us life expectancy tables to use when you calculate your withdrawal from a retirement plan or your IRA. You can find the life expectancy tables in IRS Publication 590. You will also find joint life expectancy tables that you can use if you pay your account out over your life and your beneficiary's life.

Paper Trail

Most people choose not to recalculate their life expectancy when withdrawing their IRA funds. When this is done, you simply subtract one year from your life expectancy for each year that passes. The system is pretty simple. It isn't the right choice in every situation, though. Check with your advisors.

For example, Jason has an IRA with $120,000 in it. Jason has named his wife as his beneficiary of the IRA. Jason and his wife have a combined life expectancy of 20.6 years in the year that Jason turns age $70^1/_2$. Jason's first year's distribution must be at least $5,825.24, which is $120,000 divided by 20.6.

If you fail to distribute enough from your IRA or your retirement plan account, there is a penalty. The penalty is 50% of the shortfall. If Jason only withdrew $3,000 in his first year of required distributions, his penalty would be 50% of the $2,825.24 shortfall, or $1,412.62.

This penalty is clearly meant to create incentive for us to take our retirement funds during our lifetime. You don't want to face the 50% penalty. Don't let your 70th birthday pass without starting your IRA and retirement plan distribution planning.

There are some decisions that you must make by April 1 after the year you reach age $70^1/_2$. You will need to decide on the method by which you will take your distributions. You do have options. You can choose to recalculate your life expectancy each year or not.

You should also carefully check your beneficiary designation for your retirement funds and your IRAs. The beneficiary designation indicates who will receive your retirement funds when you die. The beneficiary designation also has an impact on the required distributions that you must make from your retirement accounts.

There are many consequences to the decisions you will need to make at age $70^1/_2$. You don't get a second chance to elect your distribution method, so be sure to carefully consider your options and choose wisely.

If you are still working when you reach age 70^1/$_2$, you might not have to take out your company-sponsored retirement funds just yet. If you are not an owner in the business and you aren't related to the business owners, you can wait until you retire to take out your retirement funds from your company-sponsored plan. You will still have to start withdrawing your IRA funds, though.

Roth IRAs are an important exception to the distribution rules. You don't have to begin withdrawing Roth IRAs when you reach age 70^1/$_2$. This exception makes a lot of sense because Roth IRA distributions after age 59^1/$_2$ are tax-free if you have had the account at least five years. This is yet another advantage to the new Roth IRAs.

The Least You Need to Know

➤ The penalty that you pay for taking funds out of your certificate of deposit early is deductible on your tax return.

➤ Annuities can be used as a tax shelter. If you end your annuity early, you could face a penalty from the annuity company and a penalty on your tax return.

➤ If you withdraw retirement funds or IRA funds before you are age 59^1/$_2$, you might face a 10% premature distribution penalty.

➤ There are a host of exceptions to the 10% premature distribution penalty that might let you take your funds early without penalty.

➤ You'll have to start withdrawing your retirement funds and your IRA funds by April 1 of the year after you turn age 70^1/$_2$. The penalty for taking out too little is 50% of the amount you failed to withdraw.

IRS Forms

Form **1040**

Department of the Treasury– Internal Revenue Service

U.S. Individual Income Tax Return 1998

IRS Use Only–Do not write or staple in this space.

For the year Jan. 1–Dec. 31, 1998, or other tax year beginning _____ , 1998, ending _____ , 19___   OMB No. 1545-0074

Label

(See instructions on page 12.)

Use the IRS label. Otherwise, please print or type.

Your first name and initial	Last name	Your social security number
If a joint return, spouse's first name and initial	Last name	Spouse's social security number

Home address (number and street). If you have a P.O. box, see page 12.   Apt. no.

City, town or post office, state, and ZIP code. If you have a foreign address, see page 12.

▲ **IMPORTANT!** ▲
You **must** enter your SSN(s) above.

Presidential Election Campaign (See page 12.)

Do you want $3 to go to this fund? . . . .

If a joint return, does your spouse want $3 to go to this fund? . . . . . .

Yes | No | Note: Checking "Yes" will not change your tax or reduce your refund.

Filing Status

Check only one box.

1 ☐ Single
2 ☐ Married filing joint return (even if only one had income)
3 ☐ Married filing separate return. Enter spouse's social security no. above and full name here. ▶ _____
4 ☐ Head of household (with qualifying person). (See page 12.) If the qualifying person is a child but not your dependent, enter this child's name here. ▶ _____
5 ☐ Qualifying widow(er) with dependent child (year spouse died ▶ 19___). (See page 12.)

Exemptions

6a ☐ **Yourself.** If your parent (or someone else) can claim you as a dependent on his or her tax return, **do not** check box 6a . . . .

b ☐ **Spouse** . . . .

c **Dependents:**

(1) First name Last name	(2) Dependent's social security number	(3) Dependent's relationship to you	(4) ✔ if qualifying child for child tax credit (see page 13)
			☐
			☐
			☐
			☐
			☐
			☐

If more than six dependents, see page 13.

No. of boxes checked on 6a and 6b ___

No. of your children on 6c who:
● lived with you ___
● did not live with you due to divorce or separation (see page 13) ___

Dependents on 6c not entered above ___

Add numbers entered on lines above ▶ ☐

d Total number of exemptions claimed . . . .

Income

Attach Copy B of your Forms W-2, W-2G, and 1099-R here.

If you did not get a W-2, see page 14.

Enclose, but do not staple, any payment. Also, please use **Form 1040-V.**

7   Wages, salaries, tips, etc. Attach Form(s) W-2 . . . . | 7
8a **Taxable** interest. Attach Schedule B if required . . . . | 8a
b   **Tax-exempt** interest. DO NOT include on line 8a . . . | 8b |
9   Ordinary dividends. Attach Schedule B if required . . . . | 9
10 Taxable refunds, credits, or offsets of state and local income taxes (see page 15) . . | 10
11 Alimony received . . . . | 11
12 Business income or (loss). Attach Schedule C or C-EZ . . . . . | 12
13 Capital gain or (loss). Attach Schedule D . . . . | 13
14 Other gains or (losses). Attach Form 4797 . . . . | 14
15a Total IRA distributions . | 15a | b Taxable amount (see page 16) | 15b
16a Total pensions and annuities | 16a | b Taxable amount (see page 16) | 16b
17 Rental real estate, royalties, partnerships, S corporations, trusts, etc. Attach Schedule E | 17
18 Farm income or (loss). Attach Schedule F . . . . | 18
19 Unemployment compensation . . . . | 19
20a Social security benefits . | 20a | b Taxable amount (see page 18) | 20b
21 Other income. List type and amount– see page 18 . . . . | 21
22 Add the amounts in the far right column for lines 7 through 21. This is your **total income** ▶ | 22

Adjusted Gross Income

If line 33 is under $30,095 (under $10,030 if a child did not live with you), see EIC inst. on page 30.

23 IRA deduction (see page 19) . . . . . . | 23
24 Student loan interest deduction (see page 21) . . . | 24
25 Medical savings account deduction. Attach Form 8853 . | 25
26 Moving expenses. Attach Form 3903 . . . . | 26
27 One-half of self-employment tax. Attach Schedule SE . | 27
28 Self-employed health insurance deduction (see page 22) | 28
29 Keogh and self-employed SEP and SIMPLE plans . | 29
30 Penalty on early withdrawal of savings . . . . | 30
31a Alimony paid b Recipient's SSN ▶ _____ | 31a
32 Add lines 23 through 31a . . . . ▶ | 32
33 Subtract line 32 from line 22. This is your **adjusted gross income** . . . . . . ▶ | 33

For Privacy Act and Paperwork Reduction Act Notice, see page 52.   Cat. No. 11320B   Form **1040** (1998)

1998 Form 1040 (page 1)

Form 1040 (1998)   Page **2**

Tax and Credits

34 Amount from line 33 (adjusted gross income) . . . . | **34** |

35a Check if: ☐ **You** were 65 or older, ☐ Blind; ☐ **Spouse** was 65 or older, ☐ Blind.
Add the number of boxes checked above and enter the total here . . . . ▶ **35a**

b If you are married filing separately and your spouse itemizes deductions or
you were a dual-status alien, see page 23 and check here . . . . . ▶ **35b** ☐

Standard Deduction for Most People

Single: $4,250

Head of household: $6,250

Married filing jointly or Qualifying widow(er): $7,100

Married filing separately: $3,550

36 Enter the **larger** of your **itemized deductions** from Schedule A, line 28, **OR standard deduction** shown on the left. **But** see page 23 to find your standard deduction if you checked any box on line 35a or 35b **or** if someone can claim you as a dependent . . | **36** |

37 Subtract line 36 from line 34 . . . . | **37** |

38 If line 34 is $93,400 or less, multiply $2,700 by the total number of exemptions claimed on line 6d. If line 34 is over $93,400, see the worksheet on page 24 for the amount to enter . | **38** |

39 **Taxable income.** Subtract line 38 from line 37. If line 38 is more than line 37, enter -0- | **39** |

40 **Tax.** See page 24. Check if any tax from **a** ☐ Form(s) 8814 **b** ☐ Form 4972 . . ▶ | **40** |

41 Credit for child and dependent care expenses. Attach Form 2441 | **41** |

42 Credit for the elderly or the disabled. Attach Schedule R . . . | **42** |

43 Child tax credit (see page 25) . . . . | **43** |

44 Education credits. Attach Form 8863 . . . . | **44** |

45 Adoption credit. Attach Form 8839 . . . . | **45** |

46 Foreign tax credit. Attach Form 1116 if required . . . . | **46** |

47 Other. Check if from **a** ☐ Form 3800 **b** ☐ Form 8396
c ☐ Form 8801 **d** ☐ Form (specify) | **47** |

48 Add lines 41 through 47. These are your **total credits** . . . . | **48** |

49 Subtract line 48 from line 40. If line 48 is more than line 40, enter -0- . . . . . . ▶ | **49** |

Other Taxes

50 Self-employment tax. Attach Schedule SE . . . . | **50** |

51 Alternative minimum tax. Attach Form 6251 . . . . | **51** |

52 Social security and Medicare tax on tip income not reported to employer. Attach Form 4137 | **52** |

53 Tax on IRAs, other retirement plans, and MSAs. Attach Form 5329 if required . . . | **53** |

54 Advance earned income credit payments from Form(s) W-2 . . . . . | **54** |

55 Household employment taxes. Attach Schedule H . . . . | **55** |

56 Add lines 49 through 55. This is your **total tax** . . . . ▶ | **56** |

Payments

Attach Forms W-2 and W-2G on the front. Also attach Form 1099-R if tax was withheld.

57 Federal income tax withheld from Forms W-2 and 1099 . . | **57** |

58 1998 estimated tax payments and amount applied from 1997 return . | **58** |

59a **Earned income credit.** Attach Schedule EIC if you have a qualifying child **b** Nontaxable earned income: amount ▶ [   ]
and type ▶ -------------- | **59a** |

60 Additional child tax credit. Attach Form 8812 . . . . . | **60** |

61 Amount paid with Form 4868 (request for extension) . . . | **61** |

62 Excess social security and RRTA tax withheld (see page 37) | **62** |

63 Other payments. Check if from **a** ☐ Form 2439 **b** ☐ Form 4136 | **63** |

64 Add lines 57, 58, 59a, and 60 through 63. These are your **total payments** . . . ▶ | **64** |

Refund

Have it directly deposited! See page 37 and fill in 66b, 66c, and 66d.

65 If line 64 is more than line 56, subtract line 56 from line 64. This is the amount you **OVERPAID** | **65** |

66a Amount of line 65 you want **REFUNDED TO YOU**. . . . . ▶ | **66a** |

▶ **b** Routing number [   ] ▶ **c** Type: ☐ Checking ☐ Savings

▶ **d** Account number [   ]

67 Amount of line 65 you want **APPLIED TO YOUR 1999 ESTIMATED TAX** ▶ | **67** |

Amount You Owe

68 If line 56 is more than line 64, subtract line 64 from line 56. This is the **AMOUNT YOU OWE**.
For details on how to pay, see page 38 . . . . ▶ | **68** |

69 Estimated tax penalty. Also include on line 68 . . . . . | **69** |

Sign Here

Joint return? See page 38.

Keep a copy for your records.

Under penalties of perjury, I declare that I have examined this return and accompanying schedules and statements, and to the best of my knowledge and belief, they are true, correct, and complete. Declaration of preparer (other than taxpayer) is based on all information of which preparer has any knowledge.

| Your signature | Date | Your occupation | Daytime telephone number (optional) |
| Spouse's signature. If a joint return, BOTH must sign. | Date | Spouse's occupation | (   ) |

Paid Preparer's Use Only

Preparer's signature ▶	Date	Check if self-employed ☐	Preparer's social security no.
Firm's name (or yours if self-employed) and address ▶		EIN	
		ZIP code	

1998 Form 1040 (page 2)

Form **2106**

Department of the Treasury
Internal Revenue Service (99)

Employee Business Expenses

▶ See separate instructions.

▶ Attach to Form 1040.

OMB No. 1545-0139

1998

Attachment
Sequence No. **54**

Your name	Social security number	Occupation in which you incurred expenses

Part I Employee Business Expenses and Reimbursements

STEP 1   Enter Your Expenses

		Column A Other Than Meals and Entertainment	Column B Meals and Entertainment
1	Vehicle expense from line 22 or line 29. (Rural mail carriers: See instructions.) **1**		
2	Parking fees, tolls, and transportation, including train, bus, etc., that **did not** involve overnight travel or commuting to and from work **2**		
3	Travel expense while away from home overnight, including lodging, airplane, car rental, etc. **Do not** include meals and entertainment **3**		
4	Business expenses not included on lines 1 through 3. **Do not** include meals and entertainment **4**		
5	Meals and entertainment expenses (see instructions) **5**		
6	**Total expenses.** In Column A, add lines 1 through 4 and enter the result. In Column B, enter the amount from line 5 **6**		

Note: *If you were not reimbursed for any expenses in Step 1, skip line 7 and enter the amount from line 6 on line 8.*

STEP 2   Enter Reimbursements Received From Your Employer for Expenses Listed in STEP 1

7	Enter reimbursements received from your employer that were **not** reported to you in box 1 of Form W-2. Include any reimbursements reported under code "L" in box 13 of your Form W-2 (see instructions) **7**		

STEP 3   Figure Expenses To Deduct on Schedule A (Form 1040)

8	Subtract line 7 from line 6 **8**		
	Note: *If **both columns** of line 8 are zero, **stop here.** If Column A is less than zero, report the amount as income on Form 1040, line 7.*		
9	In Column A, enter the amount from line 8. In Column B, multiply the amount on line 8 by 50% (.50). If either column is zero or less, enter -0- in that column (Employees subject to Department of Transportation (DOT) hours-of-service limits: Multiply by 55% (.55) instead of 50%. For more details, see instructions.) **9**		
10	Add the amounts on line 9 of both columns and enter the total here. **Also, enter the total on Schedule A (Form 1040), line 20.** (Fee-basis state or local government officials, qualified performing artists, and individuals with disabilities: See the instructions for special rules on where to enter the total.) ▶ **10**		

For Paperwork Reduction Act Notice, see instructions.   Cat. No. 11700N   Form **2106** (1998)

1998 Form 2106, Employee Business Expenses (page 1)

339

Form 2106 (1998)   Page **2**

Part II **Vehicle Expenses** (See instructions to find out which sections to complete.)

Section A– General Information

			(a) Vehicle 1	(b) Vehicle 2
11	Enter the date vehicle was placed in service	11	/ /	/ /
12	Total miles vehicle was driven during 1998	12	miles	miles
13	Business miles included on line 12	13	miles	miles
14	Percent of business use. Divide line 13 by line 12	14	%	%
15	Average daily round trip commuting distance	15	miles	miles
16	Commuting miles included on line 12	16	miles	miles
17	Other miles. Add lines 13 and 16 and subtract the total from line 12 . . .	17	miles	miles

18 Do you (or your spouse) have another vehicle available for personal purposes? . . . . ☐ Yes ☐ No

19 If your employer provided you with a vehicle, is personal use during off-duty hours permitted? ☐ Yes ☐ No ☐ Not applicable

20 Do you have evidence to support your deduction? . . . . ☐ Yes ☐ No

21 If "Yes," is the evidence written? . . . . ☐ Yes ☐ No

Section B– Standard Mileage Rate

22	Multiply line 13 by 32½¢ (.325). Enter the result here and on line 1	22	

Section C– Actual Expenses

			(a) Vehicle 1		(b) Vehicle 2	
23	Gasoline, oil, repairs, vehicle insurance, etc.	23				
24a	Vehicle rentals	24a				
b	Inclusion amount (see instructions)	24b				
c	Subtract line 24b from line 24a	24c				
25	Value of employer-provided vehicle (applies only if 100% of annual lease value was included on Form W-2– see instructions)	25				
26	Add lines 23, 24c, and 25 . .	26				
27	Multiply line 26 by the percentage on line 14 . . .	27				
28	Depreciation. Enter amount from line 38 below	28				
29	Add lines 27 and 28. Enter total here and on line 1	29				

Section D– Depreciation of Vehicles (Use this section only if you own the vehicle.)

			(a) Vehicle 1		(b) Vehicle 2	
30	Enter cost or other basis (see instructions)	30				
31	Enter amount of section 179 deduction (see instructions) .	31				
32	Multiply line 30 by line 14 (see instructions if you elected the section 179 deduction) . . .	32				
33	Enter depreciation method and percentage (see instructions) .	33				
34	Multiply line 32 by the percentage on line 33 (see instructions) . .	34				
35	Add lines 31 and 34	35				
36	Enter the limit from the table in the line 36 instructions . . .	36				
37	Multiply line 36 by the percentage on line 14 . . .	37				
38	Enter the **smaller** of line 35 or line 37. Also, enter this amount on line 28 above	38				

1998 Form 2106, Employee Business Expenses (page 2)

SCHEDULES A&B
(Form 1040)

Department of the Treasury
Internal Revenue Service   (99)

Schedule A–Itemized Deductions

(Schedule B is on back)

▶ **Attach to Form 1040.** ▶ **See Instructions for Schedules A and B (Form 1040).**

OMB No. 1545-0074

19**98**

Attachment
Sequence No. **07**

Name(s) shown on Form 1040

Your social security number

Medical and Dental Expenses		**Caution:** *Do not include expenses reimbursed or paid by others.*	
	1	Medical and dental expenses (see page A-1)	1
	2	Enter amount from Form 1040, line 34 . **2**	
	3	Multiply line 2 above by 7.5% (.075)	3
	4	Subtract line 3 from line 1. If line 3 is more than line 1, enter -0-	4
Taxes You Paid (See page A-2.)	5	State and local income taxes	5
	6	Real estate taxes (see page A-2)	6
	7	Personal property taxes	7
	8	Other taxes. List type and amount ▶	8
	9	Add lines 5 through 8	9
Interest You Paid (See page A-2.)	10	Home mortgage interest and points reported to you on Form 1098	10
	11	Home mortgage interest not reported to you on Form 1098. If paid to the person from whom you bought the home, see page A-3 and show that person's name, identifying no., and address ▶	
Note: Personal interest is not deductible.	11		11
	12	Points not reported to you on Form 1098. See page A-3 for special rules	12
	13	Investment interest. Attach Form 4952 if required. (See page A-3.)	13
	14	Add lines 10 through 13	14
Gifts to Charity If you made a gift and got a benefit for it, see page A-3.	15	Gifts by cash or check. If you made any gift of $250 or more, see page A-3	15
	16	Other than by cash or check. If any gift of $250 or more, see page A-3. You **MUST** attach Form 8283 if over $500	16
	17	Carryover from prior year	17
	18	Add lines 15 through 17	18
Casualty and Theft Losses	19	Casualty or theft loss(es). Attach Form 4684. (See page A-4.)	19
Job Expenses and Most Other Miscellaneous Deductions (See page A-5 for expenses to deduct here.)	20	Unreimbursed employee expenses–job travel, union dues, job education, etc. You **MUST** attach Form 2106 or 2106-EZ if required. (See page A-4.) ▶	20
	21	Tax preparation fees	21
	22	Other expenses–investment, safe deposit box, etc. List type and amount ▶	22
	23	Add lines 20 through 22	23
	24	Enter amount from Form 1040, line 34 . **24**	
	25	Multiply line 24 above by 2% (.02)	25
	26	Subtract line 25 from line 23. If line 25 is more than line 23, enter -0-	26
Other Miscellaneous Deductions	27	Other–from list on page A-5. List type and amount ▶	27
Total Itemized Deductions	28	Is Form 1040, line 34, over $124,500 (over $62,250 if married filing separately)? **NO.** Your deduction is not limited. Add the amounts in the far right column for lines 4 through 27. Also, enter on Form 1040, line 36, the **larger** of this amount or your standard deduction. ▶ **YES.** Your deduction may be limited. See page A-5 for the amount to enter.	28

1998 Schedule A—Itemized Deductions

341

Form **8812**	**Additional Child Tax Credit**	OMB No. 1545-XXXX

Department of the Treasury
Internal Revenue Service

► **Attach to Form 1040 or 1040A.**

► **See instructions on back.**

1998

Attachment
Sequence No. **47**

Name(s) shown on return

Your social security number

Before you begin . . .

- Complete Form 1040 through line 59b or Form 1040A through line 37b.
- If you (or your spouse if filing jointly) had more than one employer for 1998 and total wages of over $50,700, see the instructions for Form 1040, line 62, or Form 1040A, line 39. Figure the amount, if any, of excess social security and railroad retirement (RRTA) taxes withheld.

1   Enter the total social security and Medicare taxes withheld from your pay (and your spouse's if filing a joint return). These taxes should be shown in boxes 4 and 6 of your W-2 form(s). If you worked for a railroad, see back of form **1**

2   **Form 1040 filers,** enter the amount from Form 1040, line 27.

   Form 1040A filers, enter -0-.   **2**

3   Add lines 1 and 2 . . . .   **3**

4   **Form 1040 filers,** enter the total of the amounts from Form 1040, lines 59a and 62.

   Form 1040A filers, enter the total of the amount from Form 1040A, line 37a, plus any excess social security and RRTA taxes withheld that you entered to the left of line 39.   **4**

5   Subtract line 4 from line 3. If the result is zero or less, **stop;** you **cannot** take this credit   **5**

6   Enter the amount from line 7 of the Child Tax Credit Worksheet in the Form 1040 or Form 1040A instructions **6**

7   Enter the amount from Form 1040, line 43, or Form 1040A, line 28 . . . .   **7**

8   Subtract line 7 from line 6. If the result is zero, **stop;** you **cannot** take this credit **8**

9   Enter the **smaller** of line 5 or line 8 . . . .   **9**

10   Do you owe the alternative minimum tax (AMT)? To find out what this tax is, see back of form.

   ☐ **No.**   Enter -0- and go to line 11.

   ☐ **Yes. Form 1040 filers,** enter the amount from Form 1040, line 51, minus any AMT used to reduce your earned income credit.

   Form 1040A filers, enter the AMT included in the total on Form 1040A, line 34, minus any AMT used to reduce your earned income credit.   **10**

11   **Additional child tax credit.** Subtract line 10 from line 9. Enter the result here and on Form 1040, line 60, or Form 1040A, line 38 . . . .   **11**

For Paperwork Reduction Act Notice, see back of form.   Cat. No. 10644E   Form **8812** (1998)

1998 Form 8812, Additional Child Tax Credit

Depreciation Class Lives

Class of Property	Types of Assets in Class
3-year	Over-the-road tractor units
	A horse that is more than 12 years old when placed in service and is not a racehorse
	A racehorse that is more than two years old when placed in service
	Breeding hogs
	Special tools used to manufacture motor vehicles (dies, molds, etc.)
5-year	Automobiles and taxis
	Light and heavy general-purpose trucks
	Buses
	Trailers and trailer-mounted containers
	Typewriters, calculators, and copiers
	Computers and peripheral equipment
	Breeding and dairy cattle
7-year	Office furniture, fixtures, and equipment
	Breeding and work horses
	Agricultural machinery and equipment
	Single-purpose agricultural or horticultural structures
	Railroad tracks
10-year	Vessels, barges, tugs, and similar water transportation equipment
	Assets used for petroleum refining
	Assets used to manufacture grain, grain mill products, sugar, sugar products, vegetable oils, and vegetable oil products

Class of Property	Types of Assets in Class
15-year	Land improvements
	Assets used to generate or distribute industrial steam and electricity
	Assets used to manufacture cement
	Assets used in pipeline transportation
	Electric utility nuclear production plant
	Municipal wastewater treatment plant
20-year	Farm buildings (other than single-purpose agricultural and horticultural structures)
	Gas utility distribution facilities
	Water utilities
	Municipal sewer
$27^1/_2$-year	Residential rental real estate
39-year	Nonresidential real estate

Glossary of Tax Terms

1040   The federal income tax return filed by individuals. You might file Form 1040, Form 1040A, or Form 1040EZ.

Accelerated depreciation   A method of depreciation that gives you higher deductions in the earlier years of the asset's life than straight-line depreciation would.

Adjusted basis   The cost of an asset increased by improvements and decreased by depreciation and tax credits. Adjusted basis is used to measure taxable gain or loss when you sell the asset.

Adjusted gross income (AGI)   The total amount of your income that is subject to tax reduced by adjustments shown on page one of your tax return.

Adjustments   Deductions that you take from gross income to arrive at adjusted gross income. Adjustments include student loan interest, IRA and Keogh contributions, medical savings account contributions, moving expenses, half of self-employment tax, penalty on withdrawing savings accounts, and alimony payments.

Adoption expenses credit   A tax credit that can be taken by parents who adopt a child. The credit can be up to $5,000 or $6,000 for a child with special needs.

Alternative minimum tax (AMT)   A separate income tax that is calculated without some of your tax deductions. If AMT is greater than your regular tax, you pay AMT instead.

Assets   Items of property that you own.

Blind   Vision of no better than 20/200 in your better eye with glasses or contact lenses or field of vision of not more than 20 degrees.

Cafeteria plan   An employee benefit plan that lets you choose from various fringe benefits. A cafeteria plan might provide health insurance, medical reimbursement, or dependent care reimbursement, among others.

Capital gain   The difference between the selling price and your adjusted basis of capital gain property.

Capital gain property   An asset that you own for investment (such as stocks) or personal use (such as your home). Does not include items that you own for purposes of resale (such as inventory).

Casualty loss   An economic loss that you suffer from a sudden, unexpected, or unusual event.

Charitable contributions   Donations of cash or property that you make to a charitable organization.

Child tax credit   A tax credit based on the number of qualifying children under age 17. In 1998, the credit is $400 per child and will be $500 per child in 1999.

Credit   A tax benefit that directly reduces your tax liability dollar for dollar.

Decedent   A person who has died.

Deduction   An expense that reduces your taxable income.

Deferred compensation   Wages, salary, or bonus that is paid in a later year instead of being paid when the compensation is earned.

Dependent   A person whom you financially support and for whom you can claim a personal dependency exemption on your tax return.

Depreciation   A deduction for the cost of an asset. You take depreciation over the life of the asset instead of deducting the entire cost when the asset is purchased.

Dividends   A distribution of corporate earnings that you receive as a shareholder. Dividends are reported to you on Form 1099-DIV.

Domicile   The state in which your legal home is located.

Donee   Someone who receives a gift.

Donor   Someone who gives a gift.

Earned income   Wages, salary, tips, or net earnings from self-employment. In essence, earned income is the fruit of your labors.

Earned income credit   A refundable credit for low-income workers.

Elderly   For tax purposes, you are elderly in 1998 if you turn age 65 on or before January 1, 1999.

Estate   An entity that wraps up your financial responsibilities and distributes your assets to your heirs after you have died.

Estimated tax payments   Tax payments that you send directly to the IRS on a quarterly basis.

Fair market value   The amount that an informed willing buyer would pay to a willing seller without having any pressure to buy or sell.

FICA tax   The Federal Insurance Contributions Act tax. FICA is the part of your Social Security tax that covers old age, disability, and death benefits.

Filing status   Your filing status determines your tax bracket and your tax rates. Filing status can be single, married filing jointly, married filing separately, head of household, or qualifying widow(er).

Fringe benefits   Things other than wages or salary that you, as an employee, receive from your employer. Fringe benefits can include health insurance benefits, the use of a company car, and so on.

Gross income   All of your income that must be included as taxable income before you take away any of your deductions.

Head of household   A filing status that you can use if you meet all of the requirements. In general, you can use head of household status if you are not married at the end of the year and you maintain a home in which your child or a dependent relative lives for at least half of the year.

Hobby   An activity that you enter into for pleasure rather than for profit.

HOPE scholarship credit   A tax credit that can be taken for the first two years of postsecondary education by some taxpayers.

Independent contractor   A worker that is not an employee.

Individual retirement account (IRA)   A certain type of personal retirement savings account. Special tax benefits are enjoyed by IRA owners.

Intangible asset   Property that is not a physical object. Stocks and bonds are examples of intangible assets.

Interest income   Earnings from savings accounts, certificates of deposits, and loans. Interest is reported to you on Form 1099-INT.

Internal Revenue Code   The laws that determine our federal income taxes.

Internal Revenue Service   The agency that collects federal income taxes. The IRS is an agency of the U.S. Department of the Treasury.

Investment income   Income that is earned from your investments such as interest and dividends.

Investment interest expense   Interest paid on loans that were taken out to buy investment property.

Itemized deductions   Deductions that you can take if they are more than your standard deduction. Itemized deductions include medical expenses, interest, taxes, charitable contributions, and some miscellaneous deductions.

Keogh plans   A retirement plan that can be used by self-employed persons. Keogh plans are also called H.R. 10 plans.

Lifetime learning credit   A 20% tax credit for qualifying postsecondary education that can be taken by some taxpayers.

Limited liability company (LLC)   A business entity that is taxed like a partnership but provides corporate-like limited liability for its owners. Your state law governs LLCs and their owners.

Marriage penalty   The higher tax that a married couple pays compared to what their taxes would be if they were not married.

Married filing jointly   The tax status used by married couples to report their income and deductions on one tax return.

Married filing separately   The tax status used by married couples to report their income and deductions on two separate tax returns.

Medical savings account   A fund that can be set up by workers of small businesses (50 or fewer employees) who use high-deductible health insurance. The fund is used to pay medical bills.

Medicare tax   The portion of your Social Security taxes that funds the federal health program for people over 65 and the disabled.

Nonrefundable credit   A tax credit that can't be more than your tax liability. If there is extra credit beyond your taxes, you might be able to carry the extra credit to other years' tax returns.

Partnership   Two or more people who join forces to carry on a business for profit.

Personal and dependency exemptions   A deduction that can be taken for each qualifying person that you support (including yourself). The deduction is $2,700 per person in 1998.

Personal property   Property that is not real estate or intangible property. Automobiles, equipment, desks, and computers are examples of personal property.

Personal use property   Property that is used in your personal life instead of being used in your business.

Property tax   A tax that you pay because you own property such as real estate, boats, cars, or assets that you use in your business.

Qualifying widow(er)   A filing status used by certain widows and widowers who have a dependent child living at home. This filing status can be used for two years after the spouse's death if the widow(er) doesn't remarry and still meets the requirements.

Refundable credit   A tax credit that is paid to you even if it is greater than your income tax.

Residential rental property   Buildings that are rented to people for their personal living quarters. Examples would be rental homes and apartment buildings.

S corporation   A corporation that has elected to be taxed under Subchapter S of the Internal Revenue Code. S corporations don't pay income tax on their own income. Instead, each shareholder reports his or her share of the corporation's profit or loss on his or her own personal tax return.

Single   The filing status used by unmarried people who have no children or dependents living in their home.

Standard deduction   A deduction that you can take instead of itemizing your deductions. The standard deduction is a fixed amount determined by your filing status.

Surviving spouse   The spouse that remains after the other spouse has died. Some surviving spouses can qualify for a special filing status that will reduce their income taxes for two years after their spouse dies.

Tangible property   Property that has physical form or substance. You can touch tangible property.

Taxable income   The result that you get after you have taken all of your tax deductions against your income. Income tax is calculated on your taxable income.

Trade or business   A business or professional activity. Merely holding investments or rental real estate can yield profits, but doesn't rise to the activity level of a trade or business.

Withholding   Income taxes that are held out of your paycheck by your employer.

Withholding allowances   The total number of allowances or exemptions that you claim on a Form W-4 that you fill out for your employer. The more withholding allowances you claim, the lower your federal income tax withholding will be.

Index

children, 18–24
    adopting, 22, 70
    death of, 23
    of divorced parents,
        24–27
    earned income, 38
    foster, 22
    hiring your, 198–99
    kiddie tax, 10–11
church employees, 296,
    297
church schools, 139
citizenship test, 24, 25
classification of workers,
    179–180
clean-fuel vehicle deduc-
    tion, 206
closing statement, 123
club dues, 167, 174–175,
    238–239
clumping technique, 78
COBRA coverage, 273
Code Section 501(c)(3),
    129
Commissioner v. Soliman,
    224
commuting method for
    valuing personal use of
    company car, 213
companions, travel
    expenses of, 245
company-owned cars,
    212–213
compensation, 203
computer expenses, 167,
    173, 174
computers, 231–232
condominiums, 98,
    99–100, 118, 191

consumer interest, 106–
    107
contributions, *see* chari-
    table contributions
control employees, 213
convenience of employer,
    home office deduction
    for employees and,
    225–226
cooperative apartments
    (co-ops), 95, 118
cosmetic surgery, 82
cost of goods sold, 185,
    186
credits, *see* tax credits

D

daycare facilities,
    home-based, 228–229
death, 16–17, 23
debt
    bad, 201
        documentation for,
        143
    see also home mortgage
        interest
debt tracing rules, 114
deduction floor, 76–77
    defined, 77
deductions, 3, 4–6, 11–13
    types of, 4
defined benefit plan, 326
defined contribution
    plans, 325–326
dental insurance, 68
dependency exemptions,
    10, 16–24, 289
    for children, 18–24
        of divorced parents,
        24–27

citizenship test, 24, 25
death and, 16–17, 23
for divorcees, 17
gross income test,
    18–19
IRS matching up, 16
joint return test, 23–24
relationship or mem-
    ber of household test,
    22–23
Social Security num-
    bers for dependents,
    29–30
support test, 19–22
dependents
    filing requirements for,
    34–35
    standard deduction for,
    38–39
    see also children
depletion, 195
deposits, lost, 151
depreciable life, 188
depreciation, 188–196
    additional first year,
    193
    asset classes, 188–189,
    343–344
    of cars, 213–216
        trading in or selling
        your old car and,
        217, 218
    of computer equip-
        ment, 232
    defined, 188
    IRS publications for,
    195–196
    listed property, 193–194
    method of, 189–191

G

H

J

T